Not So Prime Time

Not So Prime Time

CHASING THE TRIVIAL ON AMERICAN TELEVISION

HOWARD ROSENBERG

Ivan R. Dee

CHICAGO 2004

Most of the contents of this book appeared originally in the *Los Angeles Times*, whose permission to print them here is gratefully acknowledged.

Library of Congress Cataloging-in-Publication Data:
Rosenberg, Howard, 1938–
    Not so prime time : chasing the trivial on American television / Howard Rosenberg.
        p. cm.
    Includes index.
    ISBN 1-56663-577-2 (alk. paper)
    1. Television broadcasting—United States. 2. Television programs—United States. I. Title.

PN1992.5.U5R67 2004
791.45'0973—dc22

                                                                2004045538

For Carol and Kirsten

Acknowledgments

Many thanks to my editors and other colleagues at the *Los Angeles Times*, especially Lee Margulies and Betsy Sharkey, whose friendship and guidance nourished my career and helped make this book possible. Thanks also to Ivan Dee, whose insights were invaluable.

Thanks, finally, to Mom and my biggest fan always, the late, great Getzel.

H. R.

Los Angeles
April 2004

Contents

**IV. BURYING THE HYPE: TRUE HEROES AND
DEITIES UNMASKED**

Preface

In Barry Levinson's film *Avalon* several generations of a large Baltimore family gather in front of a new television set in the 1950s, eyes young and old lasered to the small screen as if waiting for the curtain to rise on a spectacular production. Television is in its infancy, and before the Krichinskys in their living room, utterly transfixing them like nothing they've seen previously, is a static, unending, black and white test pattern bearing the call letters of the network they are watching.

It's a revealing snapshot of America at midcentury and a powerful symbol, for the boisterous Krichinskys had always been defined by their verbal communications and by a storytelling grandfather passing down to the children tales describing his own boyhood in Eastern Europe.

In this scene no one is speaking, however, and no one is moving. One wonders, in fact, if the Krichinskys are even thinking as they come under the spell of this freshly unboxed technology that will alter their lives. Near the end of *Avalon*, when the grandfather starts to tell a story to a grandchild, the boy turns away to watch TV.

Simpler times, perhaps, but in some ways foreshadowing what was coming as television wired and transformed our culture.

Years later I begin observing a similar glazed-over look in the eyes of viewers before thirty-two-inch screens—silent, rapt, seduced, their brain waves flattened now by live television pictures of police pursuits on freeways, not appearing to notice or care that each of these gratuitous exercises in media flatulence played out much like the other. In effect, this contemporary audience too was watching a test pattern, a marathon freeze frame and monotone buzz of media not unlike the one that British critic and philosopher Malcolm Muggeridge aptly titled *Newzac*.

We all know that television can be a source of joy, illumination, and flat-out fun.

We know also that its creative triumphs are a slender portfolio measured against its bulging archive of thudding clunkers, many of which are described in this book. Yet that is also true of everything else on an arts and media landscape where the talented are few and the mediocre number in the multitudes.

I am supremely ticked off when I hear someone say, "It's not bad for TV," as if there were or should be a separate standard for television, less demanded of it because its screen is smallish and a few feet from our faces. Come again? One might as well say that Toulouse-Lautrec wasn't a bad painter for a dwarf or that Ellen DeGeneres tells good jokes for a woman who sleeps with other women.

Television is distinctive, not inferior by definition, and its warts should not be rationalized any more than a bad play or novel should be excused. I write some tough things about television, but that severity comes out of respect for its potential.

There's one standard of excellence, period, and pound for pound, in fact, TV has as much going for it as theatrical movies, stage, music, literature, or the fine art of your choice.

The rub is TV's reach, its pervasiveness. The public doesn't see every movie, read every book, hear every rhapsody or rapper. But television is everywhere and evermore, seeping into our pores and shaping what we think about ourselves and the rest of the planet in ways that were unthinkable when the Krichinskys sat awestruck before their first set at a time when TV's umbilical cord was still attached to Howdy Doody and Hopalong Cassidy.

Americans encounter television now in numbers far greater than those who pay their nine bucks for a blockbuster feature film or read a typical best-seller. That raises the stakes immeasurably. And the longer the mundane endures on television, the greater the chance we will become desensitized to it, and even enamored of it, dumbing down America and making third-rate the standard. That may be happening already.

How else to read the onslaught of look-alike, deceptively titled "reality" shows that have defoliated and transformed much of prime time into a cratered moonscape.

And what to think of people who, after childhoods of sucking on the mother's milk of television, take jobs in its newsrooms today, famished for . . . well, for what?

In that regard, what a difference a generation or two make.

Even now there's something thrilling about the closing scene in *Foreign Correspondent*, Alfred Hitchcock's grand 1940 movie about espionage just before World War II. "You can hear the bombs falling in the streets," reports Joel McCrea as the dashing American journalist Johnny Jones in a stirring broadcast from London during the Blitz.

The bombs we hear are German, and the danger is palpable as Johnny, a newspaperman covering Western Europe, bravely ignores it and keeps addressing America from his London studio with gorgeous Laraine Day looking on. The lump in your throat feels like a melon when he urges his countrymen across the Atlantic: "Keep those lights burning."

However embellished, at least Johnny Jones stood for something. You wonder how many young people bought trench coats and aspired to become journalists themselves after seeing this romanticized picture of a foreign correspondent whose indictment of Nazism was so impassioned.

And you wonder what calls the young to TV journalism now, beyond the lure of the camera and the wail of police sirens.

This failure to see all of television's possibilities is troubling. It's also why "critical awareness" is the message of this book and what I preached religiously while writing about television for thirty-three years, initially at the deceased *Louisville Times*, the last twenty-five as TV critic for the *Los Angeles Times*, where my final column appeared August 8, 2003.

"Critical awareness" is a fancy way of saying: Think about what you watch. Don't tolerate a program because you find nothing *less* objectionable to watch. Don't be sponged into a 9 P.M. TV audience merely because you happen to be bolted to your set (duh) at 8:59. Resist the lobotomy. Don't become their zombie. Don't be swept up in a TV programming strategy like a tuna in a net.

Think about this: For years, broadcast research has shown that the popularity of a typical local news program has less to do with its content than with the size of the audience delivered to it by its lead-in show, whether Dr. Phil, Oprah Winfrey, or "The Flintstones." Fred and Wilma passing the baton to Action News? How depressing is that! Fred and Wilma *anchoring* Action News? Don't ask.

News and entertainment now mingle on television as intimately as fun lovers snorting up together at a cocktail party, becoming interchangeable, with newscasts cross-dressing as theater and vice versa. There's probably as much "reality" in "Bachelorette" as in a typical local newscast or one on CNN, the Fox News Channel, and MSNBC. And a poll conducted in early 2004 by the Pew Research Center for the People & the Press found that one-fifth of young adults regularly got information about the presidential campaign from such comedy programs as "The Daily Show" and "Saturday Night Live." Although just half the number who relied on the Internet or tuned in traditional newscasts for campaign news, according to the Pew survey, that 20 percent would be enough to sway any election.

Television's darkest prospect has always been that it would wash over and render us passive nonparticipants in its panorama of drool, and at times we would become the buttons on the remote control and television the index finger. This absorption of humanity by electronic media—technology setting the agenda, sucking out our brains and commanding us instead of vice versa—is the ominous reality that now confronts every potato in the TV audience.

Viewers do make some choices, of course, and from an ever expanding palette. Thank you for that, cable and satellite dishes. And no thanks, for the colors on that palette are running together at an alarming rate, blues and greens merging as blue-greens, blues and purples bleeding together as mauves, narrowing choices even while creating the illusion of greater diversity. Thank *you* for that, growing media consolidation—an insidious clustering of resources that assigns more and more control and influence to fewer and fewer corporate executive suites.

How does this incestuous process work? Recently CNN did a highly advertised segment speculating on who would be named *Time* magazine's "Person of the Year." A few nights later came the payoff— an entire news special on "Person of the Year." Why would CNN, which anoints itself the nation's most "trusted" news source, squander a thick slab of time on such a trivial, even bogus news event amounting to magazine journalists polling themselves on "Person of the Year"—a self-pleasuring Golden Globes of print—as a way of advertising their own publication? Was it because—and I don't think I'm shooting in the dark here—both CNN and Time were owned by Time Warner? *Nahhhhhh.*

And recently a Los Angeles news anchor added on the air after a weightless story on recreation: "It's a nice day to go to Disneyland." Where did that come from? Was he just a fan of the theme park who wanted to share with viewers? Or was this a calculated plug because his station, KABC-TV, was owned by Disney?

Call it synergy, call it chauvinism, call it what it is, deception by newscasters who find ethics inconvenient. Whatever you call it—it stinks! And my outrage at this now-routine behavior has not diminished through the years.

Nearly all the essays in this book appear here as they did in the *Los Angeles Times* from 1986 to 2003. A few have been trimmed, a few lightly revised for clarity or because they were too centered on Los Angeles.

TV critics are the decathletes in the Olympiad of criticism, pole vaulting one moment, running (and sometimes stumbling over) hurdles the next. They are asked to write about everything because television, whatever else may be said of it, is about everything. As are the pieces here, though the bulk are tied closely to TV news and my ever-low assessment of its performance and worth to America.

For the most part, TV news has failed dismally in its self-proclaimed role as a Bethlehem Star of enlightenment, as its influence continues to widen among those who value tabloid over truth. One reason is its growing addiction to celebrities, a groupie mentality stimulated in late 2003 by new child-molestation allegations against that man-child himself, Michael Jackson, and Arnold Schwarzenegger's stunning gubernatorial charge in California, despite accusations that he had groped and sexually harassed women through the years. As for Governor Glamour's powerful allure, Los Angeles stations as apt to visit Sacramento as Mars suddenly surged with national media to the California capital now that its pitchman was a magnetic movie star with an Austrian accent, a muscular arm around their shoulder, and glib one-liners galore.

This book's subtitle refers to *chasing* trivia, making the point, I hope, that every chase is not successful. The puny and frivolous are sometimes elusive, even for U.S. television. Admirable work does on occasion rise heroically to the top, somehow squirming its way through the industry's blubbery layers of greed, cynicism, and superficiality. Some of it is cited here.

Resonating loudest, though, are the trifles, the ones much of television has come to pursue as tenaciously as those cops do fugitives on freeways. Which should give us all pause. Are these the stories tomorrow's elders will pass down to *their* grandchildren?

Not So Prime Time

I

News on a High Wire:
Clowns Without Safety Nets

Is the line blurring between mainstream TV news and tabloids?
What line?

Anything fresh is news. The challenge is not defining news but
prioritizing it, choosing what stories to include, what to omit, and
deciding what legitimately earns the most prominence. Try this: If
Saddam Hussein and Michael Jackson had been taken into custody
on the same day in 2003, the twenty-four-hour news channels, local
news, and perhaps the major networks too would have assigned the
stories equal weight by splitting the screen and showing them
simultaneously.

Bank on it. As Saddam was, they're in a rat hole.

Especially symbolic of the mainstream's slide into this abyss is the
growth in stature of Diane Dimond who, as a reporter for the tabloid
"Hard Copy," of all shows, was interviewed by CBS news more than
a decade ago about earlier child molestation charges against Jackson.
Although conventional newscasts had been quoting tabloids for years,
this interview with television's premier Jackson watcher was clearly a
watershed moment in the forging of a new hybrid.

So it was routine, no big deal, when Dimond's Jackson "scoops" for the shrill series "Court TV" earned her a gig as a regular contributor on NBC's "Today" show in 2004. You might even say it was a good fit, and a prologue for the expected sensational trials of accused murderers Scott Peterson and Robert Blake and accused rapist Kobe Bryant.

Well, ho hum, right?

When Paula Jones's new nose earns headlines, you know this is, indeed, a hyperventilating news universe. It's one where sensational crime stories grow to be Goodyear blimps, and important stories are often ignored or short-sheeted, and reporting becomes a careless, mad dash across the carcasses of the innocent. In this true-life scenario, mistakes are tolerated, rumor and innuendo assume titillating lives of their own, and relentless overcoverage creates intense interest that media use to justify *additional* overcoverage.

Nowhere is hyperbole more pronounced than among TV reporters whose beat is entertainment. Most are hopelessly enamored groupies who see themselves as extensions of the industry they cover. This makes them giddy collaborators in propaganda and susceptible to the charms of super-celebs like Arnold Schwarzenegger, whose media-massaging act, you'll read here, began long before his campaign for California governor.

Otherwise everything is fine.

Except for the little white lies and whoppers told by television, which fibs nonstop. Take the biggest lies advanced in newscasts:

One—making us an especially fearful society on the hunt for quickie panaceas—is that violent crime is the most pressing problem facing America today and that everyone, everywhere, is out to victimize you.

Another—nourishing U.S. ethnocentrism and ignorance about the rest of the globe—is that not much happens beyond our borders unrelated to violence and mayhem.

Still another, resulting from unbalanced coverage of crime and people of color, is that whites should be fearful of all African Americans and Hispanics in their midst.

No less irritating are smaller television lies perpetuated by movie after movie that gnarl history while advertising accuracy—along with newscasts that, like politicians, make self-promotion their primary agenda.

Think of anchors, for example, as gleaming hood ornaments on the chassis of news.

There's a reason why news anchors from New York to Walla Walla are paid more than anyone else on the staff, and it's not because they are smarter or better journalists. Don't be shocked if the opposite is true, in fact. I know local anchors who have had a good day when they get their shoes tied. Send them out to cover a story, a *real* story, and they might injure themselves.

The system works this way: Newscasts, both national and local, are built mostly on personalities, with focus groups and other high-priced audience research as bricks and mortar. Locally, each station advertises its news personalities as a team or close-knit family, an extension of *your* family. So you should embrace and love these warm and cuddly bunnies, and even care about their lives. It's a rip-roaring farce that I address here.

Anchors, by design and tradition, are the Mt. Rushmores of this crowd of celebrity journalists, their mere presence meant to rivet you to the screen.

That is true even in the TV news stratosphere, otherwise known as ABC, CBS, and NBC. Whatever their relative brawn as newsmen—and each is seasoned—Peter Jennings, Dan Rather, and the departing Tom Brokaw endure mostly because of their muscle as news *personalities*, the danger coming when their glamour and renown elevate them above the stories they are dispatched to cover, the messenger shining brighter than the message.

Even the iconic Walter Cronkite wasn't paid top dollar by CBS News those many years because he parachuted over Normandy with U.S. troops during World War II. He became our Uncle Walter because he was magnificently avuncular, because something indefinable in his face, voice, and manner earned America's trust. I met him a few times, once when he was still anchoring. He was an okay guy but unworthy of bronzing . . . until the camera's red light clicked on.

Meanwhile the motor beneath the chassis, too, has been corroded by deception.

Look, the network news divisions, which once ruled imperiously and still like to throw their heft around, are now decadent dinosaurs with bad tickers. Any moment, curtains—and perhaps it's time. Yet thinking about the species now inheriting the earth, as this old crowd fades from the scene, makes one more than a bit queasy.

They're not to be trusted. These newscasters with satellite dishes for brains boast relentlessly about their speed and technology, for example. What they don't reveal is how deceptively they utilize it.

Technology is great when it works for you, not against you. Southern Californians can attest that live TV is unsurpassed in covering some types of breaking stories, from massive shootouts and volatile civil disturbances to raging fires and devastating earthquakes. You may turn on the radio to learn the latest, but no one waits for the morning paper anymore.

What's more, the entire nation recalls live coverage of 9/11, that catastrophe of catastrophes when live reporting and pictures of the immediate aftermath were swiftly fed to a needy public swept up in the terror and uncertainty of that terrible day.

Most times, though, "live" is deployed strategically by newscasters as dishonest theater, a gimmick to give weight to the weightless and attract viewers by creating an aura of excitement and immediacy. Even when none exists.

As the pieces in this section affirm, moreover, "live" can be dangerous and irresponsible, often the equivalent of a newspaper printing a reporter's raw notes under a misleading banner headline. More than just a recipe for misinforming the public, even worse, live coverage is a journalistic catastrophe waiting to happen.

When one inevitably does happen, like one noted in a piece here, TV's amnesiacs wring their hands, beg forgiveness, and promise to reform. And they do, poor babies—until next time.

And count on it, there is always a next time, whether it's an act of deception or some other means of exploiting the very public they're pledged to serve. Predation is a thankless job, you know, but somebody has to do it.

Democracy is impossible without an open society, which is why media have enormous latitude under the First Amendment. Let's do keep it that way, absolutely. Yet . . . when does the free flow of information that serves the public good override the rights of individuals to personal privacy?

Sometimes that question applies to public officials accused of wrongdoing tied to their personal behavior (think Bill Clinton), often to celebrities who seek and bask in the warm sunlight of media worship only to reject coverage that sets their images aflame (think Michael Jackson).

Sometimes, too, privacy concerns apply to average citizens who are dragged reluctantly into a media spotlight by virtue of a tragedy or their connection to some other news event.

How many Americans, for example, are sacrificed unfairly on the altar of that vague ideal called "the people's right to know"? Far too many, from celebrities to ordinary citizens.

One of the most egregious media invasions of privacy I saw came years ago at the funeral of a murdered boy, when a TV cameraman leaned back on the coffin to get a dramatic shot of the distraught parents. Screw their private grief, right?

Why did the parents allow it? Why didn't they or others order the camera the hell out of there? Because they were unworldly and unaware they had that right to say no. In this case, TV abused them because it *could* abuse them.

Democracy is messy, the price of an independent press being one that's free to misbehave. Just because media may have a legal right to exploit and stalk the public as prey, though, doesn't mean they have an ethical right.

Team Coverage of Breaking News

◆ *The most insidious of abuses, almost too frightful to write about?*
This piece satirizes it.

The Michael Jackson story is continuing to arrive in dribbles as TV newscasters follow the examples of tabloids and . . .

This Just In!
Breaking News!
Hold Your Hats!
Call Everyone in Your Family to the Calendar Section!
Don't Put Down This Paper!

I'm sorry to interrupt my column, but I've just learned exclusively that allegations of journalistic ethics abuse have been made against certain TV news executives in Los Angeles.

Before I continue with my team coverage of this profoundly important, fact-free story, I want to emphasize strongly that these ironclad allegations from highly reliable sources whom I've never met nor heard of are absolutely unsubstantiated but quite possibly true while being potentially dubious. Making their publication imperative.

What follows is shocking and graphic, and may not be suitable for anyone with a mind:

"The news executives at my station callously abused my ethics," charges a reporter who requests anonymity.

I interviewed the reporter exclusively.

Please tell me what you told your therapist about your bosses.

"They abused my ethics every day. At first it was innocent, you know, assigning an occasional ambush interview, some pandering and

9

tampering here and there, overcooking a story now and then. But then . . . but then . . ."

Is this hard for you? Is it too painful? Would a glass of water help, a five-minute break?

"No, I want to go on, because at some point—I can't recall exactly when—I began to realize that something was *terribly* wrong. You see, I had always regarded my ethics as special and private, as precious and inviolate. I had been taught in school to let no one, you know, touch my ethics. But it was so harmless, so gradual. And, finally, the constant abuse took its toll. One day I looked into the mirror and saw someone who no longer had any ethics at all. I was devastated. Without my ethics I felt so dirty, so . . . *naked.*"

A second reporter told me exclusively that his own ethics had also been uncovered and fiddled with by his news director. "At first he encouraged me to blow stories out of proportion; in other words, distort what was and wasn't news. Then it became an order."

Fearing the stigma of ethics abuse, the reporter begged for anonymity. These reporters are not alone. Another ethics-abused reporter has disclosed to me exclusively that she was ordered by her superiors to lace her stories with rumors and innuendo.

"At least, that's the way it began," she said. "It was minor, rather innocuous. That's the way they operate, you know, authority figures lulling you into a state of trust. But then it graduated to something bigger, and they started asking me to actually smear peoples' reputations based on rumors and innuendo. It was ugly, and I knew I was doing something wrong, but I went along with this filth, hoping it would stop. But it didn't stop. And now . . . now I feel so . . . *violated.*

"I don't understand people who act this way," she continued anonymously. "They're insidious. They could have touched my pens, my note pads, my paper clips. But why couldn't they have kept their hands off my ethics?"

Whew! I hope that readers are as shattered as I am by these absolutely truthful possibly erroneous charges of ethics abuse.

Meanwhile, continuing my team coverage, I have learned exclusively that the above-mentioned TV news executives are in possession of stacks of photographs and videotapes. Sources say the videotapes are near a VCR where they may have been played—*recently*. Even more significant, I have learned exclusively that the subjects of these photographs and videotapes are people and, yes, *people* who are plainly . . . *visible*.

Again, I must emphasize that these appalling alleged unnatural actions—for which these news executives deserve to be tarred, feathered, and fired—have not been verified.

However, the fact that I have exclusively reported them and brought them to your attention must mean that they are credible, or else why would someone with my integrity and high standards have done it?

The obviously reprehensible but innocent-until-proved-guilty news executives alluded to in this column were given an opportunity to respond to the possibly phony but undoubtedly truthful allegations made against them, but they declined. That is their right, although if they were innocent you'd think they'd want to tell me about it exclusively.

In lieu of this, I have exclusively sought opinions about this matter from patrons of a shopping mall who have no knowledge of any of the persons referred to in this column or the charges leveled against them. But all of the shoppers agree that if the charges were true, as they may be, they'd be *horrendous*.

In another explosive revelation, meanwhile, I have learned exclusively that on more than one occasion I have shamefully engaged in the unnatural abuse of my own journalistic ethics, the most current example of which is this column. Quite candidly, I'm devastated.

[1993]

Poor Richard's Almanac of Horrors

◈ *My first response to swarming media coverage of Richard Jewell, the supposed Olympic Games bomber, was a question: What if he didn't do it?*

There's speculation he had a hero's complex.
—KCBS-TV

Call it synchronized swimming in rumor and innuendo.

Whatever the title, it stinks. If anyone has a hero complex, it's those members of the media who, swept up in their own pandemonium, leaped to conclusions about Richard Jewell based at the time only on shards of circumstantial evidence. They're the ones prancing in the limelight.

Jewell is the thirty-three-year-old security guard who was anointed a hero after alerting police to a knapsack containing the bomb that exploded in Atlanta's Centennial Olympic Park last Saturday, resulting in two deaths and 111 injuries. But a front-page story in Tuesday's *Atlanta Journal-Constitution* labeling Jewell a suspect drove hordes of TV commandos into another of their ravenous frenzies, producing a steady torrent of speculative stories whose virtual indictment of Jewell appeared to exceed anything authorities had in mind at that time.

Inevitably, the story assumed a life of its own, sucking in just about all of the media in varying degrees.

Yet the only agency that matters, the FBI, had not arrested or charged Jewell with anything or officially said that he was a suspect as of Wednesday afternoon, although it had questioned him, searched his apartment at length, and apparently shared tidbits about him with some of the media.

Even if Jewell does turn out to be the bomber, though, it won't absolve TV's clowns of summer. It won't alter the fact that their coverage of the FBI's early nosing around has been mostly outrageous and irresponsible.

Here is some speculation about that coverage:

1. By privately leaking possibly damaging information, the FBI may have been using the media to put pressure on Jewell to make him crack. If so, the media have been manipulated into being an extension of law enforcement. That should not be their role.

2. All of this wild, scattershot reporting and stalking of Jewell, and the staking out of his Atlanta apartment by the media multitudes, puts crushing pressure on the FBI, swelling public expectations and the possibility that authorities will be driven to take some premature action that could jeopardize the bomb probe.

In any case, what we have here is a striking example of the worst of journalism in the '90s, another case of O.J.itis coursing through TV veins. Another case of how TV technology is not only a means to an end but now often part of that end. Of how live TV, far from filling the traditional journalistic role of observer, now shapes, influences, and potentially determines stories. Of how this technology has goosed and accelerated reporting, too often with negative results.

Olympic sprinters have nothing on the media assigned to cover them in Atlanta. Blurring speed now drives and defines nearly everything, from those initiating it (TV and radio) to those hoping to keep up (newspapers). We see video of the Centennial Park bomb exploding, the reporting unfurling as the incident unfurls, lines of separation no longer visible, all of it leading us to expect a resolution as speedy as the minute-by-minute coverage. Here was CNN reporter Bonnie Anderson at 6 A.M. Wednesday on the fringe of the international media throng outside Jewell's apartment complex: "We'll keep you updated. The agents are inside right now." Anderson at 7 A.M.: "I believe we may have somebody coming out of the complex now." At 8 A.M.: "FBI agents have been in the apartment now for about two hours. Also within the last five minutes . . ."

Almost simultaneously, correspondent George Lewis was reporting on NBC that investigators had removed some items from Jewell's apartment. Quickly now to Paul Crawley, NBC affiliate WXIA-TV's eye outside the complex. "Today's" Matt Lauer to Crawley: "George Lewis said they have brought some things out. Have you seen anything?"

Had he seen anything? What was this, a stakeout on "NYPD Blue"? "Homicide: Life on the Street"? Couldn't be. Their scripts are more believable. What's being generated in Atlanta is almost surreal. It was only Tuesday morning that Jewell was on NBC's "Today" with an admiring Katie Couric, being celebrated as a modest, gee-whiz savior whose alert action Saturday may have limited the casualties. By nightfall, though, he had been recast as warped and demonic, a pudgy gargoyle lumbering along inside a smothering entourage of reporters, minicams, and microphones, all searching his demeanor for hints of guilt to justify the accusatory tone of their stories. As if Jewell had been fingered in a lineup, TV cameras were all over him, and networks and local stations tenaciously probed his background, questioning his Los Angeles employer and digging into his records from his days as a deputy sheriff and a security guard at tiny Piedmont College.

In Atlanta Tuesday, a CNN reporter asked some people who had returned to Centennial Park if they were pleased that "they may have caught the perpetrator," even though Jewell may not be the perpetrator. Jewell was squarely in the cross hairs of NBC's biggest guns, from correspondent Fred Francis, with his "high-level federal sources," to anchor Tom Brokaw, who assured viewers Tuesday that authorities would not have reopened Centennial Park if not "fairly sure" their man was under wraps. "We should have some resolution of this," he promised.

You were getting impatient with Jewell by this time, wondering why he didn't just get on with it and admit that he had a hero complex and had planted the bomb to gain credit for saving lives.

That was the rumor zooming across TV for two days, KCBS-TV being a typical messenger.

The headline: "Coming up, the suspect's possible motive. There's speculation he had a hero's complex." The story: "A theory is floating around that Jewell has a hero's complex," KCBS anchor Linda Alvarez began. Reporter Mary Grady had "the story," consisting of a generic interview with a psychologist about persons with hero complexes, then a review of past criminals with such complexes, then anchor Michael Tuck cautioning: "But we don't know whether Richard Jewell has a hero's complex."

Or whether he suffers from multiple personalities, one of whom could have planted the bomb without Jewell knowing it. Quick, get another psychologist on the horn.

CNN played the same game with a criminologist Wednesday, getting him to say it was "possible" that Jewell had a hero's complex. It was possible also that Jewell was innocent, something too few appeared willing to consider.

An exception Wednesday was CBS correspondent Jim Stewart, who reported that "investigators" were repeatedly advising CBS, "Don't jump to any conclusion yet." And NBC's Olympics host, Bob Costas, broached the subject of Jewell's possible innocence Tuesday night to Brokaw, who responded that if it did turn out that way, "The FBI will be very embarrassed."

But not NBC and the rest of the media, he seemed to be saying. Destroying lives was their job.

[1996]

Obsession, Not Proportion, Drives Television News

◈ *Although the cable news networks depicted themselves as social scientists, their coverage of Laci Peterson's murder yielded the same old same old.*

History versus hooey.

This week's disclosures about the ruthless and dishonest tactics of Senator Joseph R. McCarthy—as he extended the nation's Red Scare just after midcentury—evoke memories of him being famously rebuked on TV by Joseph N. Welch.

It was 1954, a time of black hearts and blacklisting in high places, and the occasion was televised hearings linked to McCarthy's charges that Communists had infiltrated the U.S. Army. When he used this opportunity to publicly attack the loyalty of a young lawyer in Welch's firm, the army's folksy, deceptively mild-appearing special counsel cut him off, with cameras rolling.

"Let us not assassinate this lad further, senator," Welch began like a preacher to a sinner. "You have done enough. Have you no sense of decency, sir, at long last? Have you left no sense of decency?"

McCarthy had a few months left as America's prince of darkness. Yet this stinging admonition, from a Boston trial attorney whose instinct for theater matched the senator's, was a history-turning moment. Combined with Edward R. Murrow's earlier "See It Now" broadcast attacking McCarthy on CBS, it was a savage blow from which the dangerous Wisconsin demagogue would never recover. News accounts gave this story the big blast it deserved.

Today it would share media time with Laci Peterson.

Just as the toppling of Saddam Hussein's statue in Baghdad—signifying the fall of his regime and Iraq's capital to U.S. forces—got less weight on TV in the long run than pregnant Laci Peterson's disappearance in Modesto, and her husband, Scott, being charged with her murder.

It's that kind of media universe, as TV's presentation of news makes it ever harder to separate the essential from the clutter, the significant from the silly, the momentous from the ordinary. It's always been the nature of TV news to render everything equal. Think cards in a Rolodex, thirty seconds of fluff followed by thirty seconds of calamity followed by thirty seconds of car chase leading to thirty seconds of global crisis, as if all were equal in news value. The twenty-four-hour news channels have built on and accelerated this process, however.

Now ABC's Diane Sawyer is no crackerjack journalist. Yet when she appeared with Larry King to promote her two-hour ABC News special detailing a scam that undermined the British version of "Who Wants to Be a Millionaire"—yes, two hours of prime time for that—CNN repeatedly billed her as "the only network anchor to interview Scott Peterson." As if, in more than thirty years in the news business, this was her achievement that would most impress viewers.

That was probably true for King's show, which these days is Laci Peterson 101. It seemed to impress CNN and King, even though Sawyer's Peterson interview was stale news that came before his wife's body was found and he had been charged with murder.

At this point, to preempt angry e-mails charging insensitivity, one is compelled to state the obvious, that the Peterson case is, indeed, newsworthy, and is, indeed, tragic and a deep sorrow for many. A young mother and her unborn child are dead, the husband and father in the dock, and two families devastated. That speaks for itself. Yet how about TV removing those black armbands for once and trying some perspective here instead of lights, cameras, teeming media hordes?

Fat chance. The medium's minions have traveled too fast and too far on this fast track for a U-turn, and taken much of the public with them.

If Lincoln had issued his document that freed slaves in rebelling states in the era of all-news channels instead of in 1863, they would have granted him half the screen, the rest to Laci Peterson's memorial. The discovery of the wheel would have shared time with Scott Peterson's bail hearing. Nero fiddling while Rome burned would have given way to Modesto.

Instead of showing us architects of history, TV encourages carpenters with fast hammers. The result is quickened pulses, impatience as a society that is incompatible with historical perspective.

Just as entertainment shows usually fix all problems before the final credits, so do news programs rev up red-herring scenarios and facile answers prematurely. Peel back the fat layers of coverage and you find news consultants, hired hands with their fingers on the pulse of ratings. The public always falls for it. As Sawyer said, people "have all the references."

As they did when much of TV repeatedly cranked up that blond-curled little cowgirl JonBenet Ramsey to the exclusion of nearly everything else, and later when it also happened with Elizabeth Smart.

It's what they do, and always have done, but now have done enough. Have they no sense of decency, at long last?

[2003]

Her Nose Makes News

◆ *Cosmetic surgery made Paula Jones and her new honker the talk of media everywhere.*

You pug, you knob, you button-head, know that I glory in this nose of mine, for a great nose indicates a great man—genial, courteous, intellectual, virile, courageous—as I am—and such as you—poor wretch—will never dare to be even in imagination.
  —"Cyrano de Bergerac"

Before and after.

When is a nose news? When it's on the face of Paula Jones, who is deeply ingrained in pop culture as the twangy Arkansas woman who publicly claimed President Clinton propositioned her while he was that state's governor, and whose sexual harassment lawsuit against him was dismissed but is on appeal. Last week her mug was everywhere.

When is a nose the butt of jokes? Same answer.

Here was Jay Leno, always on the high road, joking in his "Tonight Show" monologue on NBC, prior to Jones's remake, about her being in the presence of Clinton during her lawsuit:

"It's the first time any guy has gotten to see her twice, 'cause she's never had a second date." Hardly more mellow, here he was Thursday night finding room for Jones amid his customary Clinton one-liners:

"Paula Jones showed her new nose last night on TV. Then she showed off her old nose on 'This Old House.' She's using it to build an extension on her trailer. They're going to put the whole patio out there."

Her trailer?

Leno has compared Linda Tripp to a horse in his monologue. And Thursday night he gave his impression of Attorney General Janet Reno—as a super-macho palooka—as if seeing her only as tall timber to be chopped down.

I once wrote that Leno attacking Tripp's looks was male arrogance. It reminded me of high school, when we would ridicule the looks of girls who didn't measure up, as if we were great bargains ourselves.

Leno took umbrage at the gender reference, and he may have been right. Perhaps it wasn't a male thing, just a nasty thing.

I believe, however, that for the pugs, knobs, and button-heads who have been making fun of Jones, it's largely a class thing.

The irony is that Los Angeles is the globe's cosmetic surgery dome, and Leno has sat genially on his talk show with probably countless celebrities who have been redone from top to bottom without trashing them for what they were or still are.

Leno deserves credit for making fun of his own epic chin. But that doesn't make up for the derision he pours on others just because of the way they look. Especially when it comes to Jones's nose—noses having been used historically to demean Arabs and especially Jews, with Hitler's Third Reich and the old Soviet Union using such caricatures to dehumanize and isolate an entire people. In the German weekly *Der Stuermer* from the 1930s, for example, you find ugly cartoon after cartoon of Jews depicted as the enemies of humanity, their most prominent feature being beaklike noses that droop almost to their thick lips.

In my case, I recall vividly how some of the older kids in my elementary school would stroke their noses when they passed me in the halls, just because a guy named Rosenberg was obviously Jewish.

I was Jewish trash; Jones is trailer trash—making us both fair game in our respective generations. It's a stigma she may never outlive, no matter how many times she tries to reinvent herself. And this new nose business is just another reminder, just as some of its coverage brings to mind the ever-closer ties between mainstream media and tabloids.

As everyone on the planet is aware, Jones's new nose arrived after her new hair, new teeth, and new wardrobe. That made it news for much of the mainstream media. And for ABC's "PrimeTime Live," which on Wednesday night did a ninety-second piece featuring mostly video excerpts of an interview with the supposedly new and improved Jones going public with her nose job.

And now, announced co-anchor Sam Donaldson about midway through the ABC News series, a "first exclusive look at the new Paula Jones, after cosmetic surgery, as shown by the *National Enquirer*."

Come again?

Beyond Jones's rhinoplasty, simply stunning here are the other before/after snapshots—the ones of mainstream media that once refused even to rub shoulders with tabloids but now seem to be on the verge of joining hands with them like candidates at a political rally.

Local stations have routinely quoted or incorporated into their newscasts material from syndicated tabloid shows that they air, the effect of which is to deceptively promote those shows while narrowing the gap between the center and fringes of journalism. And with so much of mainstream media lasering in on celebrities, the bizarre and the tawdry, they are increasingly merging their news interests with those of tabloids.

"Definitely a blending has occurred," Steve Coz, editor-in-chief of the *National Enquirer*, agreed by phone Friday. "Let's go to your plastic surgery story. The [other] media, going for ratings and sales, have been going after what the *Enquirer* has been going after for years."

Now comes "PrimeTime Live," crossing a line, at least symbolically, by using material from the *National Enquirer*, however benign. "She's center stage today, sporting a new nose," reported ABC correspondent Sylvia Chase, who added her own voice-over to the Jones sound bites and pictures as a *National Enquirer* logo appeared in the upper right corner.

A small step? Perhaps. But like falling dominoes, one step inevitably leads to another.

Coz said the *National Enquirer* videotaped its Jones interview, in conjunction with its print story, as protection against it getting ripped off by other media without credit, something he says often happens. He said "PrimeTime Live" wanted some of the interview footage and was given permission to run it only after promising to burn the paper's logo into the picture. The syndicated "Extra" also ran the logo with the excerpts it carried Thursday night.

Some individual stations plucked the interview from a satellite and ran it without crediting the *National Enquirer*, Coz said. Shrewd if dishonest, it's a convenient way to use tabloid material without seeming to soil their hands.

In the *Los Angeles Times*, a brief Associated Press story, which made no mention of the *National Enquirer*'s role, ran Friday beneath two photos, also distributed by AP. One was a "before" shot from AP's files, the other was an "after" shot from "PrimeTime Live" that was cropped to exclude the *National Enquirer* and ABC logos. (A *Times* news editor said the photo was cropped to fit the available space.)

Coz said the anonymous donor whom Jones says paid for her surgery is not the *National Enquirer*. He said he "really didn't want to get into" whether the paper paid her for the interview, though.

Like other tabloids, the *National Enquirer* at times does pay for interviews. If it did pay Jones, ABC's broadcast of some of that material violated at least the spirit of the network's policy against paying for interviews.

"PrimeTime Live" producer Phyllis McGrady disagreed, saying Friday that even if the *National Enquirer* had paid Jones, she didn't believe that ABC running the material violated network policy or crossed a line vis-à-vis tabloids. "Would I prefer AP owned them? Yes. But I'm not going to sit here and dis the *National Enquirer*."

It's Jones who has been getting dissed since going public with her charges against Clinton, to a large degree because of her looks.

"If you turn to a cartoon in one of the magazines and you see this," she said in the TV interview, indicating her nose, "you know how they do. They focus on the big part—the ugly part—not the most attractive part. And they make it huge."

Actually, Jones looked fine before her surgery, and there's something a bit sad about her feeling compelled to transform herself to please her critics, as if she were grotesque. It's their attitudes that are grotesque.

[1998]

Private Lives and Public Prying

❖ *Predators trumped privacy here, making former tennis star Arthur Ashe their victim.*

> *Every move you make,*
> *Every step you take,*
> *I'll be watching you.*

These lyrics from the Police's 1983 song "Every Breath You Take" are especially applicable at a time when the news media and snoops have become nearly interchangeable, if not synonymous.

Democracy works in unison with an informed citizenry, and citizens can make enlightened decisions only if exposed to diverse information about a broad array of topics. In effect, then, a free press is a means to retaining democracy, a rung on a ladder. It's when that means becomes the end—when the public's right to know is used as justification for the media gratuitously abusing individual members of the public—that trouble arises.

What should we know, and when should we know it? The answers are not chiseled in stone.

If documented information about the private lives of political candidates is helpful to voters—the operative word being *documented*— that information should be reported, even if on the surface it seems merely titillating. Whether it's Arkansas Governor Bill Clinton in 1992 or Gary Hart in 1988, well-sourced information about a candidate's extramarital social life could reflect his attitudes about women, for example, and exposing that fact would make for a smarter electorate. So, if it is solid, put it in print, put it on the air. After all, candidates are asking for our trust, making them accountable to us.

Arthur Ashe and Linda Ellerbee, on the other hand, owe us nothing.

Is America now smarter having learned that Ashe is HIV positive or that Ellerbee recently had a double mastectomy? Are our lives somehow enriched by having their private pain exposed to leering public scrutiny? Does whatever public good that resulted from their disclosures—and none immediately comes to mind—outweigh the wrongs done to them? Hardly.

Both Ashe and Ellerbee came forward reluctantly, separately revealing intimate details about their health only, they said, after being faced with exposure by the newspaper USA Today. Feeling he had no other alternative, Ashe called a news conference (which was televised) so that he could make the announcement himself. Ellerbee's story came out in USA Today, after which she elaborated on it in a "Prime-Time Live" interview with her friend, Sylvia Chase.

"I wanted to get the information out on my own right," Ellerbee told Chase on ABC last Thursday night. With the tabloid spirit appearing to grow inside even legitimate journalism these days like a bulbous tumor, fat chance.

The right to privacy may be difficult to define, but, in most cases, responsible journalists should know it when they see it.

Although Ashe's days as a tennis champion are well behind him, his occasional work as a tennis commentator on TV gives him a quasi-celebrity status. And Ellerbee has remained in the public eye as an author, journalist, and TV personality. But does being famous automatically make one raw meat to be fed to media carnivores, who then regurgitate these morsels for the masses like predators feeding their young?

The famous have always had to coexist with media intrusiveness; it's an unavoidable condition. Yet even public figures should be allowed at least some fissures of privacy.

If Ashe's HIV status and Ellerbee's breast cancer should *not* have remained private—if that was their desire—then nothing, anywhere, anytime, should be private. Why not publish their X-rays too? What's more, if Ashe or Ellerbee were gay, would that also make headlines in *USA Today* merely because a segment of the public might find the information titillating?

How many others must be sacrificed on the altar of the "people's right to know" before we make a U-turn back to respectability?

Actually, the public's right to know absolutely everything about everything has limits. The media understand this and make judgments about it every day—pinching off the public's information intake, for example, each time they report stories using anonymous sources. Even the identities of public figures are protected when such people provide information on the condition of anonymity.

Moreover, the public's right to know rarely extends to the names of alleged rape victims, whose identities are routinely withheld by the media to protect them from the stigma still widely associated with rape. During the William Kennedy Smith trial, for example, NBC News and the *New York Times* were among the few legitimate news organizations that did not honor the request of Smith accuser Patricia Bowman to remain anonymous. Even after Bowman had appeared in open court and was identified by NBC and the *New York Times*, her name was omitted from nearly all news accounts. The list of abstainers included *USA Today*, even though it could be argued that Bowman— even as a vague accuser partially hidden behind a blue dot—was more of a public figure then than Arthur Ashe was when forced by *USA Today* into acknowledging that he was HIV positive.

Now, of course, we'll all be watching him. Every move he makes, every step he takes.

[1992]

First Amendment, Shmendment

◈ *Read here about the arrogance of newscasters who believe freedom of the press grants them the freedom to abuse.*

Increasingly, privacy is becoming a casualty of media wars.

The issue arose anew when a federal judge in New York chastised both the U.S. Secret Service and a crew from the CBS News series "Street Stories" involved in searching the home of a man indicted for credit-card fraud. The news crew videotaped the raid for a "Street Stories" segment that has not run.

U.S. District Court Judge Jack Weinstein said Monday: "You cannot, in search of news and profit, break into people's houses this way. It is simply intolerable."

Frame those words.

Rejecting the network's argument that it was protected by the First Amendment in this case, Weinstein ordered CBS to relinquish the videotape as evidence, predicting that it would lead to the acquittal of the defendant, who has pleaded not guilty.

Traditionally, most news organizations correctly resist subpoenas for unaired broadcast material or reporters' notes, one reason being that to acquiesce would give the impression that the press was an agent or extension of the government. Once viewed in that light, the press could not function freely. For example, if local stations had handed over their unaired footage to authorities in the aftermath of the Los Angeles riots, they would have looked like police snitches, thereby further endangering news crews and other journalists operating in the ravaged areas.

The principle is sound. Yet one could argue that in the New York case, by accompanying Secret Service agents on a raid, the CBS News crew was already acting in collusion with the government. Hence the tarnish was already on the image.

Whatever the legal outcome of this case, the ethical verdict is already in, for the CBS rationale for remaining in the suspect's apartment reeks of media arrogance. CBS claims that it had implicit permission from the defendant's wife to be present because she did not specifically ask the camera crew to leave. However, citing the woman's attempts to "shield her face" and that of her five-year-old child from the camera, Weinstein found the CBS argument "fanciful."

Well, if "Cops" can do it. . .

We've learned that the First Amendment is more than just an underpinning of our democracy, it's also a thick wall for media to hide behind. Be on your guard when the media cite the "people's right to know" as justification for violating the people's right to privacy.

Just because the media can do something—because they're entitled to under the law—doesn't necessarily mean that they should. For example, how appalling it was to see a TV camera (from KCBS-TV) move in for close-ups at the recent funeral of a motorist killed in one of those high-speed police pursuits that result in the deaths of innocent people. The "Action News" camera edged closer to get a full shot of the victim's sobbing little brother as he leaned his head on the casket. Other family members were devastated too.

The people's right to know? Whatever happened to the people's right to private grief?

All of this recalls media behavior during the so-called "Atlanta child murders" case in the early 1980s, where there were instances of TV camera operators leaning back on caskets during the funerals of young victims to get shots of the anguished families. Why didn't the families order these TV predators from the premises? Probably because they didn't know they could. Most were unsophisticated people who were easily cowed and exploited by the press.

A press that frequently gets full of itself.

Although it's easy to get heady in this work, the media's instructions are not inscribed on a stone tablet delivered from a mountaintop. God didn't appoint us to these jobs. A voice from a burning bush didn't proclaim: "Thou shalt report." Journalists are mortals drawing paychecks like everyone else. And when we trample on the rights of the people we're supposed to be serving, we don't honor our profession.

[1992]

When Ride-alongs Take
the Public for a Ride

◈ *It was good news when the U.S. Supreme Court said the public's right to know does not extend to TV the right to invade private property with cameras rolling.*

Always aiming for class, we welcome to this forum a new contributor, that renowned former British statesman William Pitt:

"The poorest man may in his cottage bid defiance to all the forces of the crown. It may be frail, its roof may shake, the wind may blow through it, the storm may enter, the rain may enter, but the king of England cannot enter."

Pitt did not mention Fox's "Cops" in his writings, of course. He issued his short speech about freedom from invasiveness a couple of centuries ago, having in mind bully boys sent by British monarchs, not police ride-alongs by U.S. news media and "reality" series that have been prominent on TV for a decade, earning huge profits because of their popularity and low overhead in monitoring law enforcement and emergency personnel.

Yet there is nothing at all musty about Pitt's words, which in spirit are as applicable today as ever.

Applicable to media.

The U.S. Supreme Court apparently thinks so, given its welcome unanimous ruling Monday that police, even when executing a search warrant, can be sued for bringing TV cameras and journalists into private homes to witness arrests or official ransackings. Still pending is whether the media can be sued in such cases.

Yet in effect the ruling bars such ride-alongs—cops surely won't chance being sued—even though they can still occur on the street and in other public places.

What's going on here? Isn't the "people's right to know" fundamental to democracy? Isn't it essential that we have free access to information in order to make decisions that maintain the republic in a fair and equitable manner? Yes. And so essential is it that we correctly bend over backward—enduring all kinds of media malfeasance—to preserve this principle. Far better a messy press that's free than a tidy one that's compliant.

Yet there are few greater conflicts than the need for free-information flow versus the rights of individuals to personal privacy. And on Monday the high court ruled in favor of the latter, giving a judicial framework to moral concepts that apparently never invade the noodles of media clodhoppers who callously trample others en route to perceived stories. To them, the camera's red light rules.

Have these people no humanity, no sense of justice, no sense of the good old golden rule about doing to others only what they would want done to themselves?

Nope.

So hooray this time for the Supreme Court. Cases in Montana and Maryland were the catalyst, the justices finding in each that the Fourth Amendment's ban on unreasonable search and seizure had been violated. The former had feds letting an unidentified CNN crew join them on a raid at a ranch in search of illegally poisoned bald eagles, the owner's comments to agents going directly from his lips—can you believe it?—to the news network's audio recorder. CNN later aired a documentary portraying the raid as a huge success, omitting that no poisoned eagles were found on the property. When the case went to trial, the rancher was acquitted of all charges except a minor offense involving pesticides.

"An amazing invasion" is how Justice Sandra Day O'Connor correctly summed up the second case. In that one, a fugitive search, federal marshals, and local deputy sheriffs brought a reporter and a photographer from the *Washington Post* with them on a wee-hours forced entry into a Rockville, Maryland, home that roused a partially clad elderly couple from bed. The man was photographed in his undershorts with a gun to his head, even though the pictures weren't published. The fugitive being sought was the couple's son, who was not there.

The history of ride-alongs is potholed with excesses just as perni-cious, two involving the former CBS News program "Street Stories." In one of these, a news crew went with Oakland cops to investigate a wife-beating report, then broadcast nationally the victim's face and name, and that of her young daughter, without the woman's permission. In another, CBS News personnel taped a suspect without identifying themselves while with federal agents and a U.S. prosecutor on a raid to a New York apartment looking for evidence of credit-card fraud.

And in 1997, "LAPD: Life on the Beat," a syndicated police ride-along series that recently ended production, aired without his an-guished family's permission gruesome pictures of the body of Michael Marich, a young actor who had died in his Hollywood apartment of an accidental drug overdose.

Brother!

Not that nine judicial black robes were needed to identify police and media as jerks for uniting in such ride-alongs where each acts as an extension of the other. When entering private property with cam-eras rolling, they have been appallingly indifferent to fundamental pri-vacy rights while presenting social and moral crises misleadingly with-out context and in the most narrow, emotional terms possible.

At their best, media ride-alongs and "reality" series convey how dili-gently these agencies perform most of the time, often at great peril. At their worst they create unholy alliances where cops and cameras join forces as a single snoop, the former getting to choreograph themselves as heroes for the lens, the latter getting access to action footage that in-evitably titillates viewers.

"Cops"—the only syndicated ride-along series still in production— says it already asks permission before entering private property. You'd have to bet, though, that other such series are bound to again spring up. The collusion potential is enormous, with "reality" series airing nothing they believe puts their partner subjects in a bad light. Doing so would cut off access. No access, no show.

Now, thanks to Monday's ruling, much of that access has been withdrawn anyway. And perhaps somewhere, William Pitt is smiling.

[1999]

Foreign News? It's All Alien
to the Networks

◆ *You often get the impression from American television that the world is flat and limited to the United States, and that anyone leaving risks falling off the edge.*

While President Clinton has been hobbling across Western Europe on his cane—hoping to shed Paula Corbin Jones while broadening his global profile and stumping for a widened North Atlantic Treaty Organization—much of U.S. television has been executing its own foreign policy. The usual one.

Neglect.

The chicken or the egg argument comes into play here. Are the networks and their affiliate stations reflecting viewer tastes or shaping those tastes, and then using that to excuse the nature of their news coverage? In either case, the result is less knowledge, not more.

Thursday morning symbolized the gap in foreign coverage between the regular broadcast networks and cable's all-news networks. After attending a meeting of new British Prime Minister Tony Blair's cabinet, the president held a press conference with Blair in London that was shown live by CNN, MSNBC, and the Fox News Channel, each of which afterward added a bit of analysis that gave the event some texture.

Same morning: ABC's "Good Morning America" gave the president's trip ninety seconds and "CBS This Morning" a minute (with reporter Bill Plante in London quizzed by anchor Jane Robelot in New York about similarities between First Lady Hillary Rodham Clinton and her British counterpart). On NBC's "Today," Clinton was almost invisible, his meeting with the British cabinet earning an anorexic fourteen seconds.

In fact, "Today's" best foreign coverage that morning came when it interviewed the young winner of the National Geography Bee, whose revelations included Mongolia being the largest landlocked country.

Wednesday was even more classic. Local newscasts in Los Angeles either ignored or barely noticed Clinton's trip, and nightly network newscasts gave it relatively short shrift, although "The CBS Evening News" outdistanced its rivals with a piece about a Dutchman's-eye-view of the historic Marshall Plan that poured billions of dollars into postwar Europe.

Moreover, the network morning shows that day treated the president's trip as a mere footnote to the Supreme Court's ruling that allows Jones to immediately pursue her $700,000 sexual harassment suit against Clinton. Although the ruling was a major story, so was Clinton's Europe trip, even with its carefully designed photo ops.

And even when not meriting banner headlines, the president has been doing some fascinating things worthy of attention in the United States. Yet there was "Today" on Wednesday, using the president's speech at The Hague in the Netherlands—commemorating the fiftieth anniversary of the Marshall Plan—mostly as a backdrop for the Supreme Court story and Jones's allegations of sexual crudity by Clinton in 1991 when he was Arkansas governor. CNN and MSNBC covered the speech live.

While "Today" gave the president's Europe trip brief mention, it devoted about ten minutes to the Jones spectacle. "Every day this will steal headlines from the president trying to do important work for the country," NBC's Tim Russert predicted Wednesday morning. A prophet, Russert on Thursday morning was on NBC's cable partner, MSNBC, speaking expansively about the Jones case.

So . . . what else is new?

It wasn't for gratuitous reasons that first ABC and then NBC unfurled themselves like Old Glory while televising the Summer

Olympics in the '80s and '90s. Although there was a scattering of hisses and boos, these networks knew the narrow interests of their primary audience.

After ranking so high on the global food chain for so long, the United States sees itself largely as the throbbing, pulsating epicenter of sentient life, a lush green oasis in a barren moonscape, and expects to remain so evermore. And no wonder, for most Americans see the world beyond this continent as largely a blur of teeming, anonymous masses, hot spots surfacing and disappearing according to the whims of the cameras.

Our ignorance is not total. We know Asia as a monolith that delivers suspicious political contributions to the Democratic party, and that Central America sends us illegal immigrants. Africa is where people with funny names slaughter other people with funny names. England is where Charles, Di, and other royals play, France is the Eiffel Tower, Russia is Yeltsin, and Sicily the homeland of Godfather clans like the Corleones.

The rest of Europe consists only of too-tangled-to-figure Bosnia and, for the moment, Poland, where that mysterious masked man, Michael Jackson, is scouting locations for a theme park.

Of course, out of camera range, out of mind. It's hard caring about or feeling connected, either historically, politically, or as humanitarians, to abstractions that we don't hear or know about.

News abroad was a UFO on newscasts even before the networks began decimating their foreign bureaus in the '80s for budgetary reasons. But now, with the exception of "The NewsHour with Jim Lehrer" on PBS, global network CNN, and, to a lesser extent, MSNBC, it's an even tougher sell.

We're constantly reminded by many in television that Americans are intolerant of foreign news. JonBenet Ramsey, other crime stories, and the sex scandal du jour are turn-ons. Beyond that, blotto. Lids get heavy, eyes glaze over.

If so, then TV, where Americans increasingly get most of their news, is at least partially responsible. And what TV does or doesn't do can have a big impact on public policy.

The less coverage of the rest of the globe, the more disconnected we feel. The less meaningful coverage of Clinton in Europe, the harder it is for him to sell his vision of Europe in the United States, where NATO might as well be the North Atlantic Titillation Organization.

Meanwhile, this month's international hot spot, Zaire, has now vanished from nearly all of TV. And likely will remain absent unless Michael Jackson visits.

[1997]

Let's Hear It (Again) for Old Glory

◆ *The mantra for U.S. television coverage of the Olympics is not just America first but America only.*

At a time when television's amazing technology is widening our view of the globe, NBC's flag-wrapped, America-first-and-only Olympics coverage is narrowing it.

Thursday morning:

"Next up," said Katie Couric, the "Today" co-host on sports duty in Barcelona, "more swimming—Nicole Haislett and Summer Sanders when we return."

Were Americans Haislett and Sanders swimming alone? You'd have thought so from the buildup, which was typical of the way NBC has often promoted U.S. athletes while either deemphasizing or outright ignoring their competition:

"Will Anita Nall come back?"

"The American quest continues when we come back."

Actually, Haislett and Sanders were in separate qualifying heats for Thursday evening's two hundred-meter individual event.

As it turned out, Haislett won her heat, edging What's-Her-Name from That Other Country but failing to swim fast enough to qualify for the finals. And Sanders, who did qualify, beat a bunch of swimmers Nobody Cares About Because They're Not American.

You can imagine what NBC is thinking: What a swell Olympics this would be Minus All Those Foreigners.

NBC's "world view" was demonstrated during its telecast of Saturday's opening ceremonies when acerbic host Bob Costas remarked that, following the 1988 Seoul Olympics, NBC needed to get out "the atlas to figure just where Barcelona was."

The good news is that NBC *has* an atlas.

Yet there was Costas Wednesday night, responding to tennis commentator Bud Collins's report about a player from Madagascar being concerned over an attempted coup in that African country, where rebels had temporarily seized the state-run radio facility. At least, Costas said later with a mocking smirk, "they were able to change the format of the station . . ."

If only it were as easy to revise NBC's jumbo jingoism. When a U.S. athlete mumbles anything even vaguely coherent, an NBC camera is there to record it. It has yet to interview a gold medalist who isn't an American citizen, however. (Surely it has the budget for interpreters.) And although NBC has practically made the national anthem its Barcelona theme song, rarely does a medals ceremony that isn't American get televised.

"The swimmers on the medal stand are getting to be a familiar sight," Costas said. U.S. swimmers, that is.

It's understandable that NBC would accentuate U.S. athletes and their accomplishments. After all, this is a U.S. network whose primary audience is American, making the U.S. team the home team. Plus, U.S. athletes are indeed piling up the medals.

Yet so overwhelmingly pro-American are most of NBC's telecasts that the network is close to eclipsing even the super-patriotic frenzy of ABC's coverage of the 1984 Los Angeles Olympics, where, according to legend, it was a bump on the head that caused boxing commentator Howard Cosell to begin speaking like Patrick Henry.

By packaging events to de-emphasize the time difference between the United States and Spain, NBC has rearranged reality to suit its own purposes, in some cases seeming to set up artificial rivalries for the sake of putting on a good show.

In Monday night's compulsories gymnastic competition for men, for example, NBC showed only the U.S. and Unified (formerly the Soviet Union) teams, creating an impression that this was a dual competition echoing the Cold War. Wrong. In addition to the first-place Unified team from the former Soviet Union, three other nations finished ahead of the United States in the standings. But they weren't shown or, until the end of the segment, even mentioned.

NBC hit a low in revisionist coverage Wednesday when it devoted the first twenty minutes of its three-hour morning Olympics block to the comeback of U.S. gymnast Kim Zmeskal en route to the Americans getting a bronze medal in the women's team competition. Zmeskal did rebound stirringly after falling on the balance beam.

However, viewers might have concluded that phantoms finished ahead of the U.S. women, for nowhere in the three-hour telecast did NBC mention that the gold and silver medals were won by the Unified and Romanian teams, respectively. It was the equivalent of withholding the name of the winning team from a story reporting a Dodgers loss.

"NBC Nightly News" caught the ethnocentric bug itself Wednesday when, after a lengthy story celebrating Zmeskal and her teammates, it added only as a footnote that the Americans "won the bronze medal against the former Soviets and the Romanians." That sounded like the Unified and Romanian teams had lost. NBC has allowed some exceptions to its red-white-and-blue coverage, notably the occasional inclusion of foreign Olympians in its sugary, melodramatic, tumultuously scored profiles of athletes. And it was uncharacteristically even-handed and liberal in its praise of non-Americans Wednesday night in coverage dominated by swimming and diving events that included Mark Lenzi's gold-medal performance in the men's springboard competition.

Yet American Crissy Ahmann-Leighton earlier let NBC down by not justifying the network's gold-medal buildup of her for the women's hundred-meter butterfly event. Although lightly advertised by NBC, Chinese swimmer Qian Hong won the gold, Ahmann-Leighton the silver.

"Are you really disappointed losing out to the Chinese woman?" the American was asked. To her credit, Ahmann-Leighton said that she was thrilled simply to win a medal. Any medal.

Just how thrilled Hong was, U.S. viewers will never know.

[1992]

A Lox Named Fox

I wouldn't mind the Fox News Channel so much if it would stop pretending to be fair and admit to spinning the news.

"There's a see-ya-later-buddy quality to this."
— Brit Hume, Fox News Channel anchor, on the collapse of Iraq's regime

TV pictures of Baghdad's fall included a U.S. soldier briefly draping an American flag over the head of a forty-foot statue of Saddam Hussein that was about to come down.

"No doubt, Al Jazeera and the others will make hay with that," "fair and balanced" Fox News Channel anchor David Asman said on Wednesday, expressing his disdain for the Qatar-based Arab satellite channel famous for its opinionated, non-Western news perspective.

When Fox reporter Simon Marks suggested from Amman, Jordan, that Arabs "on the street" may still regard Americans as invaders who manipulated these images, not as liberators, Asman snapped: "There is a certain ridiculousness to that point of view."

Whether he was right or wrong, the day's symbolism was historic on a level unrelated to politics or nationalism. When the statue of Hussein fell, an era of TV news appeared to topple with it.

There was a time, years ago, when even a network news anchor's raised eyebrow was correctly denounced as commentary. How quaint and musty that code of objectivity now seems as the war in Iraq winds down. And viewers face Fox's swirling sands of spin.

Fox is not the only cable news channel that seamlessly stitches opinion to news. It happens regularly at CNN, the self-anointed "most trusted name in news," where prominent anchor Lou Dobbs is easily irked by opinions he doesn't share and is allowed to slap down interviewees who express them. And some of MSNBC's minions are not far behind.

Yet story slanting and bombast have soared stratospherically at Rupert Murdoch's twenty-four-hour Fox channel under the guidance of former Republican political operative Roger Ailes since it was founded in 1996, ostensibly to combat bias in news. "Liberal" bias, that is.

Clearly, Fox is doing just fine in the eyes of many Americans, having passed older CNN in the ratings and made stars of some of its people. A recent viewers poll by Murdoch-owned *TV Guide* found vamping, hyperventilating, tabloid-bred Shepard Smith, of all people, tied with ABC's Peter Jennings, just ahead of CBS's Dan Rather, for second place in network anchor credibility behind NBC's Tom Brokaw.

And that self-inflating gasbag Bill O'Reilly and his "O'Reilly Factor" are now something of a national institution. He is a real hoot, at times rising to exquisite self-parody, as when interviewing Princeton's Peter Singer, who equated the lives of slain Iraqi civilians with those of Americans fighting there.

"I believe you are on the wrong side of this politically and morally," O'Reilly lectured him, "but I'm going to give you the last word." Then O'Reilly followed Singer's last word with his own: "You're doing a great disservice to your country, sir."

Where should journalists draw a line separating news from opinion? Throughout much of Fox, the question never arises.

Although its field reporters play it mostly down the middle—and that's significant—its New York anchor-interviewers are notorious for injecting their own views, nearly always conservative and supportive of the Bush administration. What's more, at times they press field reporters to agree.

Add to that an overwhelming dominance of right-of-center pundits and guests, and the result is pretty much a wall of conservative opinion.

Greta Van Susteren is generally fair and not jingoistic while anchoring her evening program. And Fox does use some liberal-stamped pundits as regulars. But they are nearly always relegated to the fringes of its programming schedule.

An exception is moderately left-of-center talk-radio host Alan Colmes, but he wears a bull's-eye on his chest. The hapless, sleepy, untelegenic Colmes is mowed down nightly by his forceful, articulate, camera-tailored, extreme-right counterpart, talk-radio star Sean Hannity, in their debates on "Hannity & Colmes."

In other words, Fox slants like a drunk who's guzzled a couple of six-packs. If only it did so honestly, calling itself the "conservative alternative" or something like that, instead of pretending to be what it's not by having its anchors deliver these relentless on-screen mantras: "We report, you decide" and "real journalism, fair and balanced." Fat chance.

Instead, a sample day this week found these Uncle Sams tenaciously bashing the French, the United Nations, Al Jazeera, and those in the media, especially the *New York Times*, questioning the war in Iraq. At Fox, that equals treason.

* "We report, you decide" on "Fox and Friends," an early-morning show whose three hosts tackle news with schmooze: "I want to know whether the *New York Times* is putting a picture of this on its cover," co-host Steve Doocy said about footage of Kurds celebrating the downfall of Hussein in northern Iraq. Meanwhile, co-host Brian Kilmeade wasn't buying "British intelligence" cited in London papers reporting that Hussein probably survived the recent U.S. air strike aimed at him. "So-called" British intelligence, he called it.

* "We report, you decide" with Asman, a former editorial writer for the *Wall Street Journal*: "What do you think of these armchair critics from the *New York Times*?" he asked a guest, adding about "gloom and doom" stories: "Have these news organizations lost all credibility for analyzing military strategy?"

* "We report, you decide" with anchor Neil Cavuto, who, like others at Fox, adopts White House and Pentagon war terminology—"the coalition of the willing"—to describe the U.S.-British-dominated war effort led by President Bush and British Prime Minister Tony Blair. "What's to stop us from just telling the French and Germans, 'To hell with you?'" Cavuto asked his pro-war guest. And exhuming a favorite

Fox target out of the blue, he asked: "Would you have been able to see this kind of closeness in war between Tony Blair and Clinton?"

* "We report, you decide" with anchor John Gibson, wondering "what the French are gonna do to try to screw up" Iraq's coming post-Hussein period. As for the UN wanting a central role in postwar reconstruction, Gibson added: "Americans think it's an absolute joke that the UN is so presumptuous to think that it could run Iraq. The idea that we would turn it over to the UN to fumble seems incomprehensible." When a Gibson guest argued that many Arabs oppose long-term U.S. involvement in postwar Iraq, he cut him off.

* "We report, you decide" with Shepard Smith on a U.S. tank killing two journalists and wounding many others when firing into Iraq's Palestine Hotel, where hundreds of foreign journalists were based: "I think it's now pretty clear . . . that snipers were on that roof . . . and by design, and in effect, journalists are being used as human shields," he said. That contradicted German freelance reporter Chris Jumpelt, who was working for Fox and on the line from Baghdad after being in the hotel when the blast came. The Pentagon claimed the tank was taking sniper fire from the hotel, something Jumpelt and other journalists disputed, but something Smith accepted. As if to undermine Jumpelt, Smith pointed out that the reporter was being "minded by Iraqis [who monitor] what he says." If true, then why ask Jumpelt about this in the first place?

As for those London press reports that Hussein likely survived the recent air strike, Smith didn't like those much either. "What do we know about this paper, the *Guardian*?" he asked about the famous daily. Later he announced that it and another London paper, the highly regarded *Independent*, were "decidedly anti-war," implying that they slanted their news reporting. He must have confused them with Fox, where objectivity is routinely dispatched like images of Saddam Hussein. See ya later, buddy.

[2003]

If You're Not for Yourself, Who Will Be for You?

❖ It's a sad state of affairs when the focus of your news is yourself.

"So tell me, Sheila, your piece in Calendar today on 'Milk and Honey,' is it a typical, well-thought-out, well-written Sheila Benson movie review?"

"Yes, it is."

"Reads well, does it?"

"Very well."

"And some of the descriptions you use?"

"Well intentioned . . . well acted . . . falls apart before its midpoint . . . atrocious upbeat ending in Jamaica."

"Those are excellent descriptions to use. And the review's length?"

"About 18 inches."

"Oh, I see. Not only a good read, but a short one. And that's on Page 15 of today's Calendar section?"

"Yes, Page 15."

"And you recommend that we all read your review?"

"Very much so."

"Well, always good reading you, pal. That's Page 15 today? We'll look for you in the paper."

"You, too."

If television devoted as much time to self-examination as self-promotion, its level of performance would improve dramatically.

Consider. If my above imaginary conversation with *Los Angeles Times* film critic Sheila Benson typically reflected even a small segment of newspaper content, most readers would revolt, after first falling apart with laughter over our pitifully transparent attempt to advertise and celebrate ourselves.

But television—like the chest-puffing politician who never stops running for office—gets away with its behavior because it has spent years shaping different expectations, accustoming us to its excesses. Just as we say, "Oh, well, that's politics," we also say, "Oh, well, that's television."

It's true that the Big Three networks are widening their promotional horizons to combat the ever-growing challenge from cable and videos. That does not mean, however, that they've abandoned making some promos the old-fashioned, deceptive way.

Take Wednesday morning, for example. Take it and shove it.

Here was an NBC "Today" show exclusive, the biggest out-and-out scoop since Channel 2 news in Los Angeles covered the 1981 wedding of its own top sportscaster at that time, Jim Hill.

Yes, "Today" could boast that no one else—including its main competitors "Good Morning America" on ABC and "CBS News This Morning"—had an interview with Maria Shriver about her documentary "Fatal Addictions," which was airing that very night.

That's Maria Shriver of NBC. That's "Fatal Addictions" on NBC.

For much of TV, the addiction is self-promotion.

The "Today" piece began with a lengthy clip from the documentary, followed by Bryant Gumbel's questioning of Shriver.

"Are we gonna have some success stories tonight?"

"Success stories . . . and a lot of pain."

Later, Gumbel ended it.

"Always good seeing you, pal. Ten o'clock tonight?"

"Yes."

You could live with this were "Today" also open to reporting about documentaries on opposing networks on the days they air. But don't hold your breath.

It's no big flash, unfortunately, when news programs (the "Today" show is produced by NBC's news division) present self-promotion as news—witness what happens on network morning shows and many local newscasts in ratings sweeps months. But it should be a big flash because it's a journalistic sell-out, a winking at ethics, a self-serving suspension of news standards.

In most cases, what occurs is a matter of an entertainment division having its will imposed on a news division. In Wednesday's case, it was a news division using itself to promote itself and one of its own: not only the documentary, but indirectly also the series Shriver stars on, "Sunday Today" and the new "Yesterday, Today & Tomorrow."

Never has there been a medium so incestuously promotional as television. So it seemed almost routine to hear anchor Morton Dean end a news segment on Thursday's "Good Morning America" by vowing that an investigative story on the new ABC News series "PrimeTime Live" that night "should shock you."

And in a space of about five minutes Wednesday morning, moreover, NBC viewers got a dose not only of Shriver, but also a Channel 4 news promo ("We get around . . ."), a promo applauding "L.A. Law's" Emmy nominations and a Maxwell House coffee commercial starring Linda Ellerbee and ever-mugging "Today" weathercaster Willard Scott. Running this commercial within the "Today" time period risks the possibility of some viewers confusing the clowning Maxwell House Willard with the clowning "Today" Willard, a mix-up that NBC seems almost to be encouraging.

But not its competitors. "Good Morning America" and "CBS This Morning" are running another version of the Maxwell House spot, one featuring only Ellerbee.

Meanwhile, "CBS This Morning" came up with a curious piece of its own Wednesday: Kathleen Sullivan interviewed the show's health specialist, Dr. Robert Arnot, and a woman named Nancy Hicks, who had nearly drowned in a river-rafting accident observed by Arnot while taping a "CBS This Morning" segment on rafting.

How is it that this obscure incident became a story on "CBS This Morning"? Because the show had footage of Arnot helping others revive Hicks. Would this have made the "CBS This Morning" lineup had the footage showed NBC's Shriver helping save Hicks? No. In that case you would have seen it on the "Today" show.

Always good seeing you, pal.

[1989]

The Blurred Lines of
Today's "Reality"

Talk about overselling a misleading concept, the "reality" label is applied to just about everything on television today—but newscasts.

How real is television "reality"?

Although TV has always indulged in wordspin, its tongue is especially slippery these days in deploying such white lies as "reality," self-serving euphemisms, and other glossy terms to deceptively market products and ideas. It's not only TV, of course. Just as real estate ads promote rickety houses as needing your "tender loving care," and clunkers formerly known as used cars are now "pre-owned," our old TV friend, the "rerun," has gained stature too.

It's now an "encore" in TV promos aimed at the public. The smart money in industry circles says viewers are less likely to reject an "encore episode" than something called a rerun. If it's an encore, in other words, it must be really swell.

As if all America had given this sucker a standing ovation and demanded its immediate return to the airwaves, and programmers were helpless to resist the will of the public.

When "encore" runs its course, do we get "pre-seen"?

Words help shape our perceptions, both in entertainment and the darker catacombs of human behavior. You don't need a TV columnist to inform you that "terrorist" fits anyone seeking to intimidate by crashing a jet into a high-rise or detonating a bomb with the intent to murder civilians. "Butcher" works here too.

But are Palestinians in the West Bank "soldiers" or "gunmen" when firing at Israeli troops rolling in on a mission of destruction? The two words have unequal moral standing.

And is the U.S. fighting a "war against terror," as the government and most media have said for nine months, or a "war against Islamists"? The latter was floated on CNN last week by the host of TV's most misleadingly titled program, "Lou Dobbs Moneyline." Showing you the money is hardly its only function.

"The enemies in this war are radical Islamics who argue that all nonbelievers in their faith must be killed," said Dobbs. Called to action by his epiphany, he announced he was dumping "war against terror" in favor of "war against Islamists."

Dobbs stressed that this was no war "against Muslims or Islam or Islamics," just "Islamists" and their allies, and that "if there were ever a time for clarity, it is now." Way to go.

But let's see. Not Islam or Islamics but "Islamists." Yeah, that's clarity. This is one gimmick that deserves to be buried, swiftly, with the pet rock. Next night the Dobbster was cautioned wisely on the air by former Defense Secretary William Cohen that trying to sever "Islamists" from Islam and Islamics may give people "the wrong idea" by appearing to indict all followers of Islam as terrorists. In other words, Dobbs can parse all he wants, but get real here. Most viewers hearing "Islamists" will think "Islamics," and extend that to every Muslim. Or is it Muslimist?

Meanwhile, the Fox News Channel is now calling Palestinian suicide bombings "homicide bombings," as if the former did not impose guilt. News-lite MSNBC has anointed itself "America's News Channel," even though most Americans don't know it from Shinola.

And until recently, the most misused term by this hemisphere's media was "politically correct," which too many Americans apply to anything they don't support. The smug assumption is that only their beliefs result from conviction, while the rest of us, with whom they disagree, are motivated solely by fear of controversy or what's in vogue at the moment.

Yet no reign lasts forever, and "politically correct" has been blasted from its throne by TV's latest overused and misused word of the century. "Reality."

Blame "An American Family," the pioneering 1973 PBS series that kept a camera on the Louds of Santa Barbara for weeks, becoming a "reality" prototype by capturing a marriage on the skids, while attracting such attention that the series was spoofed in a movie by Albert Brooks.

Nearly thirty years later, shows mislabeled "reality" are surfacing on TV like measles spots, as industry copycats fall over themselves trying to cash in on the "Survivor" phenomenon and join this CBS franchise's fast-spreading progeny.

Turning their heads are recent high ratings for "The Bachelor" on ABC (real guy, real babes, real dumb) and "The Osbournes," a highly popular MTV series that closely monitors the lives of rock star Ozzy Osbourne and his family, affirming that even daily minutiae can seduce a large audience.

These are called "reality" shows. But the concept of "reality" is as laughable here as on the tightly edited "Survivor" series. Try living your life in front of cameras and TV crews and see how real you can be.

Even funnier, though, is how show after show is now being sold to viewers as "reality," as producers and their networks embrace this fantasy the way politicians kiss babies.

Last week, for example, found ABC boasting that its two-parter "The Hamptons" was TV's "first reality miniseries." It's true that Hamptonians are, indeed, members of the human race (sort of). But in fact "The Hamptons" was nothing more than a documentary (a musty word banished from TV's promotional vocabulary), and a weak one from the usually accomplished Barbara Kopple. Far from being revolutionary, it was executed in a style used for decades by that master documentarian, Frederick Wiseman.

Meanwhile, TBS insists that more history is about to be made. Coming next month is its "Worst-Case Scenario," billed as TV's first "reality" magazine series. That is, if you call "reality" demonstrating "cool gadgets that help people avoid dangerous situations."

Or dangerous hyperbole, as in ABC News running radio promos last week saying its prime-time six-part series "Boston 24/7" offered "so much reality it's unreal."

ABC's profits are surely real. But reality in news? It's a troubling concept.

[2002]

Celebrating Fiction as Fact

◆ *As a history teacher, TV and its filmmakers earn a big fat "F" for rationalizing their gnarling of facts as "higher truth."*

As docudramas blur the line between fact and fiction, the reader is entitled to know what is history and what is twistery.
  —William Safire in *Scandalmonger*, his mostly true "novel" about early newspaper writer William Callender

How much of *Lincoln* is generally thought to be true? How much made up? This is an urgent question for any reader; and deserves as straight an answer as the writer can give.
  —Gore Vidal in his largely factual best-seller about Abraham Lincoln

I'm writing a screenplay—a psychological drama—about Bill and Hillary Clinton.

"Hilly and Billy" is told from the point of view of the Clintons' family therapist. Now, I've no idea whether the Clintons have a family therapist, but they could have, and obviously should have, so I've created one as a dramatic device that will liberate my story from the shackles of objective truth and give it dimension. In the business we call this dramatic license.

Don't get me wrong. I have nothing against facts, especially if they work for me. I have every right, however, to introduce this pivotal character in my TV biography without mentioning that he is fictional. Why?

Because I'm seeking a higher truth, dummy.

Kidding!

The ongoing issue of objective truth versus higher truth (code: fiction) simmers tepidly this week in "History vs. Hollywood," a four-part documentary on the History Channel that celebrates four movies about actual events or persons, and touches on the reality underpinning them.

What's not to celebrate? As entertainment, moviedom doesn't get any better than *MASH*, *Butch Cassidy and the Sundance Kid*, *Patton*, and *The French Connection*, each earning a one-hour episode from executive producer Susan Werbe. And what's not to like about hearing from narrator Burt Reynolds and others about how and why these movies were made.

On the other hand, this issue transcends fun, entertainment, and industry economics, given how many Americans get their history directly from movies and especially TV. And if that history is gnarled or false, as it often is? Well, you see the problem. If knowledge is strength, who needs ignorance?

Although much of history is subject to interpretation, art shouldn't exist in a truth vacuum. Those with a forum to sway opinion—which includes the crowd making movies—shouldn't be in the business of rewriting history by freely fabricating, however noble the motive. They have a responsibility not only to their art but also to the public reached by their art.

Even most absolutists agree that fudging truth in small ways to enhance a story isn't necessarily criminal if done judiciously. What's the harm in changing a time frame or altering or creating a bit of dialogue here and there? It's not the *Congressional Record* being filmed, after all. And "a movie can't be exactly what happened or it wouldn't be interesting," historian Ann Meadows noted in a *TV Times* story about the documentary series.

Higher truth, shmuth, though. Because of my background in journalism, I'm often accused of being too literal about these things. I've yet to see a movie biography's title include "the higher truth," however. Any work selling itself as history or even historical, though, owes its audience honesty.

Take the books by Safire and Vidal cited above. Although reading as history, each is titled a "novel."

In a section of *Scandalmonger* titled "Notes and Sources," Safire explains clearly where he has and hasn't taken liberties with history. In *Lincoln*, and also his historical novels *Burr* and *1876*, Vidal includes a brief "Afterword" spelling out the few characters and events he invented.

In contrast, docudramas engage in trickery when usually carrying only generic, fine-print disclaimers informing viewers that some characters may be composites and some characters and events fictionalized. Which ones? Sorry, you're on your own.

At the very least, everyone should follow the example of NBC when it made a movie of Vidal's book about the sixteenth president some years ago that it titled "Gore Vidal's Lincoln." His name above the title immediately told viewers this was his subjective view.

As a film titled "Oliver Stone's JFK" would have alerted moviegoers that on the screen—finding the CIA and even Vice President Lyndon Johnson possibly guilty of conspiring to assassinate John F. Kennedy—was nothing they could take to the bank. It was the filmmaker's own wildly speculative scenario.

Hardly adversarial in tone, meanwhile, the misleadingly titled "History vs. Hollywood" is much less a sharp critical analysis than a pumping in of collagen that adds mass.

Hardly belonging here, in fact, is *MASH*, the exceptional movie that led to an exceptional CBS sitcom, in the process surely raising no expectations that its Korean War vintage Mobile Army Surgical Hospital unit was anything beyond dark farce (and a hooded metaphor for the Vietnam War). Nor did the republic fall when Paul Newman and Robert Redford departed somewhat from the relatively obscure real outlaws they played in *Butch Cassidy and the Sundance Kid* or when the real French Connection drug case played out differently than in the action movie.

A bit dicier, though, is *Patton*, whose subject, General George S. Patton, Jr., remains a controversial military figure who generates considerable historical interest. Spanning his service in World War II, the Oscar-winning movie inflates some incidents and omits other negative ones that don't coincide with its theme of Patton's redemption, says an essay by Paul Fussell in *Past Perfect: History According to the Movies*. Fussell also is interviewed in the documentary.

And if the truth gap he cites doesn't matter, where should the line be drawn in docudrama separating history from myth?

Especially as the nation's pop historian—otherwise known as television—continues to air biographies galore. In coming weeks, that includes prime-time docudramas with subjects as diverse as Attila the Hun, the Kennedy wives, the Osmonds, dancer Bill "Bojangles" Robinson, and Ruth Gruber, a woman who brought one thousand World War II refugees across the perilous Atlantic to sanctuary in the United States.

It probably doesn't matter whether Attila was or wasn't the visionary and hotblooded hunk of a Hun he's cracked up to be in USA's gorgeously mounted nonsense. Or that a TV biography some years ago had smallish Bobby Kennedy towering over 6-foot-2 LBJ. And what functioning mind could buy scantily clad dancing girls welcoming Christopher Columbus to the "New World" in 1492, as a TV movie once depicted?

Yet popular art's portrayal of history does have an impact on the way we see ourselves and others, as anyone can testify who grew up believing that General Custer was heroic and most slaves in the United States were treated kindly by their owners.

Safire has the word for it: twistery.

[2001]

Paul Goes Home

◆ With cameras rolling, a Los Angeles anchorman revisited his old neighborhood, at once celebrating himself and affirming just how big a buffoon he had become.

Once again those news zealots at KNBC are humiliating the competition. Their latest spectacular scoop came this week.

"Tonight," KNBC news anchor Paul Moyer announced near the end of Monday's 5 P.M. newscast, "a trip to the area where I grew up in the South Bay."

A check of other stations that night revealed that, in an intolerable lapse of news judgment, not one had aired a story about Moyer's reminiscing about growing up. The embarrassment of it all: another Channel 4 exclusive.

It wasn't only Moyer who was going home again on Channel 4, however. In separate segments this week, the station was also featuring Linda Alvarez and reporter Vikki Vargas returning to their old Los Angeles neighborhoods, a bold display of reporting trumpeted in a full-page newspaper ad featuring snapshots of the trio at age five.

They were doing this, Moyer explained in a TV promo, "to see what's happened to the city we love."

A little belatedly, one would think, given their tenure on the air. Moyer in particular has been around forever. You'd have thought that before this week he'd have made a call, asked a friend, written a letter, inquired by fax, done *something*, to discover what happened to the city he loved.

On the other hand, he has been busy. Only recently, Channel 4 sent him to South-Central Los Angeles to find out what was happening there. One of the things happening there, as viewers could see from the long shots and close-ups on Channel 4, was Moyer standing on the sidewalk in his shirtsleeves while getting the skinny from the locals. The laserlike concentration. The empathy on his face. He was a bro, and they knew it.

And now, demanding that Moyer earn his estimated $1.4-million-a-year salary, Channel 4 had ordered him back to his old neighborhood to do the same kind of in-depth investigating there. It was dangerous work. But being a journalist, a pro, he came through.

"Torrance High School, my alma mater . . ."

Not only that, but the ever-probing Moyer showed viewers his year-book picture where he was listed as Paul Moir. It was clear he was on to something big. He discovered he had changed his name.

Relentless, he was now on campus, doing a stand-up with his former high school principal. And then:

"Baseball was my passion . . ."

Really on a mission now, Moyer found a picture of himself in his high school uniform. He took to the mound and displayed his pitching motion, then asked his old coach if he could have made it to the big leagues. The silly palooka. He *had* made it to the big leagues—the big leagues of journalism.

"Then there's the street where I grew up . . ."

Not only that, but across the street he found a neighbor still living in the house where he had been when Moyer was a boy. Moyer and his camera crew approached the front door. He knocked. The door opened on cue, and a couple stood there, surprise frozen on their faces as if none of this had been planned in advance. "Remember me?" Moyer asked.

"What brings you over here?" asked the man.

It was a good question, and if Moyer had been honest he would have answered that the November ratings sweeps had brought him there, as Channel 4 sought to increase its news audience by promoting its news personalities with bogus efforts like this. But he didn't give that answer, affirming that, like many of his colleagues, he has elevated obfuscation to a gleaming art.

They don't pay him the big bucks for nothing.

Meanwhile, did I ever tell you about the time when I was three years old and got my head caught in my "toidie" seat and Mommy had to have it sawed off? It happened in the city I love.

[1992]

Propping Up the Berlin Wall

◆ *When the wall tumbled, it became an immediate background prop for news anchors and others who traveled there hoping the Brandenburg Gate would translate into ratings.*

It looks very suspicious. How did the TV networks get the East German government to open its borders and raze parts of the infamous Berlin Wall during the November ratings sweeps?

Tom Brokaw was already in West Berlin with the "NBC Nightly News" when Thursday's historic announcement was made, symbolically getting the jump on his biggest competitors, Dan Rather of CBS and Peter Jennings of ABC, just as Brokaw and Jennings were left in the dust earlier this year as Rather and CNN's Bernard Shaw reported live from Beijing as tumultuous history was being made in China. Take *that*!

But not for long.

After completing their Thursday newscasts, Rather and Jennings were themselves airlifted to West Berlin, where they were shortly joined at the hip with Brokaw in front of the wall and famed Brandenburg Gate, telling their viewers, in effect: *"Ich bin ein Berliner"* . . . too!

The trio of icons was hardly needed to signify the enormity of this latest, loudest, deafening echo of glasnost. Instead, their presence mirrored the very star-filtered soul of TV news, for built into their images was the message that having them on the scene would somehow lift the level of reporting, which was already high. Not only that, but having them there would surely make them benefactors too, vividly etching them into the history none of us would ever forget.

Hereafter, when we think of East Germans finally gaining their freedom, our memories will also include Tom Brokaw, Peter Jennings, and Dan Rather.

All of the networks had been gathering their forces for accelerated coverage of East Germany, but as changes there began spiraling ever faster early last week, NBC brought in nine reporters from its international bureaus.

With the talent, why Brokaw too? "Brokaw is the focal point for NBC, the man people tune in for and focus on," David Miller, director of international news for NBC, said from New York, in effect also defining the institutionalized supremacy of anchors in newscasts. As it turned out, Brokaw had the lowest profile of the Big Three anchors Friday. "Yes, I have been on top of the wall several times . . .," he told viewers at one point.

Merely mentioning it was not sufficient for Jennings and Rather, who were shown Friday scaling the wall like Batman, almost as if it were their personal prop. There was Jennings on top. And there was Rather, climbing the wall "to have a better look at the other side." As we got a better look at him.

There too was Jennings peering into a car to interview an East Berliner. There was Rather, filling much of the TV picture himself while interviewing former West Berlin Mayor Willy Brandt, and again as he conversed with correspondent Eric Engberg at his side, before and after Engberg's story, almost as if he were being reported to personally.

The overwhelming bulk of the TV coverage last week and through the weekend consisted of stirring pictures and human-interest stories capturing the disbelief, curiosity, and euphoria of Germans on both sides of the wall. Nevertheless, it seemed almost that the various elements of television were chipping off sections of the story for their own purposes just as Germans were hacking away at the wall and carrying off chunks to keep for posterity, or sell.

On "The Pat Sajak Show" Friday, comedian Harry Shearer suggested a sales pitch: "It imprisoned people for . . . years, now it can be a valuable part of your living room."

Or TV program.

ABC's "PrimeTime Live" moved swiftly Thursday, setting up a Sam Donaldson interview with former President Reagan, who was not very responsive, as if this time the chopper was whirring inside his head. And among other things, the weekend brought "Saturday Night at the Berlin Wall with Connie Chung and Dan," minus simulations. In the curious, grating way that TV journalists interview each other, Chung in New York asked Rather in West Berlin to assess parallels between the freedom movements in East Germany and China. Later, Rather read Soviet leader Mikhail Gorbachev's mind concerning his scheduled summit meeting with President Bush: "Gorbachev is going to come to the summit and say . . ."

Meanwhile, Brokaw reappeared on NBC's "Sunday Today" with the program's co-anchor Garrick Utley, who had arrived from New York. "What's going to happen now in terms of the politics?" Utley, a veteran reporter who likely knows German affairs better than the man he was interviewing, asked Brokaw.

The most inventive interview of the TV coverage occurred locally, Thursday on KABC-TV Channel 7 when "Eyewitness News" restaurant critic Elmer Dills—who spent much of the '50s in West Berlin—was debriefed by anchors Harold Greene and Marianne Bannister.

It was Channel 7 reporter Gene Gleeson who had the most imposing assignment. Dispatched by the station to West Berlin, Gleeson delivered live telephone and satellite reports on developments at the wall throughout Thursday's Channel 7 newscasts.

Unfortunately, he was in Frankfurt.

Greene asked Gleeson for his "personal reaction." On a later newscast, Gleeson was asked by anchor Paul Moyer to gauge "the feeling of Germany . . ." Perhaps he thought Gleeson could do that by looking out the window.

Gleeson did sound amazingly perceptive and knowledgeable for someone initially miles from the story and having nothing fresh to report. More impressive, though, was the indelible imprint of the picture, for merely showing Gleeson on camera with a "live" label somehow conveyed the image that he was saying something unique. That was the idea.

Arriving in West Berlin on Friday, Gleeson too was able to stand with Brandenburg Gate visible over his shoulder, seeming—in a symbol of redundance—to occupy almost the exact spot occupied by Jennings. Nor was Steve Handelsman—flown to West Berlin in behalf of NBC-owned stations—any more illuminating in his reports on KNBC Channel 4.

Channel 7 commentator Bill Press confessed Friday to feeling unequal to describing what was happening in East Germany, saying: "It calls for a poet to respond to an event of this magnitude." However, with syndicated shows now also arriving in West Berlin to grab a piece of the story, you half expect to see Judge Wapner and Dr. Ruth doing stand-ups at the wall. "Inside Edition" anchor Bill O'Reilly arrived there with a crew late last week for a story scheduled to air tonight.

Quicker still was the cynical tabloid "A Current Affair." On Friday, anchor Maury Povich was in front of Brandenburg Gate beside an East German refugee whom the show planned to reunite with his brother on the other side of the wall for tonight's program. With Povich was reporter Gordon Elliott, who stood atop the wall and attacked it with a pickax "for the cause of democracy and freedom."

To say nothing of ratings.

[1989]

Out of the Anchor Chair, into the Fray

◈ *When Dan Rather told Larry King from Jerusalem that "Danger is my business," I knew this was a gathering of network anchors I had to write about.*

> Cannon to the right of them,
> Cannon to the left of them,
> Cannon in front of them
> Volley'd and thunder'd;
> Storm'd at with shot and shell,
> Boldly they rode and well,
> Into the jaws of Death,
> Into the mouth of Hell
> Rode the . . . network anchors.

That's not quite the way England's nineteenth century poet laureate, Alfred Tennyson, wrote "The Charge of the Light Brigade." Nor is this the Crimea.

But good morning, America, isn't that ABC's Charles Gibson, usually genial in New York, now greeting viewers as window dressing from Jerusalem? Also MSNBC anchor Brian Williams, doing triple duty from Jerusalem and Tel Aviv on NBC's "Today" and "Nightly News" as well as on his own cable newscast? And if any viewers had two TV sets tuned simultaneously to CBS and CNN at 6:30 P.M. Tuesday, they saw a pair of bush-jacketed Dan Rathers, one on videotape anchoring "The CBS Evening News" from Jerusalem, the other live from Jerusalem checking in with Larry King.

"Danger is my business," Rather informed his rapt CNN interviewer in Los Angeles.

Cameras to the right of them, cameras to the left of them, cameras in front of them, into the bloody maw of Israeli-Palestinian violence they charged: Last week ABC's Peter Jennings and NBC's Tom Brokaw jetting in for a look, this week "Good Morning America" co-host Gibson, Williams, and battle-tested Rather surging to the forefront of their networks' coverage, as President Bush on Thursday urged Israel to "halt incursions" and withdraw from territory it has recently occupied.

It's been the biggest gathering of media Mt. Rushmores abroad perhaps since the collapse of the Berlin Wall in 1989, when Rather and Jennings were airlifted to West Berlin to join at the hip with Brokaw in front of the Brandenburg Gate, before scaling that once-notorious freedom barrier on ladders like Batman.

That historic event delivered optimism, euphoria, and chills up the spine. Now comes the Middle East, where the loudest, most deafening blast of Jewish-Arab hatred in years features relentless Palestinian suicide bombings that slaughter Israeli civilians and powerful Israeli forces grinding up defiant Palestinians while rolling across the West Bank.

The presence of news stars is hardly needed to signify the enormity of what is happening now. Network anchors by tradition, though, are not only journalist-presenters but human exclamation points. The message (a questionable one) is that having them on the scene somehow lifts the level of reporting and commitment.

So naturally KABC-TV brought Los Angeles viewers Travels with Charlie by satellite early Thursday. "Can you tell us a little bit about those [control zones]?" an "Eyewitness News" anchor asked Gibson, the station's designated expert in one of those curious TV dialogues where journalists quiz each other.

Later, Jennings too interviewed Gibson. On the Fox News Channel, commentator Tony Snow interviewed anchor Brit Hume. On MSNBC, an anchor and reporter interviewed NBC's Washington bureau chief and "Meet the Press" host Tim Russert.

And on CBS Thursday morning, prior to Bush saying he will send Secretary of State Colin Powell to the Middle East, "Early Show" co-host

Jane Clayson asked Rather from New York: "Can you tell us what will break this impasse?" To his credit, Rather said he didn't know.

By then, however, he'd already etched himself into this ugly history by reporting at length Monday and Tuesday about a Palestinian car bomber whose explosive detonated prematurely at a checkpoint between East and West Jerusalem that Rather and his crew had passed moments earlier. They peeled back, camera rolling.

Although this was a relatively minor explosion that killed only the bomber, CBS played it big because of the Rather group's close proximity and because it had footage. "There was this muffled varoom," he told Clayson, assigned by her show to debrief Rather this week. "Take care, and be safe," she later told him.

"This war is not about journalists, [and] frankly too much can be made of this," Rather said after describing the bomb incident again, this time to the inquiring King.

"Does it not give you . . . a greater understanding what it's like living day after day there?" King wondered.

"You just have to walk the ground, be here, to experience it," Rather replied.

Other feet have preceded him. The shriveled foreign presence of the networks in the last decade notwithstanding, Israel is one place abroad where they still maintain bureaus, along with veterans with the talent and experience to probe beneath the surface. As in CBS correspondent Bob Simon's notably smart and balanced story on Wednesday's "60 Minutes II" about "transfer"—a proposal for removing Arabs from the area—that has gained stature among mainstream Israelis after this latest crush of suicide bombings.

It's no wonder that Simon's piece stood out.

So-called golden ages are rarely what they're said to be, and it's not as if network news ever earned the icon status amnesiacs grant it. Television by definition is too dependent on pictures to inform the public fully, moreover. And even before he passed CBS anchorship to Rather, Walter Cronkite was accurately branding TV news essentially a headline service. That title not only still applies today, but the stories beneath the headlines seem generally shorter and thinner than ever.

The networks can still rise to an epic challenge, evidenced by September 11, when they, and ABC News and Jennings in particular, distinguished themselves in the initial aftermath of terrorist attacks on the United States in coverage that Americans tuned to by the multitudes. The present Israeli-Palestinian war is another of those times when TV's combat reporting is sometimes high, given limits placed on media by the Israelis.

Yet Brokaw, Jennings, and Rather appear to be the John Cameron Swayzes of this age, destined to be rendered obsolete, along with many of their colleagues and the eroding tradition they represent, by economics, changing tastes, shrunken news holes, and the technologies of the Internet and cable.

"Dan Rather, on the scene in Jerusalem," King announced at one point Tuesday. You can't escape the feeling, however, that this brigade's war-zone charge may be one of its last.

[2002]

The Russian Roulette of
Live News Coverage

◆ *It was live, lethal, and a moment few of us would ever forget.*

"We apologize for what you saw," KNBC-TV Channel 4 anchor Kelly Lange read from a TelePrompTer early Thursday evening. "That goes for the helicopter crew too," added Bob Pettee, the station's man in the sky.

And later that evening, anchor Hal Fishman announced on KTLA-TV Channel 5: "KTLA shares with its viewers their distress."

Oh sure.

They'll never admit it—perhaps not even to themselves—but Thursday was the day Los Angeles television stations finally got what they wanted. In their heart of hearts, this was it. Oh, mama, was it ever. Not just another routine pursuit across freeways and a meek surrender. Not just some bumps and sideswipes. Not just another foot chase. Not just someone being pushed from a moving car like a sack of potatoes. Not just a child being abducted by a motorist on the lam.

Boring!

This time it was the full payoff, the big public splatter, the full shotgun-to-the-head kablooie. And you and your children, Southern California, were able to see it live. Plus, if you happened to be watching Channels 4 or 5—whose cameras were tightest on this insidious spectacle—you were able to see it real good.

That was doubly important because Channel 5 and KTTV-TV Channel 11 interrupted their afternoon children's programming to cover what turned out to be a live suicide. And Channel 4 interrupted "The Rosie O'Donnell Show," a program popular with kids as well as adults.

"You can't even trust [that] what they show you is all right for a five-year-old at four in the afternoon," Ruth Black of West Los Angeles complained bitterly by phone Thursday about Channel 4 preempting O'Donnell's show. Black said she had been watching the program with her five-year-old son, who loves it, when Channel 4 cut in.

"The guy was on fire," she said about Daniel V. Jones, who later would end his life on TV. Black said she got her son out of the room before that happened.

But what about kids watching alone?

All viewers witnessing the climax in its entirety saw Jones flee his flaming truck, his body smoking, then later return for his shotgun. He carried it to the side of the freeway overpass, bent over, put the barrel to his head and pulled the trigger. It looked like he blasted half his head away and, as he lay dead on the pavement, that everything inside was pouring out.

Best of all, no one had to see it on tedious, musty old videotape. The suicide was live!

It was on the transition loop from the Harbor Freeway to the Century Freeway that Jones carried out his macabre media stunt. Of course it was a media stunt. However poorly he was thinking otherwise, including allowing his poor dog to perish inside his fiery truck, Jones knew his media. He knew the TV choppers would be there. Why else would he have prepared a hand-scrawled banner that he rolled out on the pavement near his truck? The one reading, "HMO's are in it for the money!! Live free, love safe or die." He didn't point that message toward the skies so that birds could see it.

And how did he know that the choppers would be there? Because it's television, dummy. They're always there—creating their own gridlock in the skies while beaming live pictures of freeway chases, however trivial or non-newsy, and often not knowing who the fleeing suspect is or what he is accused of. Flatten those brain waves. Movement and action are all that matter here. And of course, capturing it live.

This indeed may be the quintessential Southern California story, as some have reported. Even broader, though, it represents the ultimate horror of the kind of live coverage that is increasingly practiced everywhere. No safety nets. No editing process. No control, just a total abrogation of journalistic responsibility. Turn on the camera, and whatever happens zooms across the airwaves as wild and out of control as a Scud missile.

Such is news driven by technology, the human contribution here limited to flipping on the switch. In other words, you cover something not because it's necessarily worth covering, but because you have the machinery to cover it. You do it live not because doing so makes journalistic sense, but because you have the technology at your command.

And with live come all the perils. What happened regarding Jones Thursday could have happened during any of the freeway chases that stations here love to gorge themselves on, for no reason other than they can. Someone could leave his car at any time and blast himself or someone else to oblivion. It could happen tomorrow or next week or next month.

Live coverage of a volatile situation is the equivalent of playing Russian roulette. Sometimes you must play anyway because the story is potentially worth the risk, as when KCOP-TV Channel 13's live chopper pictures probably saved Reginald Denny's life by showing him getting savagely beaten during the Los Angeles riots. Or when the story is as mammoth as the North Hollywood bank shootout last year.

But this time, for a story that began as a massive traffic tie-up before it spun out of control?

"Today" co-host Katie Couric sounded skeptical herself Friday morning. "Why was it worthy of live coverage in your estimation?" she asked KCOP news director Steve Cohen. "A man on the freeway with a gun—I don't think anyone can argue that isn't newsworthy on the face," he replied. Yes, but newsworthy to what extent? Hardly newsworthy enough, even on the face of it, for the kind of live coverage that would end so disastrously.

Couric said no one from Channel 4, NBC's station here, would appear on "Today" to talk about the incident. KNBC officials said later that was company policy. If so, it's a cowardly policy that enables the station to avoid being confronted publicly about its misdeeds.

It seemed to take only minutes after Jones's suicide before it became grist for talk radio. A caller to one program argued Thursday evening on behalf of the TV coverage of the suicide: "It happened so fast, they couldn't do anything." Which is exactly the danger of live coverage.

Putting a stopwatch to a tape of Channel 5's coverage shows that eleven seconds elapsed from when Jones removed his shotgun ("There he has his gun now," veteran Stan Chambers reported) to the moment that he pulled the trigger. If that wasn't time enough to pull back a chopper or cut back to the studio, the camera shouldn't have been there in the first place.

Or perhaps something else was happening. "Many of us became observers instead of journalists," Channel 13's Cohen said on Channel 5 Friday morning.

Even as protests against violence on TV appear to surge, our capacity to tolerate and even enjoy it seems to be growing still faster. Although many are outraged by Thursday's coverage, probably just as many found it compelling, so riveting that they couldn't turn away. If so, they are as much at fault as the stations that served it to them.

So how high does the bar go from here?

It was only a few years ago that a producer of a notorious Japanese game show known for subjecting contestants to extreme ridicule and humiliation was asked in an interview how he planned to meet the rising expectations of viewers. "Someday we might have to kill somebody," he said without smiling.

Appetites do have to be fed. And so you wonder, in a U.S. society whose pop culture has already absorbed the likes of Jerry Springer and his daily slugfests, real or fake, what happens next? Will the televised suicide of Daniel V. Jones be a lesson learned by both media and viewers or will we swallow it and expect something more and even bigger next time?

As for those Channel 4 and Channel 5 apologies, the best one they could make—the only meaningful one—is to cease and desist.

[1998]

To Air Is Human, Especially When It's Live

◈ *War is dangerous, and so is its coverage when stories are driven less by news judgment than by technology.*

Living with "live" television can be perilous.

That applied in 1998 to widely telecast pictures in Los Angeles of a suicidal man checking out with a shotgun blast to the head on a freeway overpass.

Just as it applied to those controversial propaganda videos from Osama bin Laden's Al Qaeda terrorist apparatus beamed to the United States by the major networks and cable news channels as they were being shown to the Middle East on Al Jazeera, the Arabic TV operation based in tiny Qatar.

Obviously unrelated is the substance of these stories that are separated by three years. The direct connection is elsewhere—in how they were processed instantaneously for public consumption. They were sent to viewers unscreened. No safety nets. No editing process. No control.

The game—played ever more often in newscasts during the last two decades—is called Russian roulette. In other words, TV squeezes its trigger and hopes there's no bullet in the chamber.

Why do experienced journalists telecast unscreened material in volatile situations? Because they can, and because they are driven by a powerful herd instinct, the one urging them to beat or at least keep astride of the competition and not be left behind. Just as their competitors heed the same urge in keeping pace with them.

Such is news on TV these days, increasingly driven by technology, the human contribution limited mainly to flipping on the switch. You cover something live not because you have knowledge that it's worthy or safe to do so, but because you have the machinery. You habitually go live not because it necessarily makes journalistic sense but because you have the right toys at your command.

TV news executives pledged across the board last week, however, that future Al Qaeda videos accessible to them will be highly edited or paraphrased, if aired at all. And indeed, a third Al Qaeda video, carried by Al Jazeera Saturday, was not aired live in the United States, newscasters opting either to omit it or run pared-down portions later. Why the change of heart?

The epiphany was delivered by National Security Adviser Condoleezza Rice, warning that taped statements from bin Laden and his associates could contain coded calls to action or other messages intended for Al Qaeda terrorists possibly still operating in the United States. Few of us thought of that when endorsing the TV statements being shown to U.S. viewers.

There are two issues here.

One relates to the high wire U.S. media always walk in wartime while at once seeking to report independently yet not endanger lives or compromise their nation's military efforts. This tug of war between the need to know and the need to keep secret is bound to intensify as the present conflict drags on.

Journalists have an obligation to their nation but also to a free flow of information, as much as that is possible during war. Americans have the right to see for themselves whom they are fighting, for example, and watching bin Laden and others vow further violence provided at least a glimpse into the soul of terrorism.

The second issue relates to the rush to report. Given the obvious unknowns here, it was not essential or wise for TV to speed blindly around a hairpin curve and show these videos live.

Errors were inevitable. ABC News misspoke, for example, when introducing the initial video featuring bin Laden, saying it was from the Taliban and giving the impression it was in response to the initial airstrikes against Afghanistan. Some minutes passed before anchor Peter Jennings corrected that, saying the source was Al Qaeda and the taping done apparently in advance of the air assault.

This new restraint on showing future Al Qaeda videos will not extend to other areas of war coverage, of course, live telecasting being too deeply ingrained in the culture for cutbacks at this late stage.

On the battlefront abroad, here were other live camera moments:

"This appears to be . . ."

"We're not sure what this is."

"This is raw footage that you're watching, and we're seeing it for the first time along with you."

With the press still largely severed from the war and meaningful footage, moreover, expect more of what happened last week when MSNBC went to live night-scope coverage in northern Afghanistan. It was here where correspondent Kerry Sanders reported that he and his crew may have come under fire, from unknown sources, while covering the air assault from afar.

There he was, low on a rooftop, in blurry green, telling anchor Rick Sanchez by videophone about a shot being "directed in this area."

And there was Sanchez advising him to be careful. And when MSNBC reran the same report later, with added live night-scope footage of Sanders standing safely with two members of the anti-Taliban Northern Alliance, Sanchez gave him this thumbs up: "You and I have been friends for a long time. You had me worried out there."

There it was, live from the front (almost), the war (almost), tumult (almost) right up to the millisecond.

This is not in any way to diminish the real threat to reporters covering wars, only to point out that danger exists too in knee-jerk live coverage. From Afghanistan to suicides on Los Angeles freeways.

[2001]

Live From Iraq, Ready or Not

◆ *Saddam or faux Saddam? TV's inquiring minds couldn't decide.*

"War-talk" here again.

Pictures and on-the-spot reporting from Iraq remain indelibly dramatic and powerful, capturing combat in ways that are nothing less than historic. Along with Iraq, war reporting will never be the same.

Problems arise, however, when instant buzz and speculation from the war front assume gargantuan life.

As they did through some of the weekend when America's hair-trigger cable news channels again dwelled obsessively on whether Saddam Hussein was alive—making him the war's superstar even as his capital was being bashed—after lasering in on the discovery of "suspicious-looking" white powder near Baghdad. Reported on TV with great urgency Friday, was this to be conclusive proof that Hussein was hiding weapons of mass destruction?

"Will you win the war without finding its cause?" a reporter asked during a central command briefing Saturday, after the coverage had turned out to be more suspicious than the powder.

Give the war reporting its due. Embedded journalists and instant drama will be the media story emerging from this war, and there's no question that technology is more under control now than during the Gulf War in 1991 when wailing sirens and newscasts became a single voice. Yet what we're getting now affirms that the gap separating news and reporting of news—the pause that's needed to double-check and evaluate—has not only drastically narrowed but in some cases has been completely erased. The danger comes when stories begin this way: "Unconfirmed reports . . ."

The operative question: What don't they know, and when will they report it?

If a single paragraph could epitomize the folly of some of TV's live, minute-by-minute, report-everything-they-hear-when-they-hear-it coverage, this would be it:

Dramatic developments in Iraq today as sources say U.S. troops have found thousands and thousands of boxes of suspicious-looking white powder at an industrial site south of Baghdad with documents in Arabic saying how to engage in chemical warfare that proves Saddam Hussein has weapons of mass destruction that he may no longer have because we're now being told this is not a nuclear, biological training center and the boxes of white powder are explosives and not chemical agents although we're now being told that the boxes do not contain explosives but talcum powder that we're now being told is related to a plan to infect the United States with itchy rashes of mass destruction.

Live reporting—whether a gimmick to seduce and sucker viewers or when stories are rushed on the air perilously merely to beat the competition—has been one of the uglier warts on the TV news landscape for years.

But what's to worry? If the reporting process itself is the story, as the rationale goes, it's unimportant that massive errors are made while the story is gathered. If there is a story. That applied also to the Hussein hubbub that billowed like a mushroom cloud from footage of an unannounced address by him exhorting Iraqis to resist the U.S.-led advance on Baghdad. The statement he read for Iraqi TV referred to the March 23 capture of a U.S. Apache chopper, suggesting that he survived an earlier U.S. air strike aimed at killing him, his sons, and other regime leaders who were thought to have gathered in a Baghdad bunker.

So crank up the speculation and roll that tape, again and again and again throughout the day, so that TV's stoniest chin-strokers can mass in front of the camera and again apply their guesswork to this dead-or-alive hypothesis.

But wait.

Back to that shortly, for now on the screen was bonus Saddam, video-tape of him in his black beret and military uniform amid a throng of wor-shipful Iraqis who were euphoric—or pretending to be euphoric—about being near him as he strolled in downtown Iraq. Some came up and kissed his hand.

So bring back the chin-strokers.

It had to be a body double instead of Saddam, some insisted, be-cause the real Saddam fears being touched by ordinary Iraqis. But were they ordinary Iraqis? Couldn't they have been loyalists disguised as or-dinary Iraqis? Yet if they were ordinary Iraqis, perhaps they were pre-tending to kiss his hand. Even more insidious, how do we know that was really his hand? If not a fake Saddam, in other words, a fake hand.

So let's take a closer look, and roll that tape again, again and again and again, along with more speculation.

If it is Saddam, when was the tape made? Was that smoke rising in the background from recent U.S. bombing or from trenches filled with oil and set ablaze by Iraqis as a defense against U.S. bombing? Or was it a smoke bomb? Of course, the news channels could have delayed this in-depth analysis until U.S. government experts had weighed in, but the clock was ticking, so what were they to do?

"There is no way of knowing if it really is or isn't Saddam," Fox News Channel anchor Linda Vester said. "And if it is him, what will the U.S. do about it."

The bigger issue: Was that really Linda Vester?

[2003]

Publicity, Thy Name
Is Schwarzenegger

◈ *Long before he campaigned for California governor, there was no terminating Arnold Schwarzenegger's TV time on behalf of himself or the willingness of star-struck entertainment reporters to be manipulated by him.*

"The movie is a 10." That was Arnold Schwarzenegger's brutally candid appraisal of his own new film, *Last Action Hero*, delivered to a rapt Sam Rubin on Friday's edition of "The KTLA Morning News."

Schwarzenegger's live, infomercial-style sitting with entertainment reporter Rubin—who at times looked poised to climb up on his subject's lap and purr—was yet another notch in Arnold's media belt, affirming his genius at manipulating opinion about himself and his movies. You had the feeling that if the admiring Rubin could have managed it, he would have bronzed Schwarzenegger on the spot.

Although celebrityhood has always opened doors, no one wields it as artfully as Schwarzenegger. When working the media—particularly the willing television crowd—no one matches his shrewdness. Not first runner-up Madonna. Not overbearing Tom and Roseanne. Not hammy boxing monologuist Don King.

Because of his remarkable ability to charm and flatter his media marks while using them, Schwarzenegger the self-promoter operates in a rare stratosphere. His true brawn is his brain. On some level, reporters surely know when they're being Schwarzeneggered. As if having an out-of body experience, though, they are powerless to stop the seduction. Nor would most want to.

Perhaps more than any other show-biz entrepreneur, Schwarzenegger has X-ray vision into the media's symbiotic soul—understanding the willingness of many to surrender themselves, for example, in exchange for a few moments of "good TV." In Schwarzenegger's case, this means TV people getting a fame rub-off from one of the most popular and charismatic figures on the globe.

Earlier last week, Schwarzenegger granted KNBC-TV movie critic David Sheehan an audience along with an advance screening of *Last Action Hero*. Sheehan's pal-to-pal musings with Arnold about the movie aired on the Channel 4 news. And, predictably, so did the rave review.

Schwarzenegger has been running this con for years. And Friday it was Rubin who was summoned, as he and Conan the Cajoler had a televised breakfast together at Arnold's own restaurant, whose name was prominently bannered for the camera. Aired live in two parts, during the 7 A.M. and 8 A.M. segments, the verbal combat was bloodcurdling.

"You have a great personality," Schwarzenegger snarled at Rubin.

Rubin angrily countered by naming some of the Fabulous Big Names who were set to appear at Sunday's Westwood premiere of *Last Action Hero*.

"I think it will be a spectacular," Schwarzenegger stubbornly argued.

"You seem to establish a connection with your fans," Rubin viciously shot back.

"It's really the fans who lift you to this pedestal," Schwarzenegger blasted. Before Rubin could recover from the ferocity of this counterattack, Arnold added, "This is the best movie I've ever done."

Whoa! No wonder viewers complain about excessive violence on television. Only the ceremonial exchange of peace offerings remained, with Schwarzenegger giving Rubin a *Last Action Hero* cap and T-shirt, and Rubin presenting Arnold a cap bearing the title of a coming Channel 5 series.

Cut to the KTLA studio, where anchors Barbara Beck and Carlos Amezcua displayed their own *Last Action Hero* hats and T-shirts, especially appropriate attire for Amezcua, who has a cameo role in the movie.

"The KTLA Morning News" personalities can be a very funny, refreshingly unpompous bunch. But their smart-alecky irreverence and
self-effacement are often a device to euphemize their own show's
puffery and self-adulation, as if making fun of what they do somehow
hides what they do. It doesn't.

Earlier in the breakfast, Rubin praised the way Schwarzenegger
cut his food. He handed his own omelet to the actor, who promptly cut
it for him. "Do you want me to feed you too?" Schwarzenegger asked.

No, Arnold, you'd already done that.

[1993]

The Day the World Shattered

As Disney's commanders-in-chief know, war is hell when there's a Hollywood movie to promote on the deck of an aircraft carrier.

Pearl Harbor.

This was no drill. They came in high, they came in low. They came in waves, they came in formations, they came in twos and threes past the mist-ringed purple mountains, winging toward their targets, one after the other in rapid succession, swooping through the clouds like vampire bats. They dove, they circled, they hovered. They made run after run, delivering their loads, creating concussions and nerve-jangling cacophonies that sucked life from the air. They attacked, they strafed, pursuing their manifest destiny with fanatical dedication for this apocalypse, this day that will live in infamy.

But enough about the media.

They came to Hawaii from the mainland U.S., Canada, and Europe. And thanks to these swarming hordes of shameless junketeers, TV and radio buzz over Disney's $140-million *Pearl Harbor* movie crescendoed deafeningly this week, just in time for its opening in theaters today.

Memorial Day weekend aside, how bizarre that Pearl Harbor TV specials and documentaries galore—including dueling ones on ABC and NBC on Saturday night—are showing up just now, when the sixtieth anniversary of the actual attack is more than six months away. It's as if these TV productions, too, were responding to the heavily advertised launch of a Hollywood movie on hoping to bask in its publicity.

Sound general quarters!

Although this spin had been building for some time, its apex was Monday night's shrewdly choreographed-for-cameras $5-million extravaganza aboard the *USS John C. Stennis*, with media the willing color guard. The Navy aircraft carrier was brought to Pearl Harbor from San Diego for media frolics with celebs and to be transformed into an open-air theater on behalf of Disney, with stadium seating for a special premiere of *Pearl Harbor* that was carefully tailored for consumption by a pliant press.

Give Disney credit for knowing what turns on these media suckers and suck-ups, whose snap-tos and crisp salutes to Hollywood made this cosmic stunt possible. Disney made them sob by wrapping *Pearl Harbor* in Old Glory. It brought in Faith Hill to belt out the National Anthem. It had Navy SEALs parachute from a Black Hawk helicopter. It had F-15 fighters fly above the carrier in a "missing man" formation. It paraded before teary media eyes, radio mikes, and TV lenses aged survivors of the December 7, 1941, Japanese attack that killed more than 2,400 Americans and drew the United States into World War II.

Disney didn't stop there. It set off twenty minutes of massive fireworks. It displayed a vintage B-25 bomber and a P-40 fighter. It put out white party tents and brought in the Honolulu Symphony Pops Orchestra. It rolled out co-stars Ben Affleck and Kate Beckinsale like red carpets, and delivered them, along with producer Jerry Bruckheimer, director Michael Bay and the invited veterans, for interview after interview before and after this sneak peek at *Pearl Harbor* before two thousand on the carrier's 4.5-acre flight deck.

When the black, oily smoke had cleared, TV's lumps in the throat did what Disney expected them to do, what Disney had invited them there to do. They fell all apart.

"This has been a very moving and patriotic moment for me," Disney-owned KABC's entertainment reporter, George Pennacchio, blubbered live on deck after *Pearl Harbor*.

"To those veterans of the war, Hollywood again salutes you," KCAL's overcome Cary Berglund proclaimed live.

"Have you ever seen anything like this?" KTTV's Lisa Joyner gushed live to *Pearl Harbor* actress James King. Earlier Joyner had squealed like a thirteen-year-old groupie when showing viewers snap-shots of herself with Bruckheimer and the handsome Affleck.

ABC's "Good Morning America" too kissed Disney butt by run-ning a lengthy segment on *Pearl Harbor* each day this week. Co-host Diane Sawyer anointed it "the movie event of the summer," and news correspondent Jack Ford went further, granting it biblical rank as "the biggest summer blockbuster of all time."

All this before it opened.

ABC's "World News Tonight" came through too as anchor Peter Jen-nings slipped in a *Pearl Harbor* mention when introducing a story about a veteran who began composing a letter to his family while below deck of the USS *New Orleans* as it was under attack that Sunday morning. Was this story, too, designed to promote *Pearl Harbor*? The same ques-tion applies to the ABC News website using scenes from *Pearl Harbor* to illustrate its big spread on the Japanese attack. Does ABC News do Memorial Day–timed stories only about U.S. wars or military actions featured in Disney movies? Skeptics have reason to wonder about that and about U.S. sailors in whites somehow being at the front of the au-dience cheering outdoors for Thursday's "Good Morning America."

Cross-promotion—the chauvinistic practice of creating stories that favor one's own—was hardly invented by ABC News. If "CBS This Morning" or that network's stations had been faced with reporting the 1941 Pearl Harbor attack, for example, they'd have gotten to it only af-ter covering "Survivor."

Disney's ducks weren't the only quackers on the *John C. Stennis* this week, either. The media jetted in from all points and companies. In addition to Joyner and Berglund, L.A.'s non-Disney TV contingent included KNBC's Gordon Tokumatsu and KTLA's Sam Rubin, whose live *Pearl Harbor* duty ended with tape of him learning the hula.

Earlier Rubin had come up with the question of the event when asking Hill if the movie's "over-the-top hoopla" was "a little too much." Which was like wondering if L.A. freeways had excessive traffic.

It's hardly news when TV reporters on the entertainment beat behave like fans or adoring members of the industry's extended family instead of as detached observers. That certainly was the case this week when they moored themselves to *Pearl Harbor,* implying that it was motivated much less by profit than high ideals, and that all associated with the movie pitched in as a matter of honor.

Director Bay took part "primarily out of a sense of duty," Berglund reported, adding that cast member Tom Sizemore (featured also in *Saving Private Ryan*) is "again proud to honor the men and women of World War II." ABC's Ford found Affleck "moved by the message of this story," reporting also that Bay and Bruckheimer were "touched by their conversations with the veterans." Touched most, surely, will be Disney if it succeeds in convincing Americans that passing up *Pearl Harbor* would be bordering on unpatriotic. "We're getting ten times the cost of this thing in publicity," Bruckheimer told the trade paper *Variety.*

There were mentions from time to time this week of the movie's alleged historical flaws and fears expressed by the Japanese Americans Citizens League that it would reawaken anti-Japanese sentiment in the United States. But who did shipboard media turn to most often for expert testimony on the history behind the attack, including long-standing rumors that President Roosevelt had expected it? None other than an actor in *Pearl Harbor.*

Tokumatsu to Dan Aykroyd: "How much did Roosevelt know?" A better question: How much does Aykroyd know?

After all of this, before shipping home from the carrier, Rubin gave *Pearl Harbor* a "B−," a much higher grade than he and his colleagues earned by being there.

[2001]

II

Trash, You Rock . . . *Sometimes*

The most painful thing about being a television critic is watching programs you intensely dislike. *Oy!*

Take daytime talk shows, which have a proud tradition of humiliation and exploitation for profit. Oprah Winfrey's show and a few others aside, they flourished until fairly recently as television's trailer trash, locating freaky little American subcultures and granting them undue prominence through camera exposure.

These shows and their shameless hosts profited by depicting America as teeming with grimy lowbrows. How to account for their popularity? My theory: many of their viewers were mirror images of the goofy guests, seeing in them affirmation of their own resentment and dark view of the United States as a land where betrayal by those you trusted—close friends or family members— was part of everyday life.

No wonder that after watching the daytime shows cited in this section you felt dirty all over, as if emerging from a sewer.

The stench is as great when television looks the other way when it comes to imposing pain or destruction on animals, whether for food, clothing, entertainment, or so-called sport. Animals are routinely exploited and abused by humans in myriad ways—TV's

fraudulent, profiteering Steve Irwin ("The Crocodile Hunter")
heading this list—and I'm outraged when those on camera fail to
speak for creatures who can't speak for themselves. A piece in this
section addresses televised hunting and the hypocrisy of those who
gratuitously slaughter animals they claim to admire and respect.

In other words, when it comes to double standards, welcome to
TV-style capitalism.

Years ago someone said you'd have to drive a stake through his
heart to get rid of Richard Nixon. That resilience applies also to
other notorious figures, from NBA bad boy Dennis Rodman to White
House bad girl Monica Lewinsky, to say nothing of the bubba she
serviced in the Oval Office.

The principle at work here is a simple one: no matter whom you
are or what you've done, there may be a trashy comeback in your
future. You'll always collect a paycheck—frequently via the small
screen—if you can make a buck for someone else. As I mention, this
cynical union of infamy and profit is the very essence of bad
television.

Yet—go figure—some television is *best* when it's bad. Well, not
just bad, but really, *really* bad, as in atrociously, transcendently,
you-can't-believe-how-awful-this-sucker-is bad. In other words, we're
talking trash so excruciating that it's quite wonderful, all of it the
yield of assorted boobs and kazoos masquerading as literati.

The programs described at the end of this section come under
that category, and I include them because writing about them was
much more fun than watching them.

Ratting on Bill Was Her Duty

Ever phony and sanctimonious, Sally Jessy Raphael was some piece of work as a talk show host.

Oh, my. What's a poor talk show host to do?

It's always something. Take Sally Jessy (There's Nothing She Won't Do for Ratings) Raphael, for example.

Imagine her dilemma. On July 13, the first day of the Democratic National Convention, a public relations firm faxed her office a release about a woman (not Gennifer Flowers) claiming to have had an affair with Arkansas Governor Bill Clinton, who on Thursday was named the party's presidential nominee. She and her staff "went back and forth" about it, Sally said on Friday's installment of her syndicated show. "We do this with a bit of skepticism and a bit of reluctance," she said with a sigh. You could feel her anguish, her humanity.

But look, she had to stifle her own pain and do what was best for America. "Does the American public really care about the private lives of politicians?" she asked with weighty concern in introducing Sally Perdue, who said she was a fifty-three-year-old former Miss Arkansas and Pine Bluff mayoral candidate who had a three-and-a-half-month affair with Clinton nine years ago.

Actually, Perdue added, "it wasn't an affair, it was an encounter." Ooooooh, those are even worse.

Raphael immediately attacked. "Would you say you were the pursuer or he was the pursuer? . . . What I'm understanding is that you feel that he dropped you." You just knew that throughout America, from the biggest city to the smallest hamlet, people were caring.

Perdue said she was appearing on "Sally Jessy Raphael" because she didn't want her story told in a "slimy or bimbo way." Raphael, who shrinks at bad taste, nodded. Perdue also said that she was worried that Republicans would exploit her story. To avoid that, apparently, she was telling it to millions of TV viewers.

Someone in the audience asked Perdue if she wasn't damaging Clinton's candidacy. She said she would never do that. She urged Americans to vote for neither Democrats nor Republicans.

Moving in again, Raphael asked Perdue if Clinton really supported women's issues. Perdue, now firmly established as an expert on Clinton, was doubtful. "I think he's saying what people want to hear," she said.

Raphael got Perdue's daughter on the phone. The daughter lauded her mother. Raphael introduced a friend of Perdue, who lauded her.

But now Raphael was really getting tough. "We've done research," she said, citing "reports" of Perdue "extorting people for sexual blackmail." Perdue called those "very incorrect."

Some viewers may have wondered why Raphael would provide a stage for Perdue's accusations if there were questions about Perdue's own credibility in sexual matters. Raphael gave no clue, but perhaps she had shrewdly allowed Perdue to smear Clinton's character so that she could smear Perdue's character. In tabloid terms, a two-smear show is rated a blockbuster.

Raphael then introduced Rita Jenrette, a former Playboy model and ex-wife of a congressman, who immediately accused Perdue and the show of unfairly slurring Clinton. Jenrette suggested that instead of worrying about the nine-year-old alleged sexual exploits of candidates, America should be concerned about the national deficit and other epic issues. Jenrette was obviously out of touch, and Raphael let her know it.

"I can't tell you . . . how many times I have heard people say, 'I would not vote for a man who has cheated.'" Raphael suffered a momentary lapse of confidence: "It's quite possible that I don't have my pulse on the American people." She quickly recovered. "But I don't think so."

Perdue also lit into Jenrette. "I didn't pose for *Playboy*," she said.

"I'm sure you didn't," Jenrette replied.

"I was asked," Perdue shot back.

The audience was abuzz. "I urge you to maintain some decorum," said Raphael, for whom decorum is essential. The hour's quality was really soaring when Raphael introduced *Spy Magazine* writer Rudy Maxa, who proceeded to share his suspicions about the timing of Perdue's appearance on Raphael's show and the manner in which her story surfaced. "I mean, people just don't fall out of the heavens during convention week."

Mr. Cynic—just what an earnest, just-serving-America-the-best-she-could talk show host didn't need.

Raphael now was in the audience with Phyllis Goldberg, who had written a story about Perdue in the *National Alliance*, an alternative New York newspaper. Goldberg said the paper paid Perdue's air fare to New York so that she could share her Clinton story with other media. "We think he's abused his power in this situation," she said.

The *National Alliance* is an "independent" paper with an "anti-two party bent," executive editor Jackie Salit said later by phone from New York. The paper is supporting Lenora Fulani for president, Salit said. Fulani is a sharp critic of Clinton.

Is it just possible that the paper planted Perdue on "Sally Jessy Raphael" to make its case against major party presidential candidates at a time when Clinton was about to become the Democrats' standard-bearer? Did Raphael's staff fail to check that out? Or did they check it out and just not care?

In any event, Raphael ended the hour obviously assured she had done a patriotic public service by sharing Perdue's unsubstantiated story with the nation. "I tend to believe," she said, very seriously, "that there are still a great many people who look at moral character."

So, if you too want to go on her show and say you slept with a major political figure—Margaret Thatcher, Boris Yeltsin, or anyone else—send her a fax. Painful as it is for her, she's only doing her job.

[1992]

Wanna Confess? Call Montel

🔖 *Early on, serial taper Montel Williams mastered the art of exploiting while pretending to be a good samaritan.*

You say you want to be a television star? You need the attention? You crave the attention? But you're a nobody, a small fry no one knows or cares about?

Don't despair. You can still have your moment of fame in front of the camera. There's always "The Montel Williams Show."

Here's the plan: Contact the syndicated daytime talk series by calling the New York 800 number it lists on the screen. Ask for the producers. If there's resistance, mention that you have an incredible story that Williams will desperately want to put on TV, but that if he isn't interested you'll contact Sally Jessy or Oprah or Phil or Geraldo. Then you deliver the whammy.

You're a serial rapist.

Your story is that you've raped more than ninety women in a two-year period, that you know it's wrong, but you can't stop yourself. Maybe others will stop you. So you want to confess on national television, with Williams as your confessor.

Yes, yes, it's bizarre. You're groaning because you don't believe that anyone would fall for it, that anyone would be dense enough—or irresponsible enough—to grant you airtime based on such an unproved story. It would never work. Why *would* it work?

Because this is television, dummy.

You're still not convinced. After all, Williams is a powerful TV host with a big staff that would check you out. If you've raped so many women, surely at least some of them would have blabbed. Reports would have been made, investigations made. The cops would have records. You'd be exposed as a fraud. Nah, it would never work.

Ah, but here's the genius of the plan. The victims, the more than ninety women you claim to have raped? Your story is that all of them were prostitutes, women who wouldn't be expected to press charges or even complain to police about being sexually assaulted. So no paper trail. You're home free.

And what if the producers still hesitate? Then play your ace: You're not just any serial rapist. You're a serial rapist who is HIV positive.

Congratulations. You've just made it to "The Montel Williams Show." Where do we send the limo?

Is that roughly how the man—whom police identify as thirty-seven-year-old Jerome Stanfield of Baltimore—earned himself a shot with Williams titled "Confessions of a Self-Proclaimed Serial Rapist," a two-parter that aired Monday and Tuesday.

Is "Jerome," as he was identified by Williams, a phony? We don't know. The problem is that "The Montel Williams Show" doesn't know, either. But Jerome does. Immediately after taping the two segments on March 16, he changed his story and told authorities he hadn't raped anyone.

Minor detail. When the prospect of compelling television looms— television that feeds our terror over violent crime—worries about possible misinformation are elbowed into the background. So "Confessions of a Self-Proclaimed Serial Rapist" hit the airwaves as scheduled.

"The show is not doing this to make a statement as far as this man's guilt or innocence," a Williams spokesperson said. In other words, if you've got an exploitable story, even a nutcake's one that can't be verified, we'll put it on. But only after doing the responsible thing by checking to see if your name, age, and address are correct (which the Williams show said it did with Stanfield).

Misinformation? "Hoax" is the word applied to this spectacle by Officer Doug Price, spokesman for the police in Baltimore, the city where, Stanfield told Williams and a national TV audience, he terrorized prostitutes.

"I raped over ninety prostitutes at gunpoint and knifepoint," Stanfield said, convincingly. "Something inside would say I have to do this." He was joined on stage later by a woman identified as his sister, a defense attorney, a former hooker who claimed to have been raped by a number of men (but not Stanfield), and someone from Johns Hopkins University, an institution that Stanfield said had treated him for depression.

Williams said Jerome told him he had not raped since learning in 1992 that he was HIV positive. But he could rape again, said Williams, obviously frustrated. "I have a man here on the stage who says 'I want help, I want you to get me off the street, I want you to stop me from doing this,' and we can't even put him in jail. We can't lock him up. Why?"

One reason is Stanfield now says he didn't do it, and police say they have no evidence of him, or anyone else, doing what he says he did.

Part two of "Confessions of a Self-Proclaimed Serial Rapist" ended with a flourish. Williams urged Stanfield to get help. After hesitating, Stanfield said he would. Williams then summoned his own security men, who escorted Jerome up the center aisle of the packed Times Square studio as the audience applauded. Then came a shot of Stanfield being greeted downstairs by a man who identified himself as a New York City police detective, then a shot of a car speeding away, and the sound of a police siren, then a shot of Williams, getting a standing ovation from his studio audience.

Very dramatic.

But Stanfield immediately "recanted" to a Manhattan deputy district attorney and to both New York and Baltimore police detectives, spokesman Price said by phone. He said that the Baltimore detectives were in the studio for the taping after the department had refused an earlier invitation to take part in the show.

"This type of program panders to people who want attention," Price said. "It's a shocking revelation in a format that makes the story appear newsworthy, using facts the way a drunk uses a lamppost, more for support than illumination."

Price said the Williams show had a responsibility to thoroughly verify Stanfield's legitimacy before putting him on the air. "At the very minimum," he said, "they could have called us in plenty of time so we could check his story out. But they told us only that there was someone named Jerome—they didn't tell us his last name—who had raped more than ninety women in Baltimore from 1990 to 1992. That's all we had to work with. All we could do is see if there was anyone who matched that profile, and there wasn't."

Price said that subsequent digging after the taping turned up a warrant for Stanfield concerning an unpaid fine and court costs for an old burglary conviction, but no evidence of serial rapes of the city's prostitutes or any other evidence that would substantiate his story.

"If this had happened, it could not have escaped our notice," Price maintained. "And even after all the publicity about the program, there still hasn't been anybody who's come forward with information."

Not that "The Montel Williams Show" hasn't integrity. Williams introduced each segment by reading a statement, obviously taped after the session with Stanfield, that mentioned "reports" that Stanfield "may not have been telling the truth." He added: "But we have no information at this time that leads us to believe that he was not telling the truth. And because of that, we feel it is our duty and our responsibility to broadcast this program out of concern for public safety."

In other words, a voice inside told Williams that he had to do it. Please, someone stop this man before he tapes again.

[1994]

How Was Poor Jenny to Know
He Was a Ticking Time Bomb?

◈ *Jonathan Schmitz pulled the trigger after Jenny Jones and her talk show cocked the gun.*

First the verdict, now the spin.

The rutabaga on the screen is Jenny Jones, her eyes sparkless, her face as vacant as a turnip. There's no evidence of guile, nor even a glimmer of fakery as she says to Katie Couric with the sincerity of a true believer, her pale suit, blouse, skin, and hair bleeding together reassuringly like pastels in a muted still-life:

"I defend the right to have gay people on the show."

With equal innocence, she adds later: "This is about homophobia."

Say what? Can she really be this clueless, such an impenetrable dead head? Can she really believe that the lawsuit brought against "Jenny Jones" by Scott Amedure's family was about her show booking gay guests? Or about anti-gay bias? Or about elitist "snobbery" aimed at "trash TV," as she told another NBC interviewer, Jane Pauley?

Instead of about the show's stunning recklessness in mishandling one particular guest, Jonathan Schmitz?

Or is this performer—who heads a syndicated talk show formatted along the lines of those starring Sally Jessy Raphael, Ricki Lake, and Montel Williams—just good at playing dumb and dumber?

Not good enough, certainly, to sway the Pontiac, Michigan, jury that Friday found "Jenny Jones" negligent—to the tune of $25 million—in Schmitz's fatal shotgunning of Amedure shortly after its taping of an unaired segment titled "Same-Sex Secret Crushes."

But good enough, perhaps, to persuade the coast-to-coast jury she addressed during very tough interviews Sunday night on NBC's "Dateline" with Pauley and Monday morning on NBC's "Today" program with Couric.

In that infamous 1995 taping of "Jenny Jones," Amedure disclosed to the cameras and a studio audience that he had a crush on—and sexual fantasies about—his acquaintance Schmitz, who said he was heterosexual. "I thought about tying him up in my hammock," confided a smiling Amedure. Egged on by Jones, he went on about wanting to do something to Schmitz involving whipped cream, champagne, and "things like that."

Schmitz was trapped in a classic ambush-the-guest prank symbolizing the twisted Gotcha! mentality driving much of TV this decade, this one featuring the standard mortification close-up. That meant showing Schmitz cover his face with his hands out of embarrassment.

Although he appeared genial about being publicly identified as Amedure's crushee, the fuse had been lit.

A number of legal experts predict that Friday's verdict will be overturned on appeal. If so, that will not affect the ethical or moral case against "Jenny Jones," for having a legal right to do something under the wide umbrella of the First Amendment doesn't always mean having a moral right. For example, had Couric and Pauley known something embarrassing about Jones, should they have exercised their First Amendment rights and hit her with it with cameras rolling just for the fun of it? Of course not.

More than freedom of expression, good sense and common decency should prevail, whether the venue is NBC News or "Jenny Jones."

Should "Jenny Jones" and its owner, Warner Bros., ultimately bear no legal responsibility for Schmitz pulling the trigger, they still will bear a lethal responsibility for roaring through this red light without regard for cross traffic. "Jenny Jones" has been doing it. As have likeminded shows, including Sally Jessy wearing her most compassionate face to turn an exploitative TV spotlight on troubled kids under the pretense of helping them. Where are the headlines about potential damage done to them inside their heads?

Such shows don't probe the psyches of guests they purposely place in discomfort. How could they? Besides lacking the inclination, they haven't the resources. And the thought of relying on the diagnosis of one of their own pop therapists—the telegenic ones they often include in segments as window dressing—in itself is chilling.

The answer? Immediately stop producing segments that intentionally grip guests in vices of mental stress just so voyeuristic viewers can watch them squirm.

This does not include such violent movies as *The Basketball Diaries* or *Natural Born Killers* that may inadvertently tap latent violence in someone predisposed that way. The difference is that talk shows aim their cross hairs at specific targets.

What Jones and her staff learned too late was that Schmitz's volatile background included alcoholism, depression, three suicide attempts, and a hang-up about homosexuality. One so severe that three days after the taping he went to Amedure's mobile home and blew him away.

Schmitz's 1996 second-degree murder conviction for the shooting was thrown out on appeal, and a retrial is set for August 19. He has insisted that "Jenny Jones" producers misled him by saying a female would surprise him on the segment. The show's lawyers claimed it played no role in Amedure's death because Schmitz was informed his secret admirer could be either gender. If so, and if the intent weren't embarrassment, why not eliminate all doubt and tell Schmitz straight out that it would be a man?

Warner Bros. has suggested that the murder may have been triggered by a post-taping sexual encounter between the two men, which Schmitz and the Amedure family deny occurred.

After flying home to Detroit with them following the taping, Schmitz did go drinking with Amedure and a female friend who also had appeared on the show. If Schmitz was so upset, Jones asked Pauley, "why would he do that?"

"You're assuming that he's a rational, normal, stable individual, and we know he wasn't," said Pauley.

"You're assuming that I'm rational and stable, [and] you didn't check my background," said Jones. "Anything can come up that's unexpected. Does that mean we're not allowed to have a free conversation on television?"

Thus did Jones equate her straightforward "Dateline" interview with the blind-siding "Same-Sex Secret Crushes," which she euphemistically associated with "free conversation."

Pauley wondered if Jones would have gone through with the segment knowing Schmitz's history of suicide attempts.

Jones replied that Schmitz's last suicide attempt was a year prior to the taping. "There are people who have had psychological counseling, there are people with drug and alcohol problems," she said. "That doesn't always mean that somebody can't be on television."

Of course not. But should such a person be subjected to potential humiliation on television?

Jones is not the only one spinning, this being one of those cases offering something for everyone with a special interest to promote. Some gay-rights groups join her in insisting that by suing her show over Amedure's death, his family makes it seem there is something bad about being gay. Or as Jones put it to Pauley: "Why do people so readily accept that it should be humiliating for a gay man to express a crush on any other man straight or gay?"

And why do cats have four legs?

We live in a world not just of ideals but one also of gnarled minds that yield dark, even violent thoughts about homosexuals, to say nothing about prejudice against other minorities. At issue here, though, is not what others do or don't "readily accept," but the view of homosexuality that drove the troubled Schmitz. He was the one targeted by the show, the one whose father has said that his son called him after the Jones taping sobbing that "now everybody is gonna think I'm gay."

Not to worry, though, for Jones did tell both Couric and Pauley that she was sorry about Amedure's death. Meaning that deep inside the rutabaga beats a heart of gold.

[1999]

Communing with Nature
by Destroying It

◆ *Is my bias against hunters and others who harm animals showing?*
I hope so.

I remember the day I turned on TV and immediately began trembling
with excitement and fear.

Excitement because I was watching "Sportsman's Quest," one of
many wildlife series on ESPN2.

Fear, because of the danger.

My pulse was thumping, my heart beating like a tom-tom, for on the
screen, vulnerable and exposed in southern Africa, was Jay Novacek.

Sportsman in peril.

Novacek had known pain. As a former tight end for the Dallas
Cowboys, he'd been slammed to the turf by bruisers outweighing him
by seventy-five pounds. He'd been shoved, crunched, hammered,
bent, speared, trampled, pummeled, kneed, creamed.

Opponents had battered and punished him severely enough to
send him grimacing to the bench feeling as if run over by a truck.

But never had he experienced such terror, for facing him now was
a threat much greater than any he'd encountered on a football field.
Just a few hundred yards away, capable of closing the distance in seconds, was a creature so ravenous for grass and shrub sprouts that it
made my skin crawl just to hear its name.

Kudu!

Yes, the striped African antelope with long twisted, spiral horns.
Grassy areas, beware!

Thus the tone projecting danger. Why . . . the hungry kudu could mistake Novacek for a shrub sprout. It could charge him, hurl its five hundred pounds at him, impale him. Worse, it could nibble him to death.

So what was a sportsman to do?

Novacek and his professional guide stalked, they advanced, they hid, they whispered, they quietly observed. Then ready . . . aim . . . and in self-defense:

Kablooie!

"Great shot!" proclaimed the guide. As the two men later stood over the lifeless antelope, Novacek was clearly overwhelmed by his achievement. "Wow! Holy cow! Look at the sight of him! He's beautiful!"

Too beautiful to live.

That was my introduction a while ago to ESPN2's abundance of wildlife shows, that rare TV universe where premeditated killing is not merely shown—talk about your snipers in ambush—but encouraged. And where ending life is softened by such euphemisms as "take," "cull," "thin," "manage," "harvest," and, my favorite, "getting involved with the outdoors." As in another ESPN2 show, "Ultimate Outdoors with Wayne Pearson." Cue suspense music as a hunter in hiding raises his rifle and prepares to nail an elk. "Good shot!" someone shouts.

On these shows all the shots are "good" or "great." Nothing too gory. The crack of gunfire is followed immediately by footage of a dead animal lying on the ground as if in a peaceful sleep, one from which it will not awaken.

"Sweet death" is what prolific hunter Ernest Hemingway said he dispensed to the animals whose heads he had mounted on his walls. Death is as clean on ESPN2. That's because messy shots are bad for business. And business here is booming. "Sportsman's Quest" has become "Cabela's Sportsman's Quest," for example, advertising its major underwriter, a big clothing outfitter, just as ESPN2 also gives viewers "NaturalGear's Wildlife Quest" and "Kawasaki's Under Wild Skies."

At commercial breaks you also hear from a host of other sponsors, including the National Rifle Association. The line separating these shows and their commercials is sometimes blurry, as when a Natural-Gear executive recently surfaced as an elk hunter on "NaturalGear's Wildlife Quest."

It doesn't pay to get too huffy here, given the double standard of some in the anti-hunting crowd who fall all apart at humans slaying animals in the wild but think nothing of wearing and using animal products or eating those that suffered and died in a slaughterhouse.

Coming to mind as a vivid metaphor is Tony Soprano, the HBO mobster who gorges himself on meat but weeps over ducks and was so devastated by an act of animal cruelty recently that he whacked the guy he held responsible.

What some of us can't begin to comprehend, though, is the exhilaration hunters experience when arbitrarily ending the life of a sentient creature they ooh and ahh over and profess to admire.

I recall seeing an ESPN2 show's feature on adults teaching kids, ages ten to twelve, "hunting ethics" and "respect for the animals you harvest," while thinking their thrills would multiply were they learning to operate cameras in the presence of "prey" instead of guns and crossbows. Instead, a kid, so tiny his orange vest draped him like a tunic, aimed his rifle at an unsuspecting deer from behind a tree as his teacher whispered instructions. The next sound I heard—boom!—signaled a rite of passage being attained.

Meanwhile, ambushing wild turkeys on "NaturalGear Wildlife Quest" one day this week was a foursome that included host and executive producer Shane Jones, who is a noted archer, and Daytona 500 champ Ward Burton, on whose "wildlife foundation" property this hunt was held.

A shot from a blind found its target, after which there were high-fives and a round of congrats. "Incredible turkey," someone said. Then they all marched off together like Dorothy and her pals in *The Wizard of Oz*, birds slung over their shoulders.

And under those "Wild Skies," caribou-hunting actor Brad Johnson bagged himself a "beautiful bull" in Canada while getting involved with the outdoors on "Cabela's Sportsman's Quest" were Novacek and professional angler Denny Brauer, their excitement palpable as white-tail deer advanced into their cross hairs.

"Wow," Brauer whispered from his hiding placed in the brush. "If that's what I think it is, that is a monster deer coming right at us. That is the one I've been waiting for. C'mon. C'mon. Stop right there." A shot split the silence. "I got him," Brauer said.

Cut to the dead deer, whose eyes gazed vacantly as its head was held up for the camera. "Golly, I don't believe it," said Brauer. "It's the biggest deer I have ever taken. Wow, look at that deer. It's absolutely beautiful."

So beautiful it had to die.

[2002]

Transgressing All the Way to the Bank

◈ *If Caligula were alive today, he'd have his own talk show.*

Merely being famous is a ticket to stardom.

It's worked for G. Gordon Liddy, who spent a week on "Password" recently and earlier turned up on "Miami Vice." And look how well it's working for John Ehrlichman.

Nine years after completing eighteen months in prison for conspiracy, obstruction of justice, and perjury for his role in the Watergate scandal, the former No. 2 aide in the Richard Nixon White House has become a TV pitchman for Dreyer's Grand Light ice cream, exploiting—and joking about—his lack of credibility.

It's not *what* he's doing (he's paid his debt and has a right to make a living) but *how* he's doing it that's repugnant. He's making his Watergate connection work for him as one of Dreyers' six "unbelievable spokespeople for an unbelievable product" in a regional advertising campaign that's been running for several weeks.

There he is eating the stuff on TV. Would you buy ice cream from this man? Listen:

"When I said I never knew a thing about the Watergate break-in, you probably didn't believe me, did you? Well, to show you what a good guy I am, I'll give you another chance. This Dreyer's Grand Light is 93 percent fat-free, all natural, and has a lot less calories than regular ice cream. And it tastes great. So even if you didn't believe me last time, you'd better try this stuff. It's unbelievable. And, believe me, I'm an expert on that subject."

Yes, a real knee-slapper. Ehrlichman was a key player in a dark episode that anguished the nation and triggered Nixon's resignation in disgrace. And now it's funny?

Perhaps not to Dreyer's, which, according to a spokeswoman, is considering yanking the Ehrlichman spot. "We knew we would get some negative reaction, but we got a little more than we anticipated," public relations manager Diane McIntire said Monday from Oakland.

Why use Ehrlichman in the first place? Because he got famous for lying.

"We have a product we consider unbelievable, because it's a low-calorie ice cream—which is a contradiction," said Hal Riney of Hal Riney and Partners, the San Francisco advertising agency behind the "unbelievable spokespeople" campaign. Ehrlichman was initially tentative about taking part, but consented "in the spirit of good nature," Riney said. "It's a little bit of whimsy. At least I see it that way. Some of the people who hate Ehrlichman don't see it as whimsical."

If Ehrlichman making light of perjury is whimsical, what next? The imagination runs wild:

—*"This is Jim Bakker. I got into a lot of trouble buying my wife, Tammy Faye, a Rolls-Royce with church contributions. I won't do that again, now that I've driven this gorgeous new . . . Mercedes Benz!!!"*

—*"I'm John Hinckley. When I shot President Reagan, I sure could have used one of these new genuine U.S. Army . . . bazookas!!! And then a shiny Yamaha to make my getaway!!!"*

—*"I know what you're thinking. 'What's Charlie Manson, a homicidal lunatic, doing in a TV commercial?' But at least I've got the good sense to know that you need a good dandruff shampoo in prison."*

—*"It's me, Dr. Mengele . . ."*

Actually, Riney said, the ice creamers employed their own statute of limitations for their campaign, refusing to use anyone convicted of a crime in the last six months. "And [in using someone like Ehrlichman] it had to be a crime that didn't do anybody any fundamental harm—like an injury," Riney said. "Ehrlichman considers it [his criminality] a technicality."

Taking part in a White House cover-up did no fundamental harm? Somebody here has ice cream for brains.

Riney said he was never uncomfortable with having Ehrlichman josh about his Watergate role in the spot. "Not at this point in time. Watergate is pretty much forgotten. A lot of people don't even know it happened."

The other "unbelievables" spokespersons, Riney said, are a woman who claims to have boarded several UFOs, a man claiming sightings of the Loch Ness Monster, a psychic, a "little boy we made up," and Melvin Dummar, the man who insisted that Howard Hughes left him $150 million. "We considered Ivan Boesky," Riney said, "but concluded he probably wouldn't want to do it."

Susan Schultz, Dreyer's brand manager for new products, denied that the firm considered hiring Boesky, the insider-trading scandal figure who pleaded guilty to giving false information to the Securities and Exchange Commission. "We were considering Zsa Zsa Gabor, though," she said.

[1987]

The Art of Rebounding

Here is more affirmation that it's hard to keep a bad man down.

Being a famous jerk still pays.

There's Monica with her book deal, for instance, and that disgraced opportunist for hire, Dick Morris. After his own embarrassing sex scandal, Morris joined the Fox News Channel as a Beltway guru specializing in bashing Bill Clinton, the president whom he earlier had served aggressively as a key political strategist.

The culture is forgiving, with television, especially, known for welcoming bad actors from politics and sports back into the fold of respectability like redeemed sinners.

Take Dennis Rodman.

Puhleeeeeeze!

If he doesn't get all over the place, he shouldn't be in your face. And is he. Not only as a featured player for the Los Angeles Lakers—jawing, wrestling, and bad-acting his way into sportscasts—but once more as a featured shill for Carl's Jr.

Would you buy a burger from this man? An onion ring?

Carl's Jr. believes that many of you will. It has resumed airing its commercials starring Rodman that it initially benched in early 1997 after he earned an eleven-game suspension for kicking a cameraman who was courtside at an NBA game when he was with the Chicago Bulls. Carl's Jr. began airing them again, then pulled the spots anew after Rodman was widely lambasted for cursing Mormons later that year while the Bulls were in Utah for the NBA finals.

Yet memories of expletives fade, although the green of cash doesn't. Rodman's comeback in burgerdom this week, which required negotiating another contract, affirms that whoever you are or whatever your venom, you'll thrive financially if your infamy earns a profit for someone else.

Even if your modus operandi is rage or petulance, an example of that being the Miller Lite commercials that the late Billy Martin and his former New York Yankees boss, George Steinbrenner, made together, playing off of their stormy relationship. And the Bic blades spots for which former tennis great John McEnroe re-created his famed nastiness and name-calling on the court.

They were hired because of having personality flaws as visible as sinkholes, making them all the more recognizable to consumers. Just as Carl's Jr. knew the tinderbox it was getting in Rodman.

Even before the Anaheim-based chain hired him, Rodman was as notorious for his head-butting and unstable behavior on and off the court as for his brilliance as an NBA rebounder and defender. His hot-button conduct has been an issue as well since he joined the Lakers in February, and the decision to resume his spots by CKE Restaurants, which owns Carl's, came after still more Rodmanesque adventures.

They included his ejection from a game at a critical time for getting a second technical foul after giving unsolicited chiropractic treatment to an opposing player's head. And this week he was cited for flagrantly fouling Karl Malone of the Utah Jazz.

"The advertisements will not run again," CKE spokeswoman Suzi Brown vowed after Rodman, as a Chicago Bull, trashed Salt Lake City's Mormons in an off-color critique for which he belatedly apologized ("If I knew it was like a religious-type deal, I would have never said it.").

Yet what a difference a Lakers uniform makes. Especially to a company that sells burgers—largely to sports-minded males, eighteen to thirty-four—predominantly in Southern California.

"We really hadn't considered using the ads again until he was a Laker," Brown said this week. "He has been overwhelmingly accepted by Laker fans."

She saw for herself while attending the televised game at the Forum from which Rodman was tossed. "I was blown away," she said. "He tucked in his shirt, and the crowd went wild." As it did when he was ordered from the court due to that second technical foul, many giving him a standing ovation as if he were a hero for hurting his team by careening out of control.

Would Brown want her own young son regarding Rodman as a role model? "Just because he is eating a hamburger on TV, I can't see the correlation between that and being a role model," she said.

Like it or not, he is one, though, with many youngsters surely seeing in cheers for this ear-ringed, nose-ringed, heavily tattooed Vegas animal's renegade actions a green light not just for rebellion but for conduct that's dysfunctional and destructive.

Draw your own conclusions about what their unconditional worship of Rodman says about some Lakers fans. At least they are forthright about their adoration, however, in contrast to sports reporters who hypocritically slam, ridicule, and smirk at Rodman's blowups while loving every one of them.

So much of television being predicated on conflict, it's no wonder that Rodman's explosions are as highly esteemed in most newsrooms as the exotica of his strange divot of a marriage to Carmen Electra. As an exploding Vesuvius, Rodman delivers great TV pictures that make every sportscast's highlight reel. As do the hockey brawlers whom sportscasters indict sanctimoniously while taking care to exploit their violence by giving them prominence.

Thanks to Carl's Jr., Rodman's own prominence is again growing.

Of varying lengths, the Rodman spots put him inside a tattoo parlor where he bites into a Super Star burger that drips onto his arm and causes one of his tattoos—a muscleman in a tank top—to come to life. It grabs Rodman's burger and eats it. When Rodman bends over to search for the missing burger, the top of his famously dyed head displays a red-and-yellow Carl's Jr. logo.

The concept for the tattoo preceded Rodman's involvement, said Brown. "And that pretty much narrowed the field." While reaffirming that the field of commercial spokespersons is virtually unlimited.

Although Rodman is no epic villain, one can envision his Carl's Jr. rebirth being a catalyst, perhaps leading ultimately to something like this, along the lines of those former American Express spots:

"Do you know me? I'm a ruthless dictator who is accused of being a war criminal."

S-L-O-B-O-D-A-N M-I-L-O-S-E-V-I-C.

[1999]

When Crummy Acting
and Writing Equal Fun

❖ *"Dynasty" was surely a satire . . . wasn't it?*

Krystle . . . Blake . . . Alexis . . . the Carringtons.

I never cared much for ABC's "Dynasty." It had the cheekbones of Linda Evans, the cheek of trash-enchantress Joan Collins, the gleaming elegance of John Forsythe, and all those other smartly dressed people running around snarling and spitting at each other.

But rich-bashing gets old.

Many "Dynasty" viewers ultimately agreed. Once TV's most popular series, "Dynasty" slipped a bit in the ratings last season and then writhed through the first two months of this season with a 20 percent audience dip that was potentially fatal.

Were bad story lines behind the slump? Co-creator and co-executive producer Esther Shapiro promised last November that "Dynasty" stories would be "more emotional, more realistic—without losing the glamour."

Romance has definitely been the ticket.

Sammy Jo (Heather Locklear) and her bisexual ex-husband Steven (Jack Coleman) are again looking at each other with goo-goo eyes. And Dominique Deveraux (Diahann Carroll) has been saved from thugs by a handsome stud.

But last Wednesday, "Dynasty" really outdid itself.

It reached far, far beyond merely being bad to that hallowed, rarefied area of TV programming so bad that it's actually good. I was immediately hooked. If there were a Richter scale for trash, this hour would have hit 10 and kept soaring. It made "Dallas" look like *Hamlet*. It was glorious, euphoric, and simply inspired, a throwback to those exquisitely awful 1940s romance movies that make such good parodies. Only this was no parody.

Last Wednesday:

Blake (Forsythe) is suffering from temporary amnesia after being injured in an oil rig accident in the South China seas. He now believes it's 1964.

His scheming-but-getting-nicer-each-week ex-wife Alexis (Collins) exploits Blake's amnesia by taking him to a magnificent Singapore villa where there are no newspapers or TV. She takes him for walks in the garden as they relive their early years together.

Blake still thinks it's 1964. You'd think he would wonder why he has gray hair if it's 1964, but maybe Alexis has covered the mirrors.

Actually, Alexis is doing all this to induce Blake to sign away half his oil leases to her. He finally does, but by this time she's so much in love with the big, elegant lug that she rips up the leases right in front of him.

At this point the story is so real that you can hardly stand to watch.

Meanwhile, Blake's wife, Krystle (Evans), has traced him to the villa and has a confrontation there with Alexis. While these two garbage goddesses are having it out, Blake suddenly appears.

What follows is Hall of Fame material. I mean, your heart could stop.

As that hussy Alexis looks on, Krystle rushes over to Blake and gushes: "Thank God, I've found you." But nothing. Blake's a blank.

Poor Krystle is distraught. The music crescendos.

"Tell him who I am, for God's sake," Krystle pleads to Alexis, who coolly takes a draw on her Cigarillo and exhales.

"You are not going to get away with this, you're not!" Krystle declares while exiting. Alexis takes another puff.

The music builds. Cut to Krystle's limo outside the villa, where her driver is changing a flat. Krystle tells him to hurry. She is beside herself.

Back inside the villa, Blake is confused, a tortured man. Something about Krystle was vaguely familiar. Linda Evans's bad acting?

No, something else. He rubs his forehead and wonders: "Why was she carrying on like that?"

Now Alexis is speaking in a low, throaty, torrid half-whisper. "You'll never know what the past few days have meant to me, Blake . . . being with you." But Alexis cannot bring herself to extend poor Blake's torment.

"That woman," Alexis continues, "that woman is your wife."

Blake's eyes suddenly focus. You can almost see the light bulb click on above his head.

Back outside the villa, Krystle is telling her driver: "Hurry, please hurry." The music gets even bigger.

Back inside the villa. "But us," Blake whines. "What about us?"

Alexis gives him the whole scoop. How they married and split and how she just wanted to relive their past bliss and, gee, if he can't understand that . . .

Blake is furious. It's his big scene. "UNDERSTAND? HOW?"

His forehead is pounding. He buries his head in his hands as Alexis watches, her eyes smoldering.

This time the music goes off the Richter scale.

Slowly, very slowly, Blake removes his hands from his face. There's something different about him now. His expression. His eyes. They're twinkling. They're alive. Is it possible? Can it be true?

BLAKE REMEMBERS!!!!!

"Krystle! My God! It was Krystle! I've gotta find her."

Alexis is in tears. Blake rushes out. Krystle is driving off. The music is going nuts. Blake sprints across the grass, shouting Krystle's name. The iron gates to the villa open for Krystle's limo. Blake shouts her name again. She looks back and sees Blake. He shouts her name again. The music is going berserk. Krystle is out of the limo and running to Blake.

Blake is running to Krystle.

Krystle is running.

Blake is running.

The music is running.

Krystle is still running.

Blake is still running.

You're hoping they'll collide.

Blake and Krystle meet. Music. They embrace. Music. Alexis watches from the veranda, wondering whether she has lost Blake forever.

"I love you," Blake says.

"You're my life," Krystle says.

End last Wednesday's episode, start the promo for tonight's episode. Alexis is taunting Krystle: "Did Blake and I make love? And was it better with me than with you?"

I'll be watching and laughing.

[1987]

In "Ark," Noah Plays Friars Club

◆ *What I couldn't fathom was, instead of Jon Voight, why didn't they go ahead and hire Jackie Mason to play Noah?*

Aren't you staying for the orgy?
   —Lot to Noah in NBC's "Noah's Ark"

Noah and his ark have been a hot ticket for ages, from the Old Testament to John Huston in *The Bible* to a CBS special in 1993 that was exposed as hoax when a piece of wood identified on the program as a chunk of the famous boat turned out to be contemporary pine treated to look like the real thing. CBS finally admitted being duped by the independent producers of "The Incredible Discovery of Noah's Ark," which used deception in purporting to document a creationist theory that the big tub actually existed as refuge for a few humans and all animal species, two by two.

   Now comes more loopy fantasy in a Bible story as Henny Youngman might have written it. Take Lot's wife.

   Please.

   The culprit is NBC's "Noah's Ark," a laughably bad, stunningly low-burlesque, excruciatingly slow two-parter introduced with this disclaimer: "For dramatic effect, we have taken poetic license with some of the events of the mighty epic of Noah and the Flood."

   Not that you need telling, unless you subscribe to the notion that Genesis was written by Borscht Belt comics. "Noah's Ark" opens, for example, with a savage, gauging, impaling, decapitating battle between the cities of Sodom and Gomorrah, followed by this exchange between Jon Voight's Noah and F. Murray Abraham's banged-up Lot.

Noah: "What happened?"

Lot: "Some coward shot me in the back."

Noah: "Where in the back?"

Lot: "I can't sit down."

Noah (finally getting it): "Oh."

As a biblical epic, in other words, much of "Noah's Ark" is a rim shot with jokes as creaky as nine-hundred-year-old Noah. It's a regular Hayohhhhhh! As was *Wholly Moses*, a labored 1980 sendup of the Good Book with Dudley Moore but a theatrical film that at least promised nothing beyond the weightless nonsense it delivered.

"Noah's Ark," however, is pulled opposite ways by Peter Barnes's schizoid script, splitting its baggy pants when planting one pigeon-toed foot in parody, the other in Scripture while mingling cheap one-liners with serious lectures on Godliness. It succeeds on neither level, while adrift hither and yon across four hours that feel like the forty days and forty nights of rain that the Lord pours down on the wicked world after earlier fireballing Sodom and Gomorrah into oblivion.

Part one, in particular, finds Barnes getting in touch with his inner shtick. That would be fine if his script had an elevated sense of humor and the story a lead actor who could deliver punch lines without looking and sounding like he was having his nose hairs yanked out, two by two.

Instead, this room's stand-up Noah is Voight, a capable dramatic actor whose unease with comedy—at least this comedy—is palpable when he pops off with the same stoniness that he gives ponderous endorsements of the Lord.

Voight is also voice-over for a self-mocking, wisecracking, echo-chambered God, who after instructing Noah to build a flood-worthy five hundred-foot ark for his family and pairs of all animals, quips: "I think big. I made the world in six days."

And is Noah himself a card or what, muttering that his wife, Naamah (Mary Steenburgen), is such a bad cook "she could burn water."

Lot and his shrewishly whiny, kooky spouse, Sarah (Carol Kane), are part one's designated Sonny and Cher, though, bickering so tenaciously that Noah titles them "two peeves in a pod." Oh, that Noah.

Lot to Sarah: "The trouble with you is somebody once told you to be yourself."

Sarah to Lot: "My mother always said you would start at the bottom and work your way down."

The high jinks really hit the fan when Sarah falls into a vat of red dye during one of her snits at Noah's place. The bad news? She doesn't drown. Who can blame Lot for rejoicing when she's turned into a pillar of salt after ignoring an order not to sneak a look at Sodom getting waxed by the Lord?

Other highlights:

* American-sounding Noah and Naamah having three sons who inexplicably speak as boys like Oliver Twist.

* Noah and his now-strapping sons, after appearing overwhelmed by the task of building the ark, awakening in the morning to a gift from the Lord: row after row of neatly cut and stacked lumber—as if custom-ordered from Home Depot—numbered for easy assembly.

* Noah's former best friend, Lot, resurfacing later as a brutal pirate captain who leads his ragged band ("I'm takin' your ship, Noah!") in an attempt to board the ark. Where did they get their boats?

* The animals (including actors in gorilla suits) helping repel Lot and his brigands.

* Noah's sons shoveling animal manure below deck ("Is this what the Lord saved us for?") like the script at times shovels bad jokes.

* A koala bear dropping actual poo-poo (a prime-time first) when held by the girlfriend of one of the sons. Director John Irwin didn't reshoot the scene, presumably because he was striving for authenticity.

* After the ark has drifted for months, Noah being carried below twitching, hallucinating, and babbling, and everyone aboard ultimately falling into madness and despair.

As viewers may after exposure to this.

"Noah's Ark" has the size and high-toned spectacle you'd expect from executive producer Robert Halmi, Sr., a durable and prolific TV impresario who has spent much of the '90s making about an equal number of neo-classics (such as *In Cold Blood* and *Gulliver's Travels*) and clunkers (the likes of *Bye Bye Birdie* and *Merlin*). But the computer effects here pale compared with those of his recent overwrought *Alice in Wonderland*. And the ark looks less biblical than like an oversized garbage barge.

In fact, Halmi's clunkiest yet may be "Noah's Ark," which not only flops creatively but—parents be warned—is extremely violent and gory in spots, and includes substantial chatter about sex among Noah, Naamah, their sons, and the trio of nubile young maidens the hearty young men bring aboard.

Nor, as the disclaimer notes, is the script anything to build a Bible course around. Scholars estimate that at least five hundred years may have elapsed between the destruction of Sodom and Gomorrah and the great flood, for example. Yet in "Noah's Ark" they're separated by about a decade.

And although some experts say it's at least conceivable that Noah and Lot were contemporaries, there's nothing in Genesis to indicate they knew each other, nor anything to implicate Lot as an early Captain Kidd.

Not that anyone would watch this to learn about things biblical. Where is Charlton Heston when you really need him?

[1999]

A Tale of Two Miniseries

◆ *It was the best of television, it was the worst of television . . .*

Who *says* television lacks diversity? This weekend brings the best of timeslots and the worst of timeslots, the Sunday of wisdom and the Sunday of foolishness, the network of belief and the network of incredulity, the miniseries of light and the miniseries of darkness.

On Sunday we will have everything before us (Charles Dickens's "A Tale of Two Cities" on PBS) and we will have nothing before us (Judith Krantz's "Till We Meet Again" on CBS).

Yet there are striking parallels in these two works of historical fiction. Just as Dickens's two cities are Paris and London, Krantz's story is set in France and Britain, in addition to California. Both also interweave romance and violence, and both are written by famous authors (Dickens, as it turned out, writing for the ages, and Krantz, the Bob's Big Boy of contemporary literature). What's more, the "wilderness of ruin, misery, and oppression" that Dickens applies to prerevolutionary France also characterizes "Till We Meet Again," which, as a bonus, is also a wilderness of mush.

If Dickens has the overwhelming numerical edge in heartless French aristocrats and vengeance-blinded revolutionaries, Krantz gives us her own epic French cad in Bruno the snot, whose actions in "Till We Meet Again" echo the credo of the Marquis St. Evremonde in "Tale of Two Cities": "Repression is the only lasting philosophy." More about Bruno shortly. But first this new adaptation of "A Tale of Two Cities," produced as a four-parter by Britain's Granada Television and the French Dune and Antenne 2 to commemorate last July's two hundredth anniversary of the French Revolution. The stage here is "Masterpiece Theatre."

To capsulize "A Tale of Two Cities":

As the rotting nobility is about to be toppled and annihilated by the long-suffering French people, Charles Darnay (Xavier Deluc) and brilliant-but-degenerate London lawyer Sidney Carton (James Wilby) fall in love with the luminous Lucie Manette (Serena Gordon), whose elderly physician father (Jean-Pierre Aumont) has just been freed from the Bastille after being locked away for eighteen years. Lucie marries Darnay, an idealistic French aristocrat who has renounced his family name of St. Evremonde out of shame, and lives in London.

The revolution erupts, and aristocrats are paraded to the guillotine en masse. Drawn back to Paris, Darnay is unjustly held accountable for his family's crimes and ordered executed. Now it's time for Carton to rev up, as he heroically fulfills his vow to Lucie to give his life "for you—or anyone you love."

There's lots to like here. Adapted for TV by Arthur Hopcraft and directed by Philippe Monnier, "A Tale of Two Cities" is grandly staged and a nice way to spend an evening. The climactic last half-hour—in which Carton gives meaning to his life by sacrificing it—is beautifully done. Moreover, you have to admire Hopcraft's humanized Madame Defarge (Kathie Kriegel), who remains pitiless without being mindlessly maniacal. Most of the major players are fine, but it's Jean-Marc Bory who almost steals the first hour as Darnay's doomed uncle, the unredeemably cruel marquis.

What's missing is passion, a convincing portrayal of the revolution's blind fury that stained the streets with blood.

Passion—of another sort—is available on CBS Sunday. Depending on your point of view, "Till We Meet Again" is either too bad to watch or too bad to ignore. Television has rarely been funnier.

This is no less than a festival of dumbness as it traces the tumultuous lives of a mother and two daughters, and, of course, the men they love. We meet Eve (Lucy Gutteridge) in 1913 as a rebellious seventeen-year-old French girl who runs away to the big city and becomes a dance hall singer. Her friend tells her: "Soon you will conquer Paris." Two years later she is en route to entertain French troops on the Western

Front when she is forced to take refuge in a barn from German shells. Then the door flies open, and it's dashing Captain Paul de Lancel (Michael York)—heir to a French champagne dynasty—and his troops.

The soldiers sit down. Eve sings to them. The soldiers fall asleep. A sign. Even the violins sound bored.

Directed by Charles Jarrott and adapted by Andrew Paul Martin, "Till We Meet Again" is a Rolodex of clichés—one comical, badly acted scene after another. Paul's first wife shoots herself in the head, and there's no blood. Later, two hours into his first date with Eve, Paul proposes and she accepts. It's that kind of show.

Their two daughters go in different directions, Delphine (Mia Sara) as an actress in Paris, and Freddy (Courteney Cox) as a pilot in the United States and in Britain during World War II.

The family black sheep is Paul's son by his first marriage, Bruno the snot (Hugh Grant), a sniffy, malicious, power-mad snob who despises his own family, is thrilled when the Germans occupy France, and later commits unspeakable acts. Do you hear, UNSPEAKABLE!!! At least Bruno the snot gets your attention.

Although spanning forty-three years and several nationalities, "Till We Meet Again" has no sense of period or texture: Not only is Eve's face as vacant as a cantaloupe, she doesn't age except for a few gray hairs. Meanwhile, Paul and Eve are French, yet he speaks English with a British accent and she with a cultured American accent. Bruno the snot only briefly budges from France, yet oozes Oxford. This is especially confusing when the British-sounding French characters are in Britain, or California.

Of course, the accent hasn't been invented that could improve this dialogue. Here is French director Armand Sadowski (Charles Shaughnessy) rejecting Delphine's offer of a kiss: "No. First I must undress you, button . . . by . . . button." And here's that big lug Jock Hampton (Bruce Boxleitner) all ga-ga over Freddy: "You beautiful, wonderful handful!" Your eyes fill with tears.

A tale of two miniseries. In choosing one, remember: It is a far, far better thing that Charles Dickens does, than Judith Krantz has ever done.

[1989]

The Face That Launched
a Thousand Clichés

◈ *I was in awe while watching this, knowing I was in the presence of greatness.*

Barbie and Ken of Troy.

Some of us would go just about anywhere for great trash, the kind of fat blimp that appears to take itself very seriously but lands with a big splat. Fortunately, we don't have to go far.

See those sconces Helen and Paris lock eyes as she walks naked (we see her backside) among a hundred kings.

See that little twirp Menelaus demolish burly Trojans twice his size.

See that skinhead brute Achilles spend an entire evening dragging a body in circles behind his speeding chariot—maybe he should get a life—as throngs cheer mindlessly.

Now this is a war.

The USA Network's two-part "Helen of Troy" is about as bloody as television gets. And about as bloody bad. So ferociously inane is it, in fact, that it's irresistible, its gory slaughter of battling Greeks and Trojans and fuzzy romance between Helen (perfectly formed daughter of Zeus) and Paris (handsome son of Trojan King Priam) entering a bizarro realm where flaws become attributes and usual definitions of good and bad no longer apply.

Getting there is tricky. Being bad is not good enough. Then it's just bad. But being really, really bad is an art.

The Malta filming and pageantry are sweeping, Troy being "the richest city in the world—silks from Asia, spices from Arabia, rare woods from Africa." Think Cost Plus.

But if you're a connoisseur who values corn, the gods are kind to you here. You know it's going to be a self-important epic when the press kit is swanky, the principals have English accents, and men, instead of guzzling Bud and belching, gather to eat grapes.

A theatrical "Helen of Troy" landed in 1955. And cameras are ready to roll on *Troy*, a Warner Bros. theatrical release directed by Wolfgang Petersen. But TV's new Helen hits gurgling lows that will be hard to match, affirming that first-rate trash always trumps second-rate art.

It was Helen, you'll recall, who triggered a fierce war between Greece and Troy just by looking great. In this account, written by Ronni Kern and directed by John Kent Harrison, the influential face belongs to former model Sienna Guillory. When she rides her horse in slow motion, she and everything else bounces, and before the first commercial break she's reducing men to simpering lumps of testosterone.

Frankly, though, she was more fetching three years ago when sneaking up on you as an alluring newcomer in the BBC's "A Girl Like You." Here she's commanded by Greek legend to be "the most beautiful woman in the world," a crushing burden, to say nothing of having a face credited with launching a thousand ships.

"Helen of Troy" approaches world-class TV trash. The best I ever saw, years ago, was a movie that had Christopher Columbus met on the shore by nubile dancing girls. And not far behind was NBC's more recent miniseries "Noah's Ark," which tested the theory that Genesis was written by Henny Youngman. Then take "Helen of Troy."

Please.

It strays from legend in spots, but who cares when something is such trashy fun? We meet Helen when she's a headstrong nymphet in a filmy tunic, causing her Spartan stepparents great consternation. When her wispy older brother tells her, "Let's get you bathed and dressed," you know Kern's script is tunneling into rich soil. Paris (Matthew Marsden), meanwhile, is up in the rocks herding goats, unaware that he is the son of Priam (John Rhys-Davies), who ordered him killed when he was a newborn because his snotty older sister, Cassandra, prophesized he would be the ruin of Troy.

Cassandra (Emilia Fox) resurfaces as an adult with still more pop, throwing a major snit when learning that Paris survived, and chewing up the furniture before she's packed off and jailed for overacting.

Meanwhile, see Paris—his combat skills somehow sharpened as a shepherd—take out a string of tough gladiators in front of more cheering throngs, as even his brother, that great warrior Prince Hector (Daniel Lapaine), is no match for him when these two beautiful guys duke it out in their blousy garments.

When Helen and Paris's paths eventually converge, they hit it off with all the heat of two people playing a duet on the lute. As lovers, Guillory and Marsden are, well, low-wattage, falling fabulously short of lighting up the screen. Trouble builds when Paris takes Helen from Sparta (actually she swims after his boat as he heads home), and her husband, King Menelaus (James Callis), is so humiliated that he sails with his army for Troy, an invasion that his ruthless brother, Agamemnon (Rufus Sewell), uses to his own advantage.

The siege of Troy and pursuit of Helen last a decade, during which no one ages, and when the men of Sparta frolic on the beach during down time, you half expect them to break out singing, "There is nothin' like a dame!" Yet Agamemnon has a plan: The Greeks should pretend to depart, but build and leave outside the city walls something enormous that their army would hide in and then emerge and slaughter the Trojans once it was wheeled inside. But what would it be? A giant . . . bug? Nah. A giant yak? And have a Trojan yak go down in history? No, not a yak. Instead, yes, yes, a horse. When it appears magically the next morning, that doofus Priam has it brought in, and the rest you know.

How are the Greeks able to build it unnoticed? Also, if Cassandra is such a colossal know-it-all, why doesn't she foresee a hollow horse being a weapon of mass destruction? And why does Achilles, who someday would have a tendon named after him, look like Jesse Ventura?

The masterful scene to watch for, though, has the Greeks and Trojans locked in savage combat when suddenly both armies freeze, except for Menelaus, who walks forward among the motionless soldiers with his eyes on Helen, who is watching the carnage from atop Priam's castle. Meant to convey Helen's spellbinding power, this supremely comical out-of-body pause lasts about thirty seconds. Then everyone starts fighting again.

Great trash rocks.

[2003]

III

The Pols, Prez, Props of War, and Other Phenomena: Ready for Their Close-ups?

With few exceptions, politicians splash on fakery like cheap perfume. They reek of it. So what the public needs least from them are TV-tailored charades.

Thus my pleas here to severely curtail coverage of presidential nominating conventions—a thirty-second daily TV summary and half a column of newspaper space without pictures should suffice—and end huffing and puffing over televised candidate debates that conclude with no-nothing pundits calling instant winners and losers. It shouldn't matter.

The conventions aren't really conventions, the debates not really debates.

The former have been wheezing and gasping for air since 1980, and survive only because both major parties cherish them as cheerleading megaphones. Oh, yes, the parties must pass their platforms. As if anybody cares or can ever recall a single plank.

Meanwhile the twenty-four-hour news networks still cover the conventions in relative detail because they have to cover *something* when not venting about crimes of the millennium. Best-case scenario: these geezers soon will die of attrition.

More longevity is ahead for televised debates, though, because they deliver juicy sound bites and because having command of witty one-liners is now a prerequisite for leadership. Why else would the road to the White House now lead through Leno and Letterman?

I note in essays here, however, these so-called debates yield few insights, celebrate the wrong qualities, and in fact are often misleading.

As TV often is when showing America's Anchorman after he takes office.

Are Presidents *not* like anchormen? Do we not look to them for information and guidance? Do we not ask them for steadiness and team coverage during times of crisis? Like their news counterparts, do they not command the camera, especially with the Fox News Channel, CNN, and MSNBC going live for every presidential hiccup? Do they not present a public image that may conflict with who they are in private? Do they not ask us to love and respect them, to believe in their infallibility, to keep them employed?

And is television not the medium of choice to nourish this culture of image?

Although being a Quasimodo is no attribute on the stump, it's a myth, you know, that only highly telegenic candidates can be elected to national office in the video age. Tell that to Jimmy Carter and both Bushes.

Yet the importance of camera *savvy* in presidential politics is no myth. It's a powerful ally as presidents and their wannabes increasingly speak to the public through TV in speeches, press conferences, or media events, whether verbally or through body language.

Ronald Reagan and Bill Clinton were supreme at this, of course. Reagan's words were heard, but his most enduring message was himself. Rather than communicate ideas, he projected images and moods, much like television itself. Although different in technique,

Clinton was equally commanding in front of the camera as president, and the lens loved him even when much of the public didn't.

George Bush the younger remains flat and tenuous on TV, appearing a few pints short of filling a ten-gallon hat. But he is much better now than early in his reign and during the hours following 9/11, when his wobbly performance had me saying this prez wasn't ready for freeze-framing. More than a thousand e-mailers to the paper disagreed angrily. Many called me a traitor and urged doing to me what U.S. troops later would do to that statue of Saddam Hussein in Baghdad.

The war in Iraq was not only the biggest news event of 2003; it gaveled in a national forum on media ethics whose focus on television mirrored the polarizing split in public opinion over this conflict.

Credibility was under a microscope. It turned out, for example, that POW Jessica Lynch wasn't the guns-blazing hero she was said to be in self-serving early reports fueled by journalism's most notorious bobbleheads. She still got her book deal, though.

Inevitably, too, this war joined others in producing as many showboating TV types as grandstanding politicians. There were striking distinctions, though.

As the Vietnam War *was*—and World War II, the war in Korea, and the first Gulf War *weren't*—the 2003 thrust into Iraq was beamed right into homes. You woke with it, went to bed with it, dreamt of it. Forget those faux "reality" shows, *this* was "Survivor."

But these sensational TV pictures—though remarkable for their intimacy and immediacy—were not the entire story. For example:

Had the media adequately prepped Americans in advance on the issues, risks, and challenges, so they would be able to say yea or nay on the war based on knowledge instead of spin or adrenaline? Hardly. Of *course*, Saddam Hussein's military would be clobbered in the field by vastly stronger forces. Yet what then? Everyone lives happily ever after? Too rarely did TV coverage pose that question in advance of the invasion.

Meanwhile, were the United States and its slim minority of coalition partners, conquerors or liberators?

And about combat coverage: to show or not to show bodies? Would displaying dead American soldiers and Iraqi civilians undermine the war zeal at home? Possibly. Just as rarely showing such pictures kept critical information from Americans at home.

Also: to embed or not to embed? In the first Gulf War, media were kept at a distance from the action by a Pentagon hoping to avoid a repeat of Vietnam, when grim stories by free-roaming reporters helped turn U.S. public opinion against that war.

Because that restrictive 1991 Gulf War policy drew media protests, the Pentagon this time devised a system whereby reporters were embedded in combat units. Some reporters were so embedded, in fact, that they wore military uniforms.

But did this close-up really provide a clearer view than from afar? Did "embeds" get too emotionally attached to troops, becoming virtual extensions of the military instead of independent observers? More fundamentally, were U.S. journalists, in any war, Americans first or messengers first?

And in the ongoing bloodshed of the occupation phase, were Iraqis and others opposing the U.S./coalition presence terrorists, as President Bush and the military repeatedly insisted? Or were they guerrilla insurgents or resistance fighters?

No question that slaughtering civilians was terrorism. If attacking U.S. soldiers was terrorism, though, why wasn't it also terrorism when U.S. forces were the attackers?

There was much to contemplate as casualty counts mounted.

Yet on the home front, Americans—who encounter death on TV regularly in newscasts as well as crime shows—still recoil irrationally when one raises the possibility of televising capital punishment.

It's true, as I say in an essay here, that TV tends to reduce humanity to flashcards and fleeting impressions. Yet also noted in this section are TV pictures that vividly record our status as a society at moments in time: a nation united in its anguish over the *Challenger* and *Columbia* space-shuttle disasters, one at odds over Clarence Thomas and Anita Hill, and images of Martin Luther King famously keeping the dream alive at the Lincoln Memorial in 1963.

Isn't the state taking a life also momentous enough to record? Yet mention TV cameras and executions in the same sentence and a red flag goes up.

As I argue, in fact, there are sound reasons for televising executions, and these are unrelated to sensationalism. You're skeptical? Like . . . untelevised executions are tasteful minuets attended by tea-sipping society types in satin breeches? Oh, please!

Is that how condemned killer Karla Faye Tucker went out? I describe here her memorable CNN appearance with Larry King on the eve of her execution.

The media themselves are usually on trial when covering sensational crimes.

Ever in conflict are the First Amendment, protecting an open society and free press, and the Sixth Amendment, promising Americans fair and speedy trials. Yet rarely is there a valid case against openness in the legal realm, whether the accused are U.S. citizens or non-American detainees linked, however vaguely, to terrorism.

Cameras were banned from courtrooms for decades following the brazen sensationalism of newsreels and unsavory newspapers during the 1935 trial of Bruno Richard Hauptmann for the kidnapping murder of the Lindbergh baby. Yet most states now allow trials to be televised at the discretion of judges, a policy I praise in this section. Unfortunately cameras are excluded from federal courts, which is foolish as well as un-American.

In weighing this issue, one must sever what occurs inside a trial from misbehavior of the media outside the courtroom, as I do in looking at the 1995 criminal trial of O. J. Simpson for the murders of Nicole Simpson and Ronald Goldman.

As for the feds, meanwhile, I argue here for courtroom cameras should the U.S. government ever put Osama bin Laden on trial. The same applies to that arch criminal in captivity, Saddam Hussein.

Infomercials Disguised
as Conventions

◈ *Why in the world, if not for the clout of Pat Robertson, would the Family Channel grant live coverage to the GOP nomination of Bob Dole for president?*

The story here in San Diego is the fever pitch of construction.
—CNN anchor Donna Kelly, overlooking the unfinished podium inside the Republican convention hall Friday

Today's start of the televised Republican National Coronation of Bob Dole is a signal for nostalgia-niks to chew on the past.

Oh for the good old days, when a GOP or Democratic nominating convention was a show you could count on, a real rumble of action and insults, several days and nights of suspenseful infighting and intrigue over naming the party standard-bearer.

Actually, there's been no really exciting nominating convention for ages. Let's see, what was that guy's name, Grover Cleveland?

Just kidding. But it is true that no convention since 1952 has gone past the first ballot. Not for decades, in fact, has there been a truly definitive convention, one whose top nominee was not taken for granted in advance, one whose undecided delegates mattered significantly, one whose television interviews had relevance beyond filling time and justifying the coverage.

Good people disagree about whether the present system of having state primaries and caucuses cumulatively pick major party presidential nominees is better or worse than the combustible conventions, where choices for the big job were dictated by wheeling, dealing party leaders. But from an entertainment perspective, the verdict is in.

As TV shows, today's conventions are flat-out clunkers, little more than tailored-for-TV infomercials in which processions of posturing professor Harold Hills sound partisan oom-pahs on behalf of their party and its presidential nominee, who was a lock going in.

Barring something unforeseen, that will be the case for this week's Republican convention and also for the August 26–29 Democratic affair in Chicago that will go through the motions of renominating the Clinton-Gore ticket. Ready the balloons.

No longer do all major commercial networks lavish costly gavel-to-gavel live coverage on these political infomercials, though. Nor should they, given that nothing is written in stone about the media being responsible for giving presidential candidates "bounce" in the polls via days of free exposure as they near the election.

Nonetheless, with NBC, PBS, CNN, and the Family Channel scheduling large chunks of live coverage in addition to the traditional gavel-to-gavel presence of C-SPAN, the Republicans are still getting vastly more blanket TV attention than they deserve, instead of having their speeches and other endeavors covered individually and only when warranted. And the Democrats will surely receive the same gift, minus the Family Channel.

Just how the Family Channel fits into this week is something to watch, given its control by televangelist Pat Robertson—whose "700 Club" program selectively depicted the 1992 Republican convention with a doctrinaire twist—and the docket of the party politicians who will staff this GOP-paid, GOP-friendly coverage (no wonder they're calling it GOP-TV) as if they were actual reporters.

But what's to report anyway, despite NBC promos touting its own joint coverage with PBS? Tom Brokaw: "Beyond the speakers, beyond the rhetoric, beyond the platform." Yes, the great "beyond," code for babble.

One of the TV highlights of the 1992 GOP convention was the first lady disclosing in prime time—on six channels simultaneously—that what made George Bush proudest in their many years of marriage and public service was that "his children still come home." The coverage was still live when one of their grandsons revealed that the president was "the greatest man I've ever known." And still live when Barbara Bush was joined on the podium by the rest of her dozen grandchildren and their parents and finally by George himself in a hugfest for the ages.

At some point, those guiding this week's regular live coverage will probably feel guilty about overcovering one party, but instead of cutting out they will cut into something equally un-newsworthy staged by Democrats, as they did during the 1992 GOP convention, when showing the Clintons and Gores hammering nails alongside former President Jimmy Carter at a home being built for an indigent family in Atlanta.

Should the carpenters not appear this time, here are some other things to look for:

* Pundits and reporters telling you whether the podium speeches you just heard and watched—especially Tuesday's keynote address by New York Representative Susan Molinari and Thursday's acceptances by expected GOP nominee Dole and his running mate, Jack Kemp— were electrifying or dull. Being a mere mortal, you will be unable to determine this for yourself and thus will be highly appreciative of this assistance from Greater Minds.

* The same self-anointed gurus disclosing the hidden true motives of the speakers. Again, encumbered by mortality, you will be unable to see inside the brains of speakers and will be in a terrible fog until enlightened by members of the media who have this gift.

* Reporters smirking about the convention being excruciatingly dry and unproductive, begging the question: Then, why cover it?

* Democrats brought in to give their spin on what the Republicans are doing in San Diego, just as two weeks from now Republicans will be asked to comment on Democrats, as if partisan politicians publicly laud the opposition or confess their true thoughts during election campaigns.

* Reporters nosing for mountains in molehills. This is inevitable in a convention that, in all likelihood, will generate little if any significant news, especially since the GOP seems to have ended its noisy

platform dispute over abortion rights. Thus, if dissident Pat Buchanan happens to yawn during Dole's speech, expect the media response to be scorching and the footage to be rerun each time Buchanan is mentioned in a newscast, all the way to the election.

On the other hand, if Dole himself dozes during his speech, that is news.

[1996]

Judging Political Parties
by Their Stagecraft

◆ *Were these TV pundits or critics and drama coaches whom television assigned to cover Democrats preparing to coronate Bill Clinton?*

Glorious, superb, thrilling, jaw-dropping, breathtaking . . . thoroughly enjoyable.

—Michael Medved of the *New York Post,* quoted in an ad for the movie *Alaska.*

Act 2, Scene 1.

Now you know what they mean when they call it the Windy City.

Democrats assembled in Chicago's United Center are getting their shot at America through television because the Republicans already got theirs in San Diego. So. . . .

At 7:20 P.M. Monday, veteran CBS News correspondent Bob Schieffer delivered a truly disturbing bulletin from the podium at the Democratic National Convention. "You have speakers in the hall, and I don't think you can hear them that well," Schieffer observed, staking his reputation on his well-seasoned ears. "Frankly, so far, I don't think it's going that well."

Not going that well? Oh, nohhhhhh!

Curious thing. The preliminary speakers Schieffer alluded to were not deemed worthy to televise by CBS during the 7 to 8 P.M. live coverage that it, ABC, and NBC are overgenerously granting the convention.

So why should he or his network care whether delegates in the hall could or couldn't hear speakers that CBS understandably wasn't bothering to carry or whether the convention so far was or wasn't the smash hit that its partisan impresarios envisioned?

Later, after the first evening of Democratic talks had ended with President Clinton pausing in his whistle-stop tour to cheerfully rally Chicago loyalists live via satellite from Toledo after Christopher Reeve's somber televised address in the hall, columnist Mark Shields observed on PBS that the presidential cutaway "didn't work nearly as well as the cutaway to Russell, Kansas," hometown of GOP candidate Bob Dole, during the Republican convention. Tsk, tsk.

Why should it matter to Shields, in his role as PBS political commentator, how the Democrats' staged live shot stacked up against the GOP's staged live shot?

Because . . . this is what it has come down to.

Throughout recent history, we've gotten all the important skinny from movie critics, theater critics, music critics, literary critics, architecture critics, culture critics, food critics, television critics, you-name-it critics. Now, as TV anchors, reporters, and commentators mentally twiddle their thumbs while the two major political parties execute their camera-ready stagecraft en route to November 5, comes this new species: journalists who carry the weighty mantle of political convention critic.

Does it play well? Is the audience enthralled? Incredibly, the conventions being labeled show biz are being judged by the standards of show biz by the same people who continually gripe about them being show biz.

"Heart-wrenching yet inspirational," was NBC News correspondent Jim Miklaszewski's bottom line Tuesday on the Monday night speeches of Reeve, the actor paralyzed in an equestrian accident, and handgun control activist Sarah Brady and her husband, Jim, wounded in a 1981 assassination attempt against then-President Ronald Reagan.

Reeve and the Bradys were telecast live by ABC, CBS, NBC, PBS, CNN, MSNBC, and C-SPAN, the usual suspects who also gave opening-night live coverage to a Ronald Reagan video and speeches by former

First Lady Nancy Reagan and retired General Colin Powell during the Republican convention.

Was the Democrats' first evening as "heart-wrenching" and "inspirational" as the GOP opener in San Diego? For that we must wait until Miklaszewski and other critics release their Top 10 lists on election eve. In any case, his blurb on the Democrats was the equivalent of Siskel and Ebert proclaiming, "Two thumbs way, way up!" You could envision it bannered across an ad for a Democratic National Committee video of the convention. As you could columnist Christopher Matthews's assessment, delivered on ABC's "Good Morning America," of Brady rising from his wheelchair to walk haltingly to the dais with help from his wife: "The guy stands up and walks!" And Matthews is not easy to please, either.

Critics being the nit-picking dandies that they are, inevitably there were mixed reviews. "These sad and poignant stories were supposed to bind us together but left me kind of sad," Gwen Ifill of NBC News groused about the Brady Moment during the "Today" program's own traditional morning-after round table of convention critics.

Yet her verdict on Reeve was a flat-out rave: "It absolutely fit. There was an outpouring of emotion." Added Bryant Gumbel: "There may not have been a dry eye in the house!" And then this influential blurb from Lisa Myers of NBC News: "The first people on their feet were the liberals."

It's a big, crowded convention floor, so credit Myers at least with extraordinary panoramic vision and remarkable knowledge of the political bents of all of the delegates.

And credit gavel-to-gavel CNN with knowing that behind every show there's a good sidebar on how it was put together, such as the "special demonstration of that massive video wall behind the podium" that it featured Tuesday morning. How do such things work? How does Peter Pan fly on stage? These are important questions that inquiring theatergoers want answered. It's becoming ever clearer that, as much as TV newscasters complain about being managed by politicos, in their hearts of hearts they think of themselves as extensions of the very political process they are supposed to be objectively observing.

Recently, for example, a reporter being interviewed for a network TV news story about the conventions was asked what the Democrats and Republicans should do in 2000 to ensure the same level of live coverage their conventions are getting in 1996. "Should they limit the conventions to an hour each night?" he was asked.

The interviewee replied that he didn't know and didn't care, that it was not the role of the press to advise political parties how best to stage self-serving media events. Nor is it the media's role to help them.

Obviously, some in the media disagree. All this week, for example, the newer, worse-than-ever "CBS This Morning" has been hoping to attract viewers by running "exclusives" with the Clintons. On Monday it managed to brutally coerce First Lady Hillary Clinton into admitting that yes, if we really must know, if we really must demean her like this, that she really cares enormously for the nation's children. Bullied by CBS News, she just blurted it out, letting the political chips fall where they may.

Then on Tuesday the CBS News terrorists were at it again, with reporter Jose Diaz-Balart sadistically twisting the arms of Hillary Clinton's childhood friends in her hometown of Chicago until yes, if he must know, they thought she was just a swell, wonderful, extraordinary person. The first lady looked on, obviously just overwhelmed by this public display of affection she had helped engineer.

Meanwhile, there was her Tuesday night speech to attend to, and some of Hillary Clinton's self-appointed close advisers in the adversarial media were stroking their jaws about what her strategy should be.

"A little splash of humility, of humor" should be her goal, advised Matthews on "Good Morning America." Advised Cokie Roberts of ABC News: "Smile a lot. I think that is the key here."

Should she heed their counsel, some of us were already readying our blurbs to toast the likely outcome: Glorious, superb, thrilling, jaw-dropping, breathtaking . . . thoroughly enjoyable.

[1996]

And Now, for My Next
Rehearsed Ad Lib . . .

◆ *There's so much spontaneity in televised candidate debates that it takes participants a week to memorize their answers.*

Here come Bill and Bob. But so what?

Televised debates are the ultimate fiction and the biggest redundancy of presidential campaigns. They are the big cliché, the icing on the tip of the rest of the iceberg you never see.

The media love them, much of the electorate watches them. Ever growing in prominence since the pivotal Kennedy-Nixon debates of 1960, they are now the popular currency and Holy Grail of electioneering. They're even entertaining, sometimes even suspenseful or memorable, as in Ronald Reagan repeatedly telling Jimmy Carter, "There you go again," in 1980 or Lloyd Bentsen stuffing Dan Quayle in 1988's clash of vice presidential foes.

Yet they resolve nothing except which candidate gives the better performance in front of TV cameras on a given night. As if that will make the United States safer and healthier in the next four years.

Such will be the case Sunday when President Clinton and challenger Bob Dole compete in the first of their two televised debates, followed on Wednesday by another between Vice President Al Gore and Dole's running mate, Jack Kemp. The second Clinton-Dole match, on October 16, will have a town hall format that involves members of a studio audience, an atmosphere especially conducive to Clinton's folksiness. Sunday's initial encounter will be more traditional, with a single moderator.

Grinding loudly Sunday night and Monday will be the usual conveyor belts of postdebate gab, the irritating practice of reporters giving their opinions under the pretense of analysis and interpretation, a burgeoning phenomenon in much of journalism that former *Washington Post* reporter Paul Taylor calls the "punditocracy."

On television there will be pundits galore to help the multitudes who are mentally challenged sift through the complexities of the posturing they have just witnessed. You will not only hear Machiavellian myth spinners from both major parties declare stunning victory, and the debate outcast and Reform party candidate Ross Perot tell Larry King on CNN that Clinton and Dole were both slugs who avoided addressing the real issues affecting the real people (down where the rubber meets the road). You will also hear network sages reveal who won and who lost, who looked good and who didn't, who flubbed and who flowered, who got off good lines and who didn't.

And, barring something unforeseen—such as Clinton or Dole drooling uncontrollably or doing a loopy Captain Queeg with ball bearings—you will be no smarter afterward about the candidates than you were before the debate. It can be no other way.

Break it down:

For starters, how are these learned men, Clinton and Dole, spending much of their time prior to the debate? Cramming, that's how— filling their heads with stuff they hope will impress the nation, stuff they've either forgotten or never knew. But it should already be in their heads if they're such hotshots, right? Unless knowing this stuff doesn't really matter. And in that case, why pretend it does? And if it does matter? Well, every student who has crammed for a quiz knows that the burst of brilliance is fleeting. All of those smarts vanish afterward, returning your intellect to reality.

What else are the candidates doing? They're rehearsing their roles, as any other actors would do. Both are practicing looking presidential, projecting just the right stature: strength but warmth, brilliance yet plain folks, the insider's knowledge without the insider's mentality.

In addition, Dole is practicing looking young and vigorous, Clinton practicing looking younger and more vigorous. If he thought he could accentuate the seventy-three-year-old Dole's age by wearing a beanie, he'd do it. Clinton is also rehearsing ways to make the reputedly shorter-fused Dole lose his cool, and Dole is being reminded to stay cool when provoked.

What does all this have to do with the presidency? The short answer is nothing, the long answer absolutely nothing.

In fact, televised debates mostly emphasize the exact qualities that no thinking voter would desire in a president:

* They emphasize flashy TV skills over substance. It's true that the nation's medium of choice is TV and that a president who cannot communicate to the nation effectively via the small screen is at least partially disabled. Not as severely, though, as one who's seamless on camera but ragged in the Oval Office, which is the chief executive Americans may get one of these days if they are substantially influenced by who appears to triumph in presidential debates.

* They emphasize speedy answers. The candidate who weighs a question ("What would you do if . . . ?") thoughtfully before responding, a trait you'd want in a president, appears indecisive, flustered, out of touch, or flat-out musty. Crisp sound bites resonate louder than sound thinking.

* They emphasize ad-libs and a quick, agile wit—again, the stuff of good TV, but not necessarily good leadership. Just how handy is a cute ad-lib if the president learns that Russian president Boris Yeltsin is incapacitated and his nuclear-armed nation is in turmoil? Does he come up with a snappy one-liner when presented with options for long-term peace in the Middle East or economic stability in the United States?

All of this, of course, is a minority report, the emphasis placed on these debates appearing irreversible, another example of entertainment values bleeding through news.

One of the oft-made arguments for debates is that, if nothing else, they spark interest among the electorate, especially in a year like 1996 when experts say voters are largely indifferent to the presidential race. Just as likely, though, the apathetic will leave the debates feeling about the candidates as they feel about them today.

There they go again.

[1996]

Do Great Moves Make
Great Presidents?

◆ *For his next speech, would Ronald Reagan read the Yellow Pages of the phone book?*

Ronald Reagan is America's pantomime president, a Marcel Marceau of the Oval Office.

Such moves. There is a point during every Reagan TV appearance—a speech or a rare press conference like Thursday's—at which you stop listening to his words and focus entirely on his face and body language. It happens unnoticed, a moment buried in your subconscious mind when the TV trap opens and your eyes control your ears.

When Reagan is finished, you are left with the impression that he is a superior communicator. In a sense, he is. Actions and gestures, whether calculated or instinctive, can have a certain eloquence. If not eloquent, Reagan does have a sort of visual glibness that fits TV, as it did during his press conference.

In my own notes I wrote: "Nervous at first, but got stronger and stronger." Most of the pundits seem to share essentially the same conclusion.

If words, rather than TV moves, reflect the true man, though, a different picture emerges. When it comes to words, Reagan is our most imprecise and inarticulate president in the TV era, no match for Eisenhower, Kennedy, Johnson, Nixon, or Carter, and more verbally oafish than even Gerald Ford. The press conference showed that anew.

If anyone was listening as well as watching, that is. Or if anyone bothered to read the transcript.

From the White House's perspective, the object of this press conference was to show the nation that Reagan was not a babbling fool, that rumors about him not being in control of the government were untrue.

On eighteen occasions during his thirty-two-minute meeting with reporters, the President of the United States pleaded ignorance. On other occasions, even after being well rehearsed and speaking from notes, he rambled and meandered and sometimes never answered a question, either because he was being intentionally evasive or apparently was unable to focus on the question.

An example of his press conference management style came early when veteran UPI reporter Helen Thomas asked Reagan this question about roles in the Iran/contra scandal of former National Security Adviser Vice Admiral John M. Poindexter and former national security aide Lieutenant Colonel Oliver L. North:

"Mr. President, is it possible that two military officers, who are trained to obey orders, grabbed power, made major foreign-policy moves [and] didn't tell you when you were briefed every day on intelligence? Or did they think they were doing your bidding?"

Reagan replied: "Helen, I don't know. I only know that that's why I have said repeatedly that I want to find out, I want to get to the bottom of this and find out all that has happened. And so far, I've told you all that I know and, you know, the truth of the matter is, for quite some time, all that you knew was what I'd told you."

The president seemed pleased by the cute and catchy last part of this reply—as if he'd somehow shown up Thomas. But what did he mean to say? That the press had been lazy or dumb? That the press would have known nothing of this story if not for him, even though it was an Iranian publication—not the president—that blew the lid off the Iranian arms deal?

After the press conference, Thomas could be heard complaining to Reagan that he had not really answered her question about Poindexter and North.

Not that it mattered, because he sure *looked* good.

The evening proved that Reagan—after cramming for a single televised quiz from the press the way students cram for a classroom quiz—could get through it all without embarrassment.

He showed that he *was* in control—of the news media. Presidential press conferences are as much a reading on them as they are on the president. It's everybody's photo opportunity.

Much of the public seems to see the White House press corps as a single, frothing bully pressing the president to blurt out impromptu answers to shouted questions. And it is true that the shouted question and off-the-cuff reply are seldom valid and carry added peril when the president doing the answering is not in command of his words.

Yet there is also a tendency to confuse reverence for the presidential office with reverence for the office holder. The best way to show proper reverence for the office is to constantly scrutinize the office holder. And better to err on the side of toughness than on the side of gentility.

On Thursday, the press erred on the side of gentility. There were few tough questions, and the president did not get the grilling one would expect from a press corps that hadn't had direct access to the president in four months.

In fact, most of the hard questions came after the press conference was over, at that inevitable point when the reporters close in on Reagan and pepper him with questions as he appears helpless and adrift.

"Did Don Regan deceive you?"

"Did they lie to you?"

"Did Don Regan pressure you, sir, to change your testimony?"

"Did the vice president—did the vice president object to this plan in Iran, Mr. President?"

"You said that Shultz and Weinberger didn't. Did the vice president?"

"No," Reagan replied weakly.

"He didn't object to it? Thank you, sir?"

Thank you, indeed. Why wasn't that question asked during the press conference?

The curtain fell. "It was boring," former Democratic National Committee chairman Robert S. Strauss pronounced later that night on ABC. It was "show business," protested Hugh Sidey of *Time* magazine.

Of course it was. Americans are one enormous TV constituency. Show business is our life.

On CBS, meanwhile, Dan Rather noted that "the president seemed to be perspiring. Any particular significance to this?" he asked Bruce Morton. Yes, that's what presidents need in the TV age. Not better words or better thoughts, better anti-perspirant.

[1987]

When His Presence Is the Message

◆ *Bill Clinton is so polished as a public performer that you can see your reflection in his suit.*

His sturdy jaw precedes him, he smiles from sea to shining sea. Is this president a candidate for Mt. Rushmore or what?

A recent poll gives President Clinton the same 60 percent public approval rating that Ronald Reagan brought to his second term. But that is not all the two former governors share.

No presidents in the TV era have been as camera-ready.

Reagan, the onetime movie actor, could create a national swoon as president just by grinning and cocking his head boyishly. He also scored mightily with a tear in his eye, another in his voice. His televised press conferences were often convoluted, out-of-body adventures. But he ate the lens. It was less what he said than how affably and earnestly he appeared to say it that resonated loudest and lingered magically.

Clinton has his archive of enduring TV moments, from playing the saxophone with abandon to fending off personal, political, and legal attacks from his many accusers in a continuing war zone that some believe may ultimately undermine and define his second term. Yet like Reagan, Clinton seems to know instinctively when stalked at long range by a TV camera spoiling for a close-up—which is nearly always when a president is in the vicinity—and just as instinctively what to do when he's center screen, where he was during much of Monday's inaugural rite:

The chin edges forward. Read strength, determination. The eyes narrow. Read total absorption. The bottom lip fattens and pushes out beyond the lower lip. Read defiance, yet all-knowing insight. The head nods ever so slightly. Read empathy, sensitivity, and support for whatever platitude is being expressed. And when he adds one of his trademark thumbs up . . .

Love you, man.

Anyone else wearing these looks simultaneously would end up appearing rehearsed or mannered, if not like a jerk. But on Clinton, they blend artfully.

Thus what his speeches say or don't say may matter little in the pantheon of public opinion, and the many TV pundits who faulted his inaugural address Monday and Tuesday just didn't get it.

No "romance," veteran Washington journalist Hugh Sidey lamented about Clinton's rhetoric on the Fox News Channel. "Ersatz eloquence . . . content-free," charged Richard Norton Smith of the Gerald Ford Library and Museum on C-SPAN. "Not . . . very well written or delivered," Tim Russert ruled on NBC's "Today" program.

And so on and so on, the critiques having merit but missing the point. What difference did it make whether the speech was inspired or uninspired? The importance of speeches is ever overrated. Judging Clinton solely by what he said and didn't say at his inaugural ignored the other things he did that eclipsed his oratory.

Although Clinton contributed a heroic cameo to Tuesday night's emotional CBS movie "A Child's Wish," he hardly needs written lines to indelibly stamp TV. Like Reagan, his presence alone conveys a message. And he, not what he says, is that message. Again like Reagan, his demeanor and physical essence, advertising who he is (or who he wants to be seen as), bellow louder than his words. In fact, when it comes to influencing the public, a single medley of expressions from Clinton may be worth much more, to much of America, than every ugly accusation Paula Jones can muster.

He was transfixed, even mouthing lyrics during Monday's singing of "The Battle Hymn of the Republic" by a Little Rock choir. Read spiritual. At one point his hands were in a prayerful pose, tips of his fingers touching his nose and his gaze elevated, as if in divine communication, while hearing Arkansas poet Miller Williams speak of "flowering faces and brambles that we can no longer allow." Read spiritual again.

With TV continuing to be the nation's primary means of discourse, from White House lips to your ears, having an affinity with the medium is essential for modern presidents. Can't do without it. Yet this president is so very, very good at massaging opinion through TV, it remains to be seen whether historians ultimately rate him as having been as determined to safeguard the Constitution as to preserve, defend, and protect his public image.

Perhaps all of this is Clinton doing what comes naturally without forethought. Perhaps he is responding sincerely from the heart, oblivious to the cameras that are closely monitoring and scrutinizing him, pore by pore, sensitive to his every facial tic and nuance. There certainly is no question that he blossoms amid crowds and thrives on public contact, witness TV pictures of his happy late-hours ball-hopping with the first lady Monday night, ending a day that began with telecasts of the Clintons and Gores responding with great zest to a rousing church revival.

Yet it's impossible to know where old-time religion ends and old-time PR begins. After being jobbed so often by politicians, we're conditioned to be suspicious of them and to believe that everything they do is for public consumption. Thus you are left to wonder whether the president was also referring to his image when he said on CBS Sunday about the inaugural speech he was then working on: "It's like polishing a stone. You can always find one more place that you want to polish some more."

[1997]

Our President: Man or Mannequin?

George W. Bush versus Bill Clinton on camera? No contest.

If a brick could talk on television, it would sound like George W. Bush. Yet that may be better for the United States, when hearing from its president, than having in the White House another glib, facile, alluring anchorman biting his lower lip.

Our orator-elect was on TV Monday praising Martin Luther King, Jr., in a short, clunky, unpersuasive speech read so haltingly that it appeared formed from clay and baked in a kiln. Its thud was deafening.

The point is not that Bush was or wasn't speaking with genuine conviction about a civil rights icon held dear by the multitudes. Or that his agenda, a few days before his inauguration, may have been less heart-driven than political—to expand his tenuous mandate by winning over African Americans who voted overwhelmingly for Al Gore on November 7.

Bush would not have been the first politician with something up his sleeve. The point is that when working the lens in a video age, when presidents address the nation largely through TV, Bush is a long, loping Texas stride backward from the fluid communicator he's succeeding. In the eye of the camera, Clinton is the man, Bush the mannequin.

It's for other reasons, not because of his camera skills, that Bush is being sworn in as forty-third president Saturday instead of Gore. What camera skills? Although likable enough on television when affecting his folksy mode, Bush is not even Clinton lite. For which the nation may someday be thankful.

A president who is awkward and relatively transparent on camera is preferable to one willing to use his pizazz and TV mastery to potentially deceive the public, as Clinton did on some occasions, most famously when assuring viewers he "did not have sexual relations with that woman, Miss Lewinsky."

Imagine Bush trying to pull that one off on camera if he were a philanderer. Thickness in the extreme can be dangerous, of course. What the United States doesn't need in the White House is a grunting Quasimodo unable to express himself at press conferences, address the United States resolutely at times of crisis, or define clearly, in more formal settings, his policies and vision for the nation. Bush doesn't appear to fit that lowly category. He's merely bad on camera, and uninspiring, stumbling even when giving a good-ol'-boy farewell speech to Texas in Midland on Wednesday.

Although no golden orator in the classical sense, Clinton is much more effective than Bush, somehow appearing spontaneous even when reading a speech himself and not making eye contact.

Flashing back across Clinton's presidency brings evidence that he has been truly spectacular as a TV communicator, arguably better even than the doyen of charm himself, Ronald Reagan, whose message to the masses was less what he said than it was his own physical presence. Forget the words. One sheepish grin and cock of the head, and the Gipper got you.

Clinton, on the other hand, remains fluent in the language of Lower Lip. He bit his so often, hoping to project careful thought and sincerity, that you half expected it to crack open. And how seamless he was, chamoising his Populist TV persona to a schmoozy gloss during those people-oriented town hall debates that he deployed so expertly to help him at the ballot box in 1992 and 1996.

The White House charismas of Clinton and Reagan can't be taught. Presidents either have them or they don't. As if strategized, however, the style-driven video behaviors of these two presidents were also perfectly tailored to the age in which they rose to national power, coinciding with TV's own celebration of form and process over content, especially in news.

Ideologies aside, how perfect they were for a video news that, decades after being born in vaudeville theaters as newsreels near the turn of the twentieth century, continued to roll in the jugglers, acrobats, dancing girls, and acrobatic dogs.

It's a milieu that just about always has valued performers over informers, Clinton being among the best at this stagecraft. He evoked his TV magic brilliantly to confound the knee-jerk gasbaggery of pundits falling over themselves to forecast his demise for staining his administration along with a certain blue dress. "His presidency is as dead—deader—than Woodrow Wilson was when he had a stroke," deadpanned George Will on ABC when damaging revelations about Monica Lewinsky began trickling out.

Wrong.

Although drawing ridicule from late-night comics and others for his various capers, moreover, Clinton was able, through sheer force of personality, to swat away Leno and Letterman one-liners like King Kong pawing off attacking fighter planes high above New York City.

As his enemies are now aware, Clinton is a long-distance runner. Just when they appear to have him licked, he leaves them behind with a wicked kick. Because common wisdom has been that only the most telegenic of candidates need apply for the nation's top job, there's something refreshing about that not being the case with Bush. His own White House will rise or fall on more than his performances on TV, of course. Unmagnetic Harry Truman's presidency and the TV age were born almost together, after all, and he is given good marks by most historians.

As for that traveling man Clinton, CNN carried a bit of his own farewell address to the Arkansas legislature on Wednesday, and here was looking at you, kid. He was as confident, relaxed, beaming, and commanding as ever, proving that the camera still loves him, even if many Americans don't.

[2001]

Bush's Image Fails to Fill the Screen

◆ *Although his supporters say he's grown into the job, in 2001 TV captured George Bush when he still looked like a toddler.*

Television was their milieu, one of them putting you away with a sheepish grin and cock of the head, the other a seamless communicator fluent in the language of the bitten lower lip. Titans of the airwaves, they used the lens, also, to deliver strength through sheer force of personality.

Whether you liked either or not, or cared for their very different politics, Ronald Reagan and Bill Clinton had in common style, stagecraft, and video qualities perfectly tailored to the age in which they rose to national power, coinciding with TV's own celebration of form and process over content.

Reagan and Clinton had what it takes to communicate to the country effectively through a medium that inevitably favors performers over informers. The nation's forty-third president does not. Three days of George W. Bush on television this week affirm that.

None of us can know what Bush is like behind closed doors. He may be an incisive, take-charge tiger out of the public eye. Better a TV nerd who has other critical presidential skills, after all, than a glib, facile, alluring leader who has the magic but falls apart off camera and is no deeper than his pancake makeup.

Image is important in this arena, however, especially when a nation shaken by tragedy traditionally takes it cues from its highest elected leaders and how they present themselves publicly, and when so many rhetorical demands are placed on modern presidents.

None greater than those facing Bush today, when so many Americans are looking to their president for strength at this time of crisis.

The man does have heart. The pain on his face expresses eloquently his compassion and depth of feeling for the thousands of Americans who died in New York, Pennsylvania, and Washington, D.C., when those four hijacked airliners were crashed. He is aching, too, quite obviously for the anguished loved ones the dead left behind.

Yet throughout this terrible week in U.S. history, Bush has lacked size in front of the camera when he should have been commanding and filling the screen with a formidable presence as the leader of a nation standing tall under extreme duress.

Even his body language is troubling, as when TV cameras captured him returning to the White House late Tuesday after being shuttled about on Air Force One after an alert that the presidential residence and plane also had been possible targets of that day's terrorism. The Bush we saw, walking alone, appeared almost to be slinking guiltily across the lawn.

Bush has seemed almost like a little boy at times—a kid with freckles wishing he were somewhere else—when instead a national anchorman was needed to speak believably with confidence about the state of the union during one of its darkest hours.

He was at his stiffest Thursday while stumbling through a painfully long staged-for-TV conference call in the Oval Office to New York governor George Pataki and New York mayor Rudolph W. Giuliani, telling them he'd be flying to Manhattan today to speak with rescue workers and others. Loved the sentiment, but whose bright idea was the media stunt that made Bush look so bad?

Something seemed not quite right, either, when Bush was addressing the country with heartfelt words and tearing up with genuine emotion during the brief televised news conference that followed. Again, right sentiment, wrong timing.

When speaking of "hunting . . . down" the remaining terrorists and "holding them all accountable," for example, the president was clearly crying, a display of humanity that would have been admirable at other times. But in this context his tears softened his own resoluteness and the toughness of his words directed at those behind the Tuesday attacks that killed thousands.

This is not definitive, of course. Surely no chief executive has been less magnetic than Harry S Truman, whose own presidency was born almost together with television, a medium he surely would not have mastered had he run for a second full term. Yet his backbone turned out to be a steel girder, and historians generally adore him.

The camera was not especially friendly, either, to Presidents Johnson, Nixon, Ford, Carter, and George Bush the elder. History will judge Bush the younger, too, on far more than his TV performances, actions speaking louder than sound bites.

Yet even though the White House charismata of Reagan and Clinton can't be taught, Bush should somehow find a way to rise to the occasion. These are times when America needs a president they can look up to, not just one who will share in their mourning.

[2001]

When No News Is Big News

◈ *Although it would later come back to haunt him as U.S.*
casualties in Iraq mounted steadily, George Bush made photo-op
history this day in 2003 because the media believed that everything a
president did was big news.

Atop the Calendar copy desk . . .

I'm standing here, surrounded by thrilled *Los Angeles Times* copy
editors, to thank them for editing this column announcing that I have
nothing to announce. Nothing other than the tide has turned and the
major mistakes and misspellings in my column have ended, but that
there is still work to be done, for typos will continue to appear.

This is historic, for I am the first TV critic to write a self-serving
fantasy about saying absolutely nothing of note while standing atop a
newspaper copy desk in downtown Los Angeles. And I can tell from
the adoring faces of young copy editors, who have been coached to
cheer my every word, that this is a big boost for their morale and a day
they will not forget.

In other words, the mood here is one of optimism tinged with en-
thusiasm colored by buoyancy marked by joy despite the possibility
that what appears evident, obvious, and irrefutable is merely illusory.

Which is why TV is covering this column live.

Yikes!

Amazing, isn't it? Watching CNN's patsies do giddy cartwheels
on the deck of the aircraft carrier *Abraham Lincoln* for a couple of
hours prior to President Bush's arrival there Thursday evening affirmed how easy it remains for the White House—any White House,

regardless of party—to command attention and manipulate the major media.

Light the flame, the moths will come. As they have since the invention of media stunts, even those less bold and imaginative than this one.

Other majors joined CNN at sea Thursday, of course, and Bush's address would be beamed live also by the Fox News Channel, MSNBC, NBC, ABC, CBS, and just about any other call letters that came to mind.

The president's message: Major combat in Iraq had ended. Which is what the White House had advised the media a day earlier that he would say. And also what Defense Secretary Donald H. Rumsfeld had declared in Afghanistan hours earlier.

Which meant there was no real need to repeat it—except for dramatic effect in front of cameras—and that doing so would not constitute news. Except that Bush would be the rare president to make a speech on a moving aircraft carrier, and to boot, a carrier returning to an emotional welcome in San Diego after active duty in the war on Iraq. To say nothing of a president arriving in the co-pilot seat of a navy jet and debarking for cameras in a green flight suit. A former pilot in the reserves, he reportedly had even taken the stick himself.

Get out! It was brilliant.

So brilliant that a day later CNN's Carol Costello had upped Bush to "commander-in-chief of the free world," which must have been news to the rest of the free world.

Would Bill Clinton's White House have gone for the same brass ring as Bush? Absolutely. In fact, he gave a speech on a carrier at sea in 1993. And Al Gore, had he been elected president? Count on it. Self-promotion is Paragraph 1, Article 1 of the politician's manifesto.

White House planners knew that no one would be able to resist this photo op for the ages, with Bush greeted euphorically by the sailors he had sent to war, and even sleeping over before jetting back to California. Although the timing of his speech (9 P.M. in the East) disrupted network prime-time schedules, it gave him powerful lead-ins from CBS's "Survivor" and NBC's "Friends."

And speaking of friends . . .

"The president is a former pilot so he knows exactly what he's doing up there," crowed CNN's Kyra Phillips from the deck. What he was doing was making photo-op history.

And as the president strode off after landing, CNN's Miles O'Brien added: "I tell you, that's the fighter pilot's strut."

More likely the strut of someone knowing he'd succeeded in using TV to send a missile whistling across the bow of Democrats hoping to topple him in 2004. As many are noting, Thursday provided a cornucopia of flattering images for Bush campaign commercials. Not that he wasn't sincere in his remarks to sailors and everyone else tuning in, but when opportunity presents itself, you take it.

As he did Friday when the all-news channels covered live his lengthy address touting his embattled economic package before an effusive throng at United Defense Industries in Santa Clara. As Bush spoke, he was paired split-screen with pictures of sailors debarking happily from the *Abraham Lincoln* in San Diego.

Take that, Democrats.

Their opportunity, such as it was, came in a Saturday night debate at the University of South Carolina that ABC News televised live and excerpted Sunday morning on "This Week with George Stephanopoulos." How meaningful was it? Nine candidates were crowded into ninety minutes like hoboes in a boxcar. You do the math.

The Democrats were barely a footnote compared with the Bush spectacle, which was all they deserved to be as participants in one of those pointless shallow exercises that typify national political campaigns.

If this is to be the unofficial start of Campaign 2004 (to share time with the Laci Peterson case, naturally), reform should be addressed before the coverage gets out of hand. Candidates won't change unless media change. And media can change.

Read on, as Moses leads them through this wilderness toward the promised land:

* Unclutter the airwaves and stop covering non-news.

* Report in depth candidates' positions on issues, not just their insults. If there's no news to report, don't report it. You will lose nothing

but will gain the affection of viewers for liberating them from campaignspeak, and also gain air time to cover legitimate stories you've neglected. As in, everything else.

＊ The common wisdom in some circles is that everything a president does is newsworthy. Ignore it. The president is not automatically news, even when he wants to be. Other candidates are not news merely because they are candidates.

＊ Bush tooting his own horn is not news. Democrats calling the president a toad is not news. Old Glory is not news just because candidates use it as background for speeches. Red, white, and blue balloons are not news. One-liners are not news.

＊ Candidates manipulating the media are not news, even when you point out that they are manipulating the media.

＊ Blah blah blah is not news.

＊ What a candidate says today is not news if he said it yesterday.

＊ In lieu of actual campaign news, devote twenty seconds at the end of each newscast to a terse review of candidates' activities that day ("George Bush" kissed babies, Democrat X wore a hard hat while touring a plant), and leave it at that. Once a week, run an accelerated montage of candidates' image stunts, if only to ridicule them.

＊ Report polls only monthly, and after the election, report which was the most accurate.

＊ Remember, a sound bite doesn't exist if not heard and a sight bite if not seen. Everyone will benefit from this restraint. Everyone, that is, but professional pundits who have made their reputations appearing on TV to pontificate about campaign news that isn't news.

Will TV heed this advice? Absolutely. And if you buy that, Moses would like to sell you this nice condo in Baghdad.

[2003]

White Meat or Dark?

◈ *Bush junior would learn from an earlier commander-in-chief,*
described below, that Thanksgiving with the troops makes for great
pictures and symbolism.

This year the Thanksgiving Day parade had human floats. Those top
bananas Dan Rather, Tom Brokaw, and Peter Jennings along with
"Good Morning America" were already in the Persian Gulf region
cheering up the troops, and Willard Scott himself had only recently
gotten back.

"In the main, the guys are holding up real well," Rather of Arabia
reported on "CBS This Morning" earlier this week.

So watching second banana George Bush chow down in Saudi
Arabia early Thursday morning amid a sea of sand and camouflage
seemed almost anti-climactic.

But there he was in his shirtsleeves, accompanied by First Lady
Barbara Bush wearing her own desert camouflage and congressional
leaders wearing their biggest smiles. Bush first delivered pep talks at
army and air force installations. However, it was his "centerpiece"
speech to Marines at about 4:45 A.M. and his subsequent Thanksgiving
meal with them that got live coverage on ABC and CNN and exten-
sive tape coverage later that morning on all the networks.

NBC's Jim Miklazewski noted at one point: "This is about messages." And symbols.

There was nothing more symbolic, in fact, than CNN's intercut-
ting live coverage that morning of British Prime Minister Margaret
Thatcher en route by limo to deliver her resignation to the queen with

pictures of Bush en route by military vehicle to that Marine encampment said to be about two hours from the Kuwait border.

Two leaders, two rituals: Thatcher stepping down, Bush stepping it up. His Thanksgiving visit showed anew how a president, through careful orchestration, can command media attention and make it virtually impossible for the camera to ignore him. This event also showed how growing skepticism about the U.S. military buildup in the gulf region can be reduced to barely audible Muzak by dramatic pictures of the commander-in-chief breaking bread with his troops in a distant land. Ronald Reagan could not have managed it better.

The setting—sand and guns in the background—was perfect. The speaker, sprinkling his talk with emotional buzz words calculated to whip up support while boosting morale, echoed a politician on the stump: "Let me just say how pleased Barbara and I are to be here. . . . And let me say this . . ."

There were rousing cheers from the troops.

You could spot the sound bites and sight bites that later would follow on all the newscasts: Bush waving, shaking hands, smiling, giving autographs, issuing a horseshoes challenge, posing for pictures, and chatting. Between mouthfuls of food—and hardly oblivious to the minicam in his face—Bush carried on a continual conversation with troops closing in on him. About Iraqi president Saddam Hussein: "The problem is he talks about all this negotiation, but he won't get out of Kuwait." About possible war with Iraq: "I guarantee you there won't be any more Vietnams. . . . We'll fight to win!"

Today the holiday season, tomorrow the dying season. TV seemed to be hopping on this tank Thursday, with the emphasis far less on the philosophy of war than on the process of war.

As the gulf dilemma drones on and on, TV has been especially brilliant in conveying the emotional and human side of the story. The impact of military mobilization on the home front, particularly the strain on families, has been reported with great sensitivity and insight. And satellite technology has made it possible to reunite loved ones by electronically reaching across the seas.

Except for brief comments from the father of a Marine on "CBS This Morning," however, voices of dissidents opposing Bush's gulf policy were all but excluded from Thursday morning's coverage. The symbolism and emotion of the moment were just too powerful.

As the pictures showed Bush greeting troops, Middle East expert and ABC consultant Judith Kipper questioned Bush's anti-Hussein rhetoric, saying it personalized the conflict and that the president should "slow down." But she was cut off by Peter Jennings:

"Let's get away from politics now. . . . For any U.S. servicemen here to be able to spend a moment with his or her president is clearly a moment to be remembered."

Later on NBC, correspondents Miklazewski and Katherine Couric sat side by side in Saudi Arabia and commented on the Bush visit during the "Today" program as if they were co-hosting the Macy's Thanksgiving Day Parade telecast that Willard Scott and Deborah Norville would co-host later.

Before leaving the air, "Today" managed to squeeze in one last guest, and just like that, Miklazewski was gone and Couric was joined by O. J. Simpson of NBC's "NFL Live." It seemed that Simpson had been in Saudi Arabia preparing a feature for Thursday's Detroit-Denver telecast that was about to follow on NBC. He was ebullient.

"Morale is up, everyone is very positive," Commander Simpson said. "The big question is, 'When are we gonna go home?' not 'Why are we here?' Let's get it on or get out."

It was that sort of holiday.

"So that is Thanksgiving Day for President and Mrs. Bush," Peter Jennings had said earlier, wrapping up ABC's live coverage. It had been a feast in the desert—turkey, roast beef, and ham.

Lots and lots of ham.

[1990]

D-Day and the Resonance of War . . .
Now and Then

◈ *How different real combat is from the war movies that kids of my generation learned from and imitated with our toy guns.*

"I ducked my head under the sharp cracking that was going overhead."
—War correspondent Ernest Hemingway with U.S. troops under fire in a landing craft approaching France, June 6, 1944

Good morning, Normandy!

This is an invasion. The D-day documentaries, black-and-white newsreel footage, and testimonials from military veterans and former riveting Rosies are this spring's blitzkrieg, dusting off memories while massing on television in such force that you can hardly keep count.

With the fiftieth anniversary of the Allies' liberating invasion of France so near, U.S. media are hitting Normandy with everything they've got, waves and waves of camera crews scurrying across its beaches like sand crabs. Although the elements of spectacle are ever present, it's encouraging, at least, to see television cover an event not of its own making.

The invasion cost the lives of 23,000 American troops. "Only those who were there know how horrendous it was," ABC's Peter Jennings reported on videotape from the French coast during Wednesday night's "Turning Point." Surely most on the home front never understood the horror.

Especially the children. Reared on simplified war movies that were as dispensable as popcorn and isolated from the actual killing fields by their geography, that generation of American kids sealed themselves inside an impenetrable play world where war was a dreamy reality at best and death was an abstraction.

There was no television to speak of during World War II and the immediate postwar years. No slaughters in Los Angeles, Bosnia, Haiti, Sudan, Gaza, or Rwanda that anyone could see, no nightly pictures of rotted, fly-buzzed corpses baking in the sun. No wretched victims dying right there on the screen, nothing on a mass scale that could convey to the very young just how gory and grim war was. That wouldn't happen until Vietnam.

"Real war is never like paper war," Hemingway wrote, "nor do accounts of it read much the way it looks."

To many kids of that era, it looked this way: Bang-bang, you're alive.

I remember playing lots of baseball with my friends as a kid in Kansas City, Missouri. Just as vivid are my memories of having fun playing guns.

For us, only one thing could compare to the crack of a bat hitting a ball, and that was the crack of gunfire, at least as we innocently imagined it. We provided our own sound effects, even our own danger (dum-de-dum-de-dum-de-dum) music. There was something very romantic about the fantasy of both shooting someone and pretending to get gunned down yourself, grunting and clutching your chest in mock agony while keeling over, then getting back up and starting the game again. To us, war was a game, an exercise in heroism minus real casualties.

Some things stay in your head. One afternoon in the winter of 1949, my neighbor Jody Aldrich and I returned from the Fiesta Theater excited and energized after watching a Saturday matinee of *Battleground*, a movie about Americans fighting and dying in the Battle of the Bulge. Hearts pounding, we tore into our houses and in only a few minutes were back outside with our plastic guns (I think mine was a

Thompson submachine gun), brown infantry helmets, and other soldier gear, refighting World War II in the snow. Being two years older
than I, Jody pulled rank and, as a result, I got killed probably a dozen
times that afternoon, hitting the white ground so often that my clothes
took on a glacial rigidity. What fun.

It all came back to me while watching "Turning Point." I con-
trasted my childhood war games with the recollections of Normandy
survivors, their voices at times cracking with emotion after all these
years.

"I curled up as small as I could."

"Twenty or thirty G.I.s who had gotten up ran smack into a shell."

"They were just mowed down."

"Men were getting hit, you know, drowning."

"His eyeballs . . . were hanging down."

Reuniting America with its dead sons, the ninety-minute program
ended with an overview of white crosses at Normandy's military cemetery, where so many soldiers are buried beneath a bit of the ground
they fought to free.

During "The MacNeil/Lehrer NewsHour" on PBS Tuesday, artist
and Normandy survivor Tracy Sugerman asserted that the memory of
what happened there will be "dusty and meaningless" to today's children and future generations. A disturbing thought. Yet, sadly, he's
right, and it's something that cannot be changed by all the history les-
sons in the world. Time is too great a barrier to overcome, rendering
us all uncaring amnesiacs when it comes to the major crises experienced by our predecessors.

Thus a lot of people are probably tiring of *this* history lesson that is
now preoccupying so much television, even though it memorializes a
seminal event of a war that changed the twentieth century. It must
seem as abstract to them as it was to war-playing kids in 1949, especially
compared to the contemporary violence that intersects their lives
nightly via their favorite newscast. On CNN Thursday came this report
from Rwanda: "We saw nine bodies. When we got closer, we could see
five were alive, barely alive. Then we witnessed a government soldier
shooting one."

In the 1990s, business as usual.

Unfortunately, it's hard for many to get worked up over Normandy when there's so much in the present that competes for our attention and fear, as television relentlessly reminds us of today's killing fields both abroad and in the United States, where even children—no longer the innocents of yesteryear—have access to firearms. And instead of toys, these guns are real.

Bang-bang, you're dead.

[1994]

Looking to the Past to See the Present

◈ *It's ironic that an HBO miniseries about World War II would provide a more intimate glimpse of combat than news coverage.*

With every fresh stroke, the chance of life grew less and less for those who were not yet killed.
—Leo Tolstoy, *War and Peace*

America at war.

The ache ran deep Wednesday when the television screen showed a terrifying display of deadly firepower sending panicked U.S. troops running for cover in a distant land. Your heart sank when some didn't make it.

The counterattack against terrorism?

Wrong war. Instead it was episode seven of "Band of Brothers," HBO's extraordinary nonfiction miniseries tracing Easy Company of the 101st Airborne in World War II, from training for invading Normandy through Germany's surrender.

Ever palpable today is the angst gnawing at Americans caused by mysteriously spreading anthrax as they fight a war against fear.

Yet how strange—with no speck on the globe potentially beyond TV's panoramic eye—to be excluded from the hotter war going on across the seas. How odd to feel nearer to wars of many years ago than the critical one waged now against the Taliban regime in Afghanistan, almost entirely out of media view.

If not the Napoleonic conflict of Tolstoy's novel, the war in 2001 is still historic and hard to forget. But also one whose violence and pain abroad are easy to ignore, given the knowledge gap separating it from a public distracted at home by the anthrax spores of October.

In contrast, look again at Ken Burns's great PBS documentary series "The Civil War." Pop in the episode on 1862's bloody Battle of Antietam, and swiftly feel the fire of words and old photographs bringing the conflict alive.

Or absorb again the emotional thunderbolts of "The Great War and the Shaping of the 20th Century." That fine PBS work memorialized World War I's slaughter of wave after wave of young men: The body counts in the millions. The shellshocked twitches and disfiguring stumps of survivors. The scarred moonscapes where armies dug their ditch cities. The intricate tunnels at Verdun and terror beneath the ground where poison gas swirled through the earthen, candlelit, putrid-smelling warrens that entombed French and Germans who fell to the choking fumes.

Even closer to the heart is the war personalized in "Band of Brothers," which pay-channel HBO says is averaging an impressive six million–plus viewers an episode, compared with zero Americans at home being granted more than a teasing glimpse of the present combat in Afghanistan.

In early January 1945, Easy's young paratroopers were in Belgium's Ardennes Forest, poised to attack the occupied town of Foy, when the Germans shelled their positions, cutting some of them to pieces.

Wednesday's repeat episode brought it home. Filling the screen at one point was Joe Toye (Kirk Acevedo), on his back but raising himself just enough so he could see the bottom part of his leg, which lay in the snow, a yard away from the upper part. Trying to drag Toye to a foxhole, Bill Guarnere (Frank John Hughes) was blasted too, his own leg reduced to crimson pulp. Traumatized by the sight of fallen friends, Lieutenant Buck Compton (Neal McDonough) dropped his weapon and helmet in a vacant daze, then sat with head buried in hands.

Soon a second withering assault began, and as two Americans shouted encouragement to an exposed comrade crawling frantically toward their foxhole, a German shell blew them apart.

That you felt. The arbitrary nature of death in war, you felt. As you do in coming episode eight when a soldier, in the wrong place in the wrong time, is killed by German mortar fire while carrying a sack of potatoes from one building to another.

Wars are not conducted for the entertainment of couch blobs snug in their homes, and President Bush has repeatedly stressed that this one will require great patience from Americans and be fought in part beyond public view. So, fellow citizens, get used to it.

Yet the disconnect remains disturbingly surreal, and the battle against Osama bin Laden and his Al Qaeda terrorist network is as sanitized on TV as the Gulf War in 1991.

Although the September 11 terrorist attacks were a horror that won't soon fade, the question asked in 1991 remains valid today: How can Americans fully appreciate the full, terrible nature of distant war—as when Vietnam gore was beamed into their homes decades earlier—if what TV shows them is largely sterilized?

Of no help is the Taliban, which abhors press freedom and allows in cameras only to publicize U.S. misfires or for some other propaganda advantage. And the Pentagon is tightly censoring information it's parceling to Americans on an impersonal, need-to-know basis.

That includes fancy graphics and computer-driven pictures from the air of bombing raids showing Nintendo-like targets going splat. It includes officers in uniforms briefing the press with visual aids while speaking the arcane tongue of "engagement zones," followed by retired officers in suits using Telestrators to brief viewers on the briefings.

Whether the coverage we're getting reflects the war's air focus, legitimate concerns for security, or Pentagon paranoia—or all three—does not alter the reality that warfare is being defined for Americans via second- and thirdhand experiences.

Primary sources beyond accounts spoon-fed by the government? They're rare when media are relegated mostly to the war's fringes.

After a U.S. bomb inadvertently hit that Red Cross warehouse in the Afghan capital, Kabul, for example, CNN went to its correspondent Walter Rogers in northern Afghanistan, who naturally had seen nothing. He turned to a Red Cross spokesman, who also had seen nothing, but could relate what he had "heard" of a bomb hitting the structure.

Meanwhile, CNN's Christiane Amanpour got her "exclusive" interview with Defense Secretary Donald Rumsfeld this week, but in Islamabad, Pakistan, she was relying on "sources" for word of heavy bombardments of Afghanistan cities that yielded "potential heavy casualties" in Kandahar.

Just as the Fox News Channel on Thursday illustrated "reports coming out of new attacks" by drawing circles around cities on a map.

As for close-up combat coverage, there was this. "The battle draws on for hours," reported NBC's Jim Cummins, with the 101st Airborne. Yes, the same 101st Airborne whose World War II duty is depicted in "Band of Brothers." Except this week's combat on NBC, captured in hazy green nightscope, instead of being real was a "live action exercise" in Fort Polk, Louisiana.

If these men do see action in Afghanistan, will you and I get even a peek at them? Will a Joe Toye or Bill Guarnere be among them? A Buck Compton? A thoughtful Harvard man like David Webster (Eion Bailey), who more than any other soldier in "Band of Brothers" sees the horrors of battle through the observant eyes of Tolstoy's Pierre Bezuhov in *War and Peace*?

In a poignant voice-over, Webster wonders if Americans back home will "ever know what it cost the soldiers to win this war."

Whatever that cost in this year's fight against terrorism, it appears we'll be learning of it from "sources."

[2001]

A New War, but the Same Old Tube

◈ *Need a feel-good upper? From the ashes of tragedy, we bring you flawed common wisdom and false assumptions.*

In the teeming marketplace of ideas, common wisdom is what everyone "knows" to be true.

Today's common wisdom is that America and Americans "will never be the same." That's a given, in a sense, for both individuals and nations are the sums of many experiences and influences, a life residue thickening like waxy yellow buildup on kitchen linoleum. That old refrain about "the same-old same-old" notwithstanding, today is never quite like yesterday.

By implication, though, "never . . . the same" means change that is neither slow-building nor fleeting, but dramatic and lasting—as in, U.S. air travel will never be the same. True. Families and friends of victims of the terrorist strikes will never be the same. True. Survivors who experienced hijacked airliners slamming into the twin towers of New York's World Trade Center will never be the same. True. Visitors to the smoking rubble, beneath which are unknown numbers of anonymous bodies, will never be the same. True.

Here's more common wisdom: U.S. television, which beamed those terrorist acts and their aftermath to the world, also will never be the same. Yes, forever transformed, eternally sensitized, responding now to a public whose TV tastes are governed by fresh perceptions arising from one of the most traumatic events of our time.

Talk about a cosmic impact. Television, after all, is just about everyone's extended family. It's the electronic campfire around which we all gather into the wee hours to hear and witness tales of life that shape how we see ourselves and the world. Watching TV, it's been said, is what Americans do more than anything but work and sleep.

But, alas, the terrorism-triggered revolution of TV is vastly overstated. Short-term changes, yes. Long-term, no. New Yorkers are estimating that their cleanup will take six months to a year. In returning to normalcy, TV's own cleanup will end much sooner.

From picture tube inventor Philo T. Farnsworth to the present, in fact, lasting change in TV has flowed not from outside events, however extreme or cataclysmic, but from new technologies, economic forces, and regulatory shifts.

Videotape changed TV permanently. Color did. Cable did. Satellites in the heavens did. Portable lightweight cameras did. Digital signals did.

There are overlaps. The Vietnam conflict changed TV indelibly, for example, but only because of technology that allowed newscasts to cover the war as they did, with the military's cooperation, thereby nourishing doubts about the conflict's wisdom.

For the roots of today's coarsened TV, look not to sliding moral values but to another fluidity that came into play in the mid-1980s. It was there, at this crossroads of burgeoning cable and a softening economy, that an ever-expanding number of TV entities found themselves competing for a shrinking advertising dollar. And the major networks, fearful of not holding viewers, began turning increasingly to violence, raunchspeak, and sex to keep pace with their relatively unregulated nonbroadcast competitors.

Of even greater importance is the present loosening of federal regulations governing media ownership, which threatens to further stunt TV diversity. The concentration of influence narrows TV's voices to the very few.

The recent terrorist holocaust won't equal any of this in leaving a permanent stamp on TV. Mark down as a wonderful oddity the highly competitive TV industry's recent lovefest in airing a star-laden telethon to raise money for the New York relief effort. It recalled World War I, when pockets of U.S. and British troops briefly celebrated with German soldiers on Christmas Eve, after which both sides returned to their trenches and resumed slaughtering each other.

One can predict, of course, that viewers shaken by the recent real-life calamity may now be less inclined to fret about indulged adventurers playing to TV while facing small hardships in pursuit of big paydays. In other words, ratings may slip irrevocably for faux reality trifles along the lines of "Survivor" and its offspring.

Yet who's to say, if that happens, that such shows wouldn't have vanished during this period anyway through attrition? History teaches us that prime-time genres, from quiz shows to westerns, have natural life cycles, and that frequently what goes and comes around on this carousel at some point goes around again.

What of other TV neighborhoods?

We can expect late-night comics Jay Leno, David Letterman, and others, whose monologues usually take no political prisoners, to continue shying away from their customary presidential slams—those merciless jokes about a thudding President Bush, for example, remaining patriotically on the spike. No "Saturday Night Live" digs at the president either, or gags about airlines or New York, which has been elevated by catastrophe to icon status.

The sensitivity bar also has been lowered in other regions of TV entertainment. Wiped immediately from TV's skyline were New York shots of the twin towers and stories about terrorist violence, Arabs, Muslims, and other subjects even indirectly related to last month's events, the single exception to date being a special episode of NBC's "The West Wing." Yet all of this is temporary. Americans may never be the same, but they want their television to be, their mixed messages about the medium's extreme violence aside. Recent strong ratings for escapist prime-time fare suggest that time, the great healer, is already at work, and that viewers are craving a return to the structure and routine of their lives.

In TV's news arena, the networks and twenty-four-hour news channels have been hemorrhaging dollars to finance their expanded coverage of the New York story and its lingering ache, a financial outpouring that may cripple their ability to cover future major stories, especially abroad. The networks, however, have been closing bureaus and curtailing coverage for years, and have been obsessed with celebrities. How could they possibly do worse?

On another front, the downside of the temporary grounding of private choppers was the shrinking of traffic reports, and the blessing was an absence of gratuitously televised freeway chases that bump important stories from the air. Those restrictions have been eased, however, and expect the choppers to be up and whirring everywhere soon.

Echoing Bush about the U.S. fight against terrorism, CNN at one point called its coverage "A New Kind of War." The common wisdom here, however, is that America won't have a new kind of television. Not for much longer, anyway.

[2001]

War as a Sales Tool

◈ *Wars are like enormous whales that are carved up by Eskimos and their entrails and every piece utilized for a specific need and function.*

Meeting the press on TV last week was President Bush's national security adviser, Condoleezza Rice.

"The important thing is to complete the mission," said Rice, deploying "mission" again and again in answering questions from reporters about America's anti-terrorism campaign. What is that mission regarding television's teeming, throbbing bazaar of doctrines and personalities?

Operation Enduring Promotion.

As the U.S. economy sags, merchandising through TV has rarely been as vigorous, ironically. That takes in not only the usual sponsor-paid ads, including those new thirty-second spots boosting terrorism-scarred New York as again a swell place to visit, but especially the unpaid, unidentified ones that have always been ground zero for newscasts and talk shows.

Propaganda of all kinds, from newscasters saluting themselves to national leaders lobbying the public, is the furniture of TV. Commercials start at the top these days, notably Bush's nationally televised speech Thursday that many commentators correctly labeled a "pep talk" by a president understandably selling wartime confidence and his economic stimulus package.

It was a masterfully designed sales pitch before a boisterous and supportive Atlanta audience of uniformed military, law enforcement officers, firefighters, postal workers, and health-care workers who spent as much time on their feet applauding as in their seats.

"Let's roll!" Bush ended with a bang, shrewdly adopting the reported last words of Todd Beamer, one of the passengers said to have heroically fought terrorist hijackers on the jet that crashed in Pennsylvania on September 11.

It's not only the White House that's adopting the war effort as an emblem, though. On Friday, ABC's "Good Morning America" and hosts Diane Sawyer and Charles Gibson ran themselves up the flagpole when telecasting from the returning aircraft carrier *Enterprise*, which launched the first air strikes against Afghanistan.

"This is the first time an entire U.S. broadcast has come from a U.S. carrier at sea," someone said. A nice idea were it not for Admiral Gibson being decked out in Navy threads.

Meanwhile, CNN keeps running thunderous promos that sell its war coverage as "Saving Private Ryan II." And what juxtapositions. One day anchor Kyra Phillips was selling CNN's extended live coverage of police chasing a flaming lumber truck in Dallas as significant news—expressing dismay that the driver was endangering other motorists (duh)—and the next crouching on one of those floor maps while reviewing U.S. battle military strategy in Afghanistan.

Speaking of selling, Bush administration advisers were to have met with Hollywood leaders here Sunday, reportedly to lobby for TV and movies that rallied around the war effort in ways inoffensive to the fragile international coalition assembled by the United States.

"You might see Julia Roberts speaking Farsi," a straight-faced Bryce Zabel, chairman of the Academy of Television Arts and Sciences, told a TV reporter. Yes, Iran would love her.

The naive faith in good old American know-how turning every tide was alive also in the administration's decision recently to hire legendary advertising executive Charlotte Beers to counteract Osama bin Laden's anti-U.S. propaganda said to be influencing Arabs and Muslims abroad.

Madison Avenue or Middle East—what's the difference, right? "I'm not as awed by the bin Laden propaganda machine as the world is at this point," Beers told NBC's Andrea Mitchell last week. "She got me to buy Uncle Ben's rice . . .," Secretary of State Colin Powell told Mitchell.

That's the ticket. Instead of leaflets, the U.S. should be dropping boxes of Uncle Ben's.

Maybe what's needed is more of a hard sell. Take Bill O'Reilly's biggest fan, Bill O'Reilly. If you tuned in the host of Fox News Channel's "The O'Reilly Factor" one night last week, you would have heard him cap one of his patented harangues with another pitch for viewers to buy his best-selling book *No Spin Zone*. He also found time to mention his website and a special Internet deal for an autographed copy of the book with a free bumper sticker and a three-month trial subscription to a magazine that carries a column he writes—an incredible offer—for a single low price.

Two nights later he ended his show with another infomercial, this one advertising his coming appearances on other shows, including NBC's "Today," where on Friday he renewed his attack on the September 11 Fund, which he bitterly charges has mishandled money collected for families of those who died in the terrorist attacks.

O'Reilly reacted badly when co-host Matt Lauer suggested that he may be less interested in going on shows to talk about that issue than in promoting his book. Lauer said that O'Reilly's publicist told "Today" that "Bill will not appear unless you show the book."

"That's publicists," O'Reilly tossed it off.

If O'Reilly was selling his book, another cable news star—Geraldo Rivera—was selling himself as a serious war correspondent. Rivera is about to leave his CNBC show to cover the war in Afghanistan for the Fox News Channel. Looking terrific, the warbound Rivera talked about it on Friday's syndicated "Live with Regis and Kelly."

Rivera, a loud advocate for more heat and passion in news reporting, spoke of his anger following the September 11 terrorist attacks. "I couldn't sit at my comfortable anchor desk and watch as younger men and women went off to protect us," he said. He added that he would leave this week for the former Soviet republics in the north and "work my way down." He said he anticipated about a six-week gig. "I'm a war correspondent now," he said.

Although the U.S. military can't locate bin Laden, it was a given on this show that a personal showdown with Osama was in Geraldo's future. "If anyone can find Osama bin Laden, Geraldo can," promised Kelly. "What would you do if you found him?" she wanted to know.

Instead of interviewing him, Rivera said, "I would want to tear his beard off. I deputize myself to be part of the posse that brings him in." He said he would contact the U.S. military and "call in the artillery, call in the big planes."

It won't be easy, with all those caves for Rivera to search.

Regis: "Take care of yourself." And, above all, keep on looking great. As for all you other journalists thinking of heading for Afghanistan with an itch to take out bin Laden?

Let's roll.

[2001]

Seeking Symbolic Moments
in the Tides of History

❖ *When Saddam Hussein's statue came down in that square, wishful thinking was erected in its place.*

Television is moments.

It was such moments—converging sights and sounds that instantly convey lasting impressions of dramatic change—that helped make television so memorable in earlier times, from bloody combat and dashed lives in the jungles of Vietnam to the 1989 fall of the Berlin Wall and collapse of dictator Nicolae Ceausescu in Romania. To say nothing of a solitary dissident boldly defying the Chinese military by using his body to block a column of tanks in Beijing's Tiananmen Square.

Where Wednesday's Baghdad event ranks in this hierarchy of cosmic images remains to be seen, as does the long-range result of a U.S.–led invasion that has toppled and possibly even killed Saddam Hussein. Unknown is whether today's euphoria will endure or become tomorrow's frustration and sorrow.

When recalling Iraqis' gaining freedom from Hussein's oppressive regime, however, memories will surely go to TV pictures of his forty-foot statue being pulled down in Baghdad's joyous Firdos Square. Here was a freeze frame for the ages, a poster in the making, a signature for a shift in history whose ultimate consequences are a blur.

Symbols don't come more powerful, unless it's other TV pictures of the statue's head being dragged through the city with a noose around its neck, and Iraqis, including children, hitting it and a huge photo of Hussein with shoes, slippers, and sandals—an insult among Arabs. All the while, TV was rolling, still cameras clicking away, the world watching.

The war's live pictures from media with sand-swept combat units are something you talk about. If Vietnam was the living-room war, after all, this is the living war, thanks to technology and the Pentagon's decision to embed media in combat units as intimate witnesses.

But Wednesday's pictures you remember.

As you do the jubilance of Iraqis in that square, as some vented their anger by pounding the statue's base with sledgehammers before a Marine armored recovery vehicle helped bring it down. Why, there must have been thousands there.

Or so it seemed much of the time.

"You can see it on the screen," a news anchor cried out from somewhere.

But see what? If the emotion spoke for itself as people let off steam, the pictures spoke half-truths. With a camera fairly tight on the square, teeming, cheering Iraqis pressed against the edges of the TV screen, as if Baghdad's multitudes had poured from their homes and hiding places to celebrate Hussein's demise in this city of nearly five million.

When the camera occasionally pulled back, however, it was apparent there were maybe three hundred, about the size of a healthy demonstration in front of the federal building in Westwood, once again the camera creating its own misleading universe. And when cameras occasionally widened to shots of Iraqis parading elsewhere in the streets, their visual impact also shrank.

Perhaps it meant nothing, perhaps it meant everything. Perhaps many Iraqis were still too frightened or skeptical to publicly join the early-evening celebration, or many decided not to take part for other reasons. Perhaps those multitudes would turn out in Baghdad today, just as a much larger crowd of Arab Americans took to the streets in Dearborn, Michigan, on Wednesday in support of Hussein's removal.

In any case, Wednesday's contrast between dominant TV images and street reality provided a cautionary note about putting too much faith in TV pictures and how well the United States and this power transfer would be accepted in a post-Hussein scenario. That ambiguity was something to consider.

Meanwhile, these stirring pictures were replayed repeatedly. TV chipped off sections of the story, just as chunks of Hussein's statue were probably carried off for posterity, and human-interest pieces were worked up capturing Iraqi curiosity and happiness. Taking a lead from the Pentagon and the White House, though, much of the early coverage was more wary than giddy, as if TV too feared overstating what had happened.

When it came to history's pantheon of epic TV footage, nothing Wednesday matched seeing hundreds of thousands of citizens demonstrating in Prague in support of ending Czechoslovakia's Communist government. Or Ceausescu and his wife after their execution, the close-up of him on his side with his eyes open, staring vacantly.

Nothing Wednesday was as exhilarating as witnessing the dismantling of the Berlin Wall via TV and seeing throngs of ecstatic Germans attacking it with pickaxes and celebrating the demise of this symbol of oppression.

As for Baghdad, it was only a statue, after all, not the real Hussein, whose fate and whereabouts are unknown. And what of TV pictures of a U.S. soldier briefly draping an American flag over the statue's head, as if the U.S. were a colonial conqueror? However fleeting, that will be a symbol too.

[2003]

Talking the Talk Before
Taking the Walk

◈ *Before Karla Faye Tucker was put to death for killing with a pickax, with Larry King she looked and sounded as demure as the girl next door.*

They're saying now that despite her growing fame and list of testimonials, it will take a miracle to save Karla Faye Tucker from dying February 3. If she were behind bars in California, it would take a dozen miracles.

That's because unlike Texas, where Tucker is on death row, California effectively bars inmates' one-on-one interviews with the media at state prisons. And the thirty-eight-year-old Tucker's slender hopes of escaping lethal injection indeed flow mainly from her sympathetic national television chats, in which she comes across as extremely likable, contrite, earnest, totally transformed, and devoutly Christian while acknowledging her guilt and offering no excuses. If she were in California, she wouldn't be having those chats.

Sister Helen Prejean, a foe of capital punishment and author of the book that yielded the movie *Dead Man Walking*, told Fox News Channel's Catherine Crier recently that if Tucker is put to death, "what we are saying is that the saving of a person, the changing of a person, the redemption of a person doesn't matter."

Television has made it possible for viewers themselves to assess Tucker's level of redemption, for she is the first condemned murderer in memory to present her case for life on national TV. Her case is . . . herself.

She looked as demure as the girl next door last week when CNN's Larry King faced her for an hour across a plexiglass barrier in prison, the same partition that separates her from her visiting husband, a prison minister she married in 1993.

Tucker's attorneys are challenging the legality of the Texas clemency process. But it's favorable TV exposure that has elevated her far above the typical cause célèbre, attached a haunting human face with dark curls to every subsequent TV and newspaper story about her, and increased pressure on Texas governor George W. Bush to save her life in a state that leads the nation in executions.

Most court-watchers believe he won't, given the precedent that would set in Texas, and how he would be opening himself to charges that he commuted Tucker's sentence to life because of her gender. Moreover, he has never commuted a death sentence or delayed an execution.

Without Tucker's TV celebrity, however, her window of opportunity would have been even narrower.

Thus in California, her execution most likely would have been a thundering slam dunk. California is one of fifteen states that, encumbered by advanced myopia, have restricted or choked off media access to prisoners, and vice versa. One rationale for imposing this state's restrictions in 1995 was that sensational coverage by tabloids and other segments of media tended to reward notorious criminals with celebrityhood. A sound bite making the rounds among state legislators then: "You shouldn't do the crime and end up on 'PrimeTime.'"

Who in the world would look forward to more of Charles Manson on TV, where, before 1995, Los Angeles newscasters and some national programs regularly granted him camera access from prison during ratings sweeps periods, and then heavily promoted his inevitable rantings to inflate their ratings? You made your macho bones in local news by boldly going "one on one with Charlie."

Yet penalizing the many for the sleaze of the few is not only unfair but also unenlightened, thickening the barbed wire around legitimate information trickling from the state's tax-funded prison system. As for prisoners on death row the likes of Tucker, moreover, why shouldn't an

1

inmate facing death, female or male, Christian, Muslim, or Jew, have a shot at taking his or her case to the people via the medium that reaches the most people? Even if the overwhelming majority of these doomed cons are poseurs who will tell any lie to save their lives, a few may not be.

Rarely has TV been used as aggressively on behalf of saving a life as with Tucker, who has spent fourteen years in prison after taking part in a grisly double murder that found her, accompanied by her boyfriend, wielding a lethal pickax against Daniel Ryan Garrett and Deborah Ruth Thornton in Houston, then later boasting on tape that she had an orgasm each time her weapon struck her male victim. Seldom has homicide been as gruesome. But that was another Karla Faye Tucker, she, her lawyers, and others have maintained on TV and elsewhere.

Yes, Americans appear queasier about executing women than men, which is subtext for the photo ops granted Tucker. Yes, she would be the first woman to be executed in Texas since 1863, and the first in the United States since 1984. Yes, even conservative Pat Robertson, usually a zealot for capital punishment, is urging fellow Republican Bush to commute her sentence, citing her "authentic spiritual conversion." And yes, Robertson looms as a kingmaker of the religious right, whose support Bush would covet if he makes a run for the White House in the coming presidential season.

All of that notwithstanding, without Tucker's TV exposure, her crusade to live beyond February 3 probably would not have risen above the level of footnote.

Clearly, her lawyers have sought to exploit their client's telegenic qualities by using TV in a way that would have been barred to them in California, where Governor Pete Wilson last year vetoed a bill that would have revoked those state regulations that all but pinch off one-on-one media access to prisoners. Under existing rules here, reporters may question inmates only at random during prison tours, ask them to call collect, or seek access to them during regular visiting hours—but without pens, notebooks, tape recorders, and, of course, cameras.

In Tucker's case, the TV lens is her only means of selling herself, in effect, directly to the public, in hopes Americans en masse will lobby the Texas Board of Pardons, whose recommendation for commutation the governor needs before he can act himself, even though he subsequently could ignore it.

In addition to King, Tucker has done interviews with "60 Minutes" on CBS and with Charles Grodin on CNBC, a portion of which also aired on NBC's "Today" program. Although media requests are still pouring in, Tucker plans only one more interview, with Robertson's "700 Club" program, a spokeswoman for one of her lawyers, David Botsford, said by phone from Austin on Tuesday.

Christian broadcaster Robertson discovered Tucker only after she found Christ, an earlier supportive story that the "700 Club" did on her foreshadowing the publicity that was coming. The big national TV push for Tucker began with last month's highly favorable segment on "60 Minutes," one of TV's most watched programs. It didn't hurt her cause that "60 Minutes" even seemed to exaggerate the size of her constituency.

King followed recently with his two-parter, whose sound bites resonated beyond CNN. The second half was a round-table that included Tucker's attorneys, Thornton's embittered widower, a Board of Pardons member, and Robertson, who never adequately explained why he had embraced Tucker after ignoring countless men on death row who also claimed contrition and Christian rebirth well before being executed.

Part one was especially indelible, though, with King facing Tucker alone in an interview of amazing intimacy, given its physical awkwardness. It was a powerful connection that Tucker made through her plexiglass, a smiling, gentle, God-evoking advertisement for herself that surely many viewers found impossible to reconcile with the monster whose evil crime she is expected to die for.

[1998]

Ultimate Reality

◆ *How can we televise executions? How can we not?*

Growing national debate over the death penalty—coming when voyeurism is ever browning the television landscape in both news and entertainment—makes this an ideal occasion to revisit a related hot-button issue.

Lights! Cameras! Execution!

If the TV lens is to be our designated peeper this year and after— from "gotcha" footage on newscasts to "Survivor" and Wednesday's coming "Big Brother" on CBS—then have it count for something beyond frivolous diversion. Keep the fluff. But have TV also witness what nearly 75 percent of U.S. states authorize and polls say more than 70 percent of Americans favor.

Capital punishment. The needle, the chair, the gas chamber, whatever.

Are we really a nation of voyeurs, as many claim these days, citing a pattern of public snooping whose most recent subjects range from the hanky-panky of President Clinton to the rat-eating thrills of fame-seeking survivalists on CBS? Or is "Survivor" a huge hit because, as "Politically Incorrect" host Bill Maher says, "People enjoy watching other people lose"? Televising an execution would be a test. Welcome to a reality show that actually is real.

The purpose, to reiterate, would not be a media stunt or grisly tit-illation, but visual access to a policy whose full extent reaches the public now only through the thick filters of TV and movie drama (*Dead*

Man Walking) and the handful of news media let in as eyewitnesses ("About two chest heaves, he turned purple, that was it").

Having it on TV in living purple would be too ghastly, you say? The way news footage of fatal crashes at air shows, aerialists falling to their deaths, and the possibility of a televised Robbie Knievel jump going bad are not too ghastly?

A little consistency, please.

If the multitudes could handle gruesome live pictures of a Los Angeles motorist blasting himself in the head with a shotgun a couple of years ago, and Jack Kevorkian's death-giving appearance on "60 Minutes," they surely could handle prison officials imposing on condemned inmates a policy of state-performed legal killing that most Americans cheer.

After all, the 1998 audience for the since-imprisoned Kevorkian giving a lethal injection to a man with advanced Lou Gehrig's disease almost matched the estimated 24 million who saw last week's episode of "Survivor." Advertised in advance, that "60 Minutes" segment aimed a piercing laser at the issue of so-called mercy killing. The footage of Kevorkian and his consenting subject got people talking, widening the debate beyond the abstract and theoretical.

Just as, especially now, televising an execution would sharpen the dialogue about the death penalty, which is increasingly in the news because of publicity about the potential of enhanced DNA and the many clemency appeals confronting Texas governor George W. Bush as he aims for the White House. Both Bush, a shoo-in for the Republican nomination, and his likely Democratic foe, Vice President Al Gore, favor the death penalty.

If they despise government in the shadows as much as they insist, they should not resist putting executions on TV, where everyone can see them. Just as, if there is nothing to hide, other Americans who endorse the death penalty should not oppose the camera's presence in state killing rooms.

Nor should the pro-choice crowd, moreover, oppose televising legal abortions (the video technology is available), however emotional the impact.

To review once more, these telecasts would occur on a state-by-state basis and require the subject's permission (which might preclude abortions). They would be videotaped, tightly structured, and presented in context. When it comes to executions, no romanticized eulogies or metaphorical walks into a sunset for the doomed inmate. Instead there would be a review of the case with ample material about the crime or crimes, the victim or victims, and no exclusion of brutality, terror, and suffering.

Here's betting the audience would be larger than you might expect. The purpose would be knowledge, though, not ratings. Whether an execution or an abortion, in other words: you asked for it, you got it. If you're a true believer who can stomach what you see, so be it.

There's no question of TV's power to influence. The Independent Film Channel last year ran Randy Benson's devastating short film about a rudimentary animal shelter in rural North Carolina where up to forty dogs a week, many of them pets given up by locals, were euthanized after just one day's grace. Killed not by relatively humane lethal injection but by locking them into a bin (often atop dogs killed earlier) and turning on poison gas.

The squeals of the dying dogs were unbearable but important to hear to understand the agony of their deaths. Since that film aired, creating a stir, the shelter has been replaced by a modern facility where animals are killed by injection. These were innocent dogs, though, accused of nothing but being dogs, in contrast to humans condemned to death for heinous slayings.

George W. Bush has presided over 135 executions in Texas, more than any governor in history. His latest denial of a stay went against Jessy San Miguel, a confessed murderer who Thursday became the fifth inmate there to die of lethal injection in June. His death closely followed the much higher-profile execution of Gary Graham, who drew wide support while maintaining his innocence to the end. Would televising his execution have changed opinions about the death penalty, pro or con?

And what of Karla Faye Tucker, who attracted enormous public sympathy while claiming on death row in 1998 that she had been reborn long since taking part in a grisly pickax murder years earlier? What would have been the impact had this soft-speaking Texan—looking as demure as the girl next door after claiming to have found Christ—received her needle on TV instead of out of public view, after on-camera interviews with CNN's Larry King and others had attached to her name a haunting face and dark soft curls?

How much earlier, moreover, would Florida have switched to lethal injections (as it did this year under Governor Jeb Bush) if its ancient electric chair, nicknamed "Old Sparky," had been televised torching condemned men as it killed them?

Who would want to watch this macabre reality other than sick voyeurs? Who wouldn't, if the goal is public awareness?

[2000]

Timothy McVeigh: The Closed Circuit

◈ *When a killer's crime is public, his execution should be too.*

If confessed mass murderer Timothy (not "Tim," as some TV people chummily call him) McVeigh is executed June 11 or on any other date, I want to see him die.

Not necessarily in person at the U.S. Penitentiary in Terre Haute, Indiana, where McVeigh is still on death row after getting a stay, although that would be fine. Already picked, though, are the few media members and others who will be watching there through a glass window, as provided by law.

I'd settle, instead, for seeing McVeigh die on closed-circuit TV. The federal government is offering that option in Oklahoma City, where in 1995 McVeigh detonated a truck bomb that killed 149 adults and 19 children at the Alfred P. Murrah Federal Building.

McVeigh has been quoted as callously labeling the kids he blew apart "collateral damage" in his quest to avenge the government's 1993 raid on Branch Davidians near Waco, Texas, in which seventy-five perished.

Nonetheless, watching him die won't be pleasant, I'm fairly sure. I can take it, though, and I know you can too. We're veterans of death on TV, after all, as far back as seeing Jack Ruby gun down Lee Harvey Oswald in Dallas in 1963. And especially after seeing live news coverage three years ago of a deranged Los Angeles motorist blowing away half his face with a shotgun on a freeway overpass. What sight could be worse than that?

186 | NOT SO PRIME TIME

Surely not McVeigh's final act. As I understand it, he'll be strapped down on a gurney as prison technicians give him a series of injections, including a muscle relaxant designed to protect him from the pain of death and two more shots, one to stop his breathing, another to stop his heart and kill him.

I'd take witnessing that any day over seeing death by shotgun, however speedy, with a victim leaving his brains on the pavement.

As a U.S. citizen, moreover, I have as much right as my fellow citizens to watch McVeigh die on TV. Correct?

Obviously not.

I asked for a seat at the closed-circuit telecast, but the U.S. Bureau of Prisons said no because I wasn't a survivor of the bombing or a relative of a victim. Thanks to Attorney General John D. Ashcroft, only they are being given entry to this special telecast of McVeigh dying by injection in the first federal execution in nearly four decades.

And of course, there'll be no national telecast or authorized additional showing of any kind now that a federal judge has turned back an Internet company's efforts to offer live video of the execution on the Web at $1.95 a pop.

Sound and video recording devices are banned by law from federal executions. Ashcroft made an exception for McVeigh, approving the closed-circuit telecast to accommodate a reported 285 surviving victims and family members who said they wanted to watch the bomber die, a group too large for the small witness room adjacent to the execution chamber in Terre Haute.

Call it curiosity, even twisted voyeurism. I want to view McVeigh's execution, however, because I want to see for myself, and not hear from others, what it's like for the government to put someone to death.

I'm against capital punishment, whether McVeigh drifts off serenely or departs as gruesomely as Florida murderers who at times flamed up like Roman candles when dying in an electric chair nicknamed "Old Sparky." But I'm avidly for televising executions, believing the public should confront the reality that polls say it endorses, that it's hypocrisy to approve actions one hasn't the courage to witness, that averting eyes from the consequences of one's deed—as McVeigh himself appears to have done—is cowardly.

Besides, governments in democracies are meant to do things in the open. So I applaud, on both philosophical and humanitarian grounds, Ashcroft arranging this special viewing in Oklahoma City. If McVeigh is to die, and watching him die brings these folks peace, closure, or whatever, give them the best seats in the house.

But help me on this part. If the execution is fit viewing for them, why isn't it for the rest of us? If watching it won't harm them, why will it harm us? If they have earned this opportunity, why haven't all Americans, many of them also carrying deep emotional scars from the bombing? If it could grant them serenity, why wouldn't it all across the land? Why is what's good for them not good for everyone else?

I can't imagine agreeing with McVeigh about anything except that his own execution will be an act of state barbarism and that, as he has urged, it should be televised nationally and not limited to a select group in Oklahoma.

Ashcroft is said to oppose anything that would generate more exposure for McVeigh, believing the ultimate photo op would be a national telecast of his death, his final words becoming a dangerous manifesto of his gnarled beliefs.

But McVeigh long ago became a martyr to his comrades and others potentially in that camp. As far as self-serving publicity, that genie too is out of the bottle, with him already having his say at length in *American Terrorist: Timothy McVeigh and the Oklahoma City Bombing*, a book by two *Buffalo News* reporters claiming to accurately relate his life and events surrounding the bombing. And McVeigh's recently rerun "60 Minutes" interview with Ed Bradley was not only widely watched but also inexplicably so soft (as if challenging him would be unfair) that the questions could have been ghost-written by Larry King.

So any TV forum available to McVeigh at his execution would pale compared with what he's already gotten. In other words, if the survivors and families are to see him die, no valid case can be made for excluding others who want the same chance. Equal opportunity: That too is what this nation promises its citizens.

[2001]

Let's Bring Cameras to Death's Door

◈ *We pay money to watch grisly slayings in movies with popcorn and drinks in hand, but turn away from killings we endorse as government policy.*

Dead issue walking?

Thumbing through the files of Apparent Lost Causes, it's time again to call for televising executions. Oh, nohhhhh! Oh, yes! The catalyst this time is the on-again, off-again scheduled execution in California of convicted killer Thomas M. Thompson. He was to be executed Tuesday after his bid for clemency was denied by Governor Pete Wilson. However, the execution was blocked Sunday by the Ninth U.S. Circuit Court of Appeals.

But if Thompson is ultimately executed, pool cameras—offering coverage to any station or network interested—absolutely should be inside the killing room.

Why televise something so inevitably grisly? Because capital punishment is the will of the vast majority of Americans, say the polls. And because it is public policy in California, affirmed at the ballot box. Thus the public should have the opportunity to view the full extent of that severe policy instead of being able to experience it only through movies, as in Sean Penn getting strapped in and bowing out vividly in *Dead Man Walking*. Or through the accounts of reporters who are among the designated observers, as in those checking in on newscasts after freeway killer William G. Bonin died by lethal injection in San Quentin last year: "About two chest heaves, he turned purple, that was it."

On the other hand, you may argue, there are lots of things we sanction, if only tacitly, without desiring to witness them. We approve surgery, for example, but may be too queasy to watch it being done. Also, most people eat meat but haven't the stomach to peek inside a slaughterhouse, even through a TV lens.

Yes, but the difference is that cameras are not banned by government regulation from those venues, which have been televised on occasion. Cameras are banned from executions of convicted killers.

This wouldn't foster a return to an earlier age of public hangings or beheadings, when you brought the family and made an outing of it. Once again, details would have to be worked out, and there would be strict ground rules. The condemned person's approval would be mandatory (although you could make a good case against that), and the telecast would have to provide context. No romanticized eulogies for the condemned or metaphorical walks into the sunset.

That is, the telecast should not only review the legal aspects of the case and show the condemned person's death but also must stress the full heinousness of the crime resulting in execution and the suffering of the victim or victims and their loved ones. In the case of Thompson, who continues to claim innocence, the victim was Ginger Fleischli, whose 1981 rape and murder landed him on death row.

Wouldn't this be, well, tasteless? Get serious.

It's not as if televised executions would be blemishing a pristine medium, not as if TV is exactly squeamish about showing viewers or exploiting things violent, ghastly, or bloody. On the contrary, increasingly these days, anything goes, to the extent that public criticism received by some newscasts several years ago, after airing tape of a woman being shot to death by her estranged husband in a Florida cemetery, now seems almost old world.

You had the impression, for example, that several Los Angeles TV stations were hoping for a shootout with cops (although they'd never admit it) when they aimed their live cameras at a fugitive motorist for more than half an hour Wednesday as he sat like a stone inside his truck with a reportedly loaded spear gun at his side after a long pursuit.

And really now, didn't some stations here revel in and make serial murderer Bonin's demise serve their own brand of pageantry, with one newscast, for example, titling it "Date with Death" and captioning both foes ("Dreading the Moment") and supporters ("Awaiting the Moment") of capital punishment?

The issue of media appetites and human wreckage as an abstraction is not new: Witness Haskell Wexler's stunningly wise 1969 film *Medium Cool*. It opens with a Chicago TV crew being first on the scene at a serious freeway accident and being so emotionally detached from a moaning, semi-conscious woman sprawled half outside her car that they first get their shots and then call an ambulance.

But watching someone who is dying go through contortions and turn purple like a lab specimen? Well, televised executions perhaps would be just the jolt to make even the firmest capital punishment advocates change their positions.

Or just as likely, such telecasts would further desensitize viewers, just as the *Medium Cool* crew was inured, and have no impact on the status quo. After all, TV is already so deep in spectacle and boorish excess, there's not much that shocks us anymore.

[1997]

O. J. on Trial

◈ *Coverage of this case was so pervasive that Simpsonspeak became our national language.*

At last, something to overshadow that other obese spectacle, the Super Bowl. Inscribe it in stone: O. J. Simpson VII.

Or does it just seem like seven years, instead of merely a bit more than seven months, since the start of the overblown odyssey that has consumed so many of the media, and much of the nation, since the discovery of the bodies of Nicole Brown Simpson and Ronald Lyle Goldman outside her Brentwood townhouse?

How overblown?

* So overblown that Tuesday's long-awaited opening statements in O. J. Simpson's murder trial seemed almost anti-climactic coming after months of wild speculating, fantasizing, and rumormongering. The exception came late in the day when Judge Lance A. Ito angrily aborted Tuesday's session—prior to defense attorney Johnnie L. Cochran, Jr., delivering his opening statement to the jury—reportedly after learning that at least one alternate juror had been caught by the Court TV pool camera as it roamed the courtroom.

At least temporarily, the lapsed-telecasting issue threatened to eclipse the trial itself, and it remained to be seen whether Ito would now permanently boot TV from the courtroom, something the defense apparently would oppose. Cochran's co-counsel Robert L. Shapiro gave the dispute a cosmic spin: "The world has a right to hear our opening statement."

Earlier a sweeter, gentler, softer, frillier Deputy District Attorney Marcia Clark had presented the "how" of the homicides, following

Deputy District Attorney Christopher A. Darden's depiction of Simpson as an uncontrollably jealous man who slew his gentle Desdemona and her friend, Goldman.

As for the prosecution's side, at least, hadn't we heard the thrust of all of this previously? Thus, was it worthy of the mass simulcasting—all these screens showing identical pictures—by ABC, NBC, CBS, three cable channels, and six local stations?

* So overblown that the Simpson-Goldman case has become a common denominator, a shared national language by which many Americans now communicate, the case having been indelibly branded into their psyches. *Simpsonspeak* has penetrated even the world of hoops where, in the course of his radio/TV play-by-play announcing of Monday night's Los Angeles Lakers–Charlotte Hornets game, good old Chick Hearn weighed in, saying about a disputed referee's call: "Judge Ito wouldn't have changed that call. Boy, is he some smooth man?" Will Simpsonspeak also seep into Sunday's Super Bowl telecast that Ito has given jurors permission to watch?

* So overblown that early Monday morning the usually circumspect Aaron Brown, one of four ABC News correspondents now assigned to cover the case full time, promised on radio that the Simpson trial would be "the biggest trial ever." That's an upgrade from trial of the century.

As Ito likes to advise hyperventilating lawyers: It's time to take a deep breath. Is the Simpson trial bigger, in terms of lasting impact, than the Nuremberg tribunal that sent Nazi war criminals to the gallows? Bigger than the Adolf Eichmann trial? The Scopes Monkey Trial or those trials that have led to landmark Supreme Court decisions that have dramatically altered U.S. society? Bigger than the trials of those four Los Angeles police officers accused of criminally beating Rodney G. King, the first of whose verdicts sparked rioting in some sections of Los Angeles? Of course, anointing it as the "biggest trial ever" was one way to justify months of the biggest coverage ever—as part of that steady media drum roll leading to Tuesday's opening statements. No wonder that probably many more Americans knew in advance about those opening statements than about that evening's live TV coverage of the State of the Union speech by President Clinton.

Say what you want about the Super Bowl, but at least its kickoff begins on schedule, whereas an array of tedious legal skirmishes caused the long-awaited opening statements to the jury to be rescheduled to Monday from last week, then rescheduled again to Tuesday.

Not so tedious, however, as to alter preset plans by much of television to preempt regular programs to carry the opening of O. J. Simpson VII live on Monday. These electronic media folks were anticipating the start of opening statements but instead found themselves rouged, mascaraed, and gowned to the hilt with no place to go. Rather than withdraw, however, everyone went with full-blown live coverage anyway.

It's just a hoot that television, which zooms to breaking news with astonishing speed, often becomes trapped in the quicksand of its own technology in seeking to remove itself from a story when there is no story. At least not one that merits this level of mobilization, or the attention to minutiae reflected in ABC News correspondent Cynthia McFadden's comment to anchor Peter Jennings during Tuesday's lunch break: "Jurors No. 620, 1427, and 2457 were each taking notes at various points."

By that time, prosecutor Darden already had described Simpson to the jury as a man whose private face differed dramatically from his public face. TV's inquiring minds wanted to know which face was on exhibit during the prosecution's opening statements.

At one point Tuesday, Shapiro looked directly at the camera as it shot Simpson in close-up, then whispered something to his client, who nodded and then resumed taking notes on a legal pad. Was it rehearsed behavior? And was that a thin smile on Simpson's face at another point or merely a neutral expression? TV's in-house facial experts warmed to this long-range speculation with a fury, and KCBS-TV Channel 2, for one, promised to "analyze his expression for clues" to what Simpson was thinking. Twitch by twitch, presumably.

You'd expect nothing less from coverage of the biggest trial ever. We have a right to hear it. The world has a right to hear it.

[1995]

The Year of Simpson

◈ *It was hard separating outlandish TV coverage of this gory tragedy from Jay Leno's Dancing Itos.*

In June 1994, Los Angeles media were obsessed with O. J. Simpson. In June 1995, Los Angeles media are obsessed with O. J. Simpson.

oh.

As a TV reporter mused recently about Monday's first anniversary of the murders of Nicole Brown Simpson and Ronald Lyle Goldman, the best thing to emerge from this case may be the Dancing Itos, the troupe of bearded Judge Lance Ito clones whose stunningly choreographed musical numbers epitomize the aggressive late-night lunacy that has drawn NBC's Jay Leno within lethal striking range of CBS' David Letterman.

The frolicking Itos really outdid themselves recently as background dancers (this time wearing Hasidic hats) for an inspired version of *Fiddler on the Roof*, featuring a look-alike as Simpson defender Robert Shapiro singing, "If O. J. were a poor man . . ."

Always topical, the Dancing Itos were scheduled to appear on Thursday night's Leno show as the chorus line for a "Shapiro" adaptation of "New York, New York." Substitute lyrics: "Mistrial, mistrial."

Just as Leno's robed rogues are neither judges nor real dancers, the Simpson double-homicide case is in no way a primer on society, even though some in the media speciously argue otherwise to justify their year of relentless panoramic coverage. A mirror of spousal abuse and race relations in the United States? Nonsense.

Has coverage of this gory tragedy transfused us with deep knowledge? Are we any smarter about ourselves and our neighbors now than we were before all of this began? On the contrary, the case, to say nothing of the hot-lit Simpson trial with its severely depleted, agonizingly se-questered jury, is a three-headed freak from which little of value can be learned. If anything, it's a diversionary side road. Sheer commerce, not sociology, drives the reporting out there on the TV midway.

What the Year of Simpson does offer—with much more, obviously, to come—is a nasty snapshot of U.S. media, especially newscasting in the mid-1990s, an era in which Brentwood has outranked Bosnia in too many newsrooms. There have been weeks this year, for example, when NBC's "Nightly News" led every other night with the Simpson trial, if only to alert America that nothing newsworthy had happened in the courtroom, while ending each of those programs with a summary of what didn't happen. And addicted CNN, inhaling its heady Simpson ratings like a hophead snorting coke, plunged nose first into this case from the start. As a twenty-four-hour news network, at least it has time for other stories.

Is it just possible, though, as a thoughtful observer suggested recently, that the Simpson case will become a ratings litmus test for future stories, that the hunger level has been irrevocably raised, that the standard of O. J. must now be met and salacious appetites fed to merit serious cover-age? Under this scenario, important stories without such muscular ratings legs may get downplayed even more than they have in the past.

More than mere legs, almost from its outset this story had wheels, about a dozen sets of them, as a near monolith of TV channels trans-mitted global live pictures of a fleet of police cars pursuing fugitive Simpson in a white Ford Bronco on Los Angeles freeways. The low-speed chase looked like the start of the Indianapolis 500, with Simpson and his pal, A. C. Cowlings, just ahead in the pace car.

The media's fast lane to Rockingham and Gretna Green Way in 1994–1995 included greasy pit stops with William Kennedy Smith, Amy Fisher and Joey Buttafuoco, Tonya Harding and Nancy Kerrigan, John and Lorena Bobbitt, the Menendez brothers, and Michael Jack-son. These were primers, the prep course culminating in Simpson.

The story that has produced a cottage industry of camera-ready lawyers and boosted CNN and Court TV, while ironically energizing opposition to TV cameras inside courtrooms, also has nourished the nation's paranoia about violent crime at a time when FBI figures show a decrease in violent crime for the last two years. And much of the public, while decrying violence in the media, lapped it up. The call of Simpson proved irresistible.

The so-called honorable mainstream press and the so-called disreputable tabloids arrived side by side at these big shows of shows in Brentwood and at the Criminal Courts Building. And side by side they have remained, in effect, this Kato-izing union of interests giving the once-disdained, anything-goes media muckers an undeserved patina of legitimacy that may endure indefinitely.

The possibility of a mistrial has intensified bitterness and cynicism about our legal system and its jury process. When it comes to news gathering, though, the case's primary legacy indeed may be this intermarriage of media, whereby journalism's snide and journalism's snooty have for months toiled shoulder to shoulder in grubby pursuit of the same story, one that would have been widely reported in past times but hardly to the extent that it is getting covered today.

The more Simpson, the less time, resources, and appetite for news that really matters. Note in Los Angeles, for example, that stations that can find Simpson's mansion in Brentwood blindfolded still don't know the way to the governor's mansion or the Statehouse in Sacramento.

Meanwhile, the newlyweds are smooching. Tabloid "think tanks" increasingly get calls from TV panel shows and interviewers seeking talking heads with inside scoops about the Simpson case. And both print and TV tabloids are routinely becoming Simpson points of reference on so-called legitimate newscasts. *As "Hard Copy" reported last night* . . .

And if "Hard Copy" is run on your station, you at once promote a sister program and remain atop the Simpson sizzle.

Colleges may someday bump Journalism 101 for Tabloid 101, and why not? The faces in both camps are becoming a blur as they pursue the same story. It's the kind that tabloids happen to be more adept and experienced at, having come into existence solely for the purpose of dipping into dirt and tapping their fat bank accounts to pay the oilcans they interview.

And now, class, our distinguished guest speaker from the National Enquirer . . .

It could happen. On television, in the year of Simpson, it is happening.

[1995]

The Case for Cameras in Courtrooms

◈ *No one advocates barring print reporters from trials, so why discriminate against television?*

Some of the media have hurt their cause by whipping themselves into a disgusting frenzy over the alleged behavior of Paul Reubens, alias Pee-wee Herman. Nevertheless, arguments against televising the William Kennedy Smith trial—which promises to be one of the most sensational court cases of the decade—are almost too ridiculous to bother rebutting.

Almost!

CNN and especially the new Courtroom Television Network both hope to provide wide coverage of Smith's Florida rape trial, which has been postponed indefinitely by a judge in West Palm Beach in hopes of creating a sort of cooling-down period.

Although Florida is one of forty-five states that allows cameras inside courtrooms, Smith's lawyers have asked Judge Mary E. Lupo to bar TV on grounds that cameras would swell the proceedings into a "sensationalized Hollywood-style mockery of the justice system." Their words mock reality.

You don't have to look far to find overwrought, predatory media reporting that would appear to validate their fears of increased "carnival-like" coverage. It ranges from the McMartin case here to the frequently leering, snickering stories about Reubens—whom many in the media have symbolically convicted of indecent exposure even though he denies the charge—to the stereophonic din of irresponsible coverage surrounding Smith (a nephew of Senator Edward M. Kennedy), who has pleaded not guilty to charges of raping a twenty-nine-year-old Florida woman.

All of which has little if any bearing on the issue at hand.

The media circus outside the courtroom—plus the hawking of T-shirts with crude depictions of Senator Kennedy outside the Florida courthouse—will continue, regardless. When it comes to cameras *inside* the courtroom, however, the arguments offered by Smith's attorneys are ones long-ago discredited in Florida—which has liberally allowed televised trials since 1979—and other states.

One of the arguments is that the presence of TV transforms participants—witnesses, lawyers, judge, and even the jury—into actors performing for the camera. However, there's just no evidence to support the claim that people inside the courtroom automatically turn on when the red light turns on. And since when, moreover, do trial attorneys require the presence of a camera to encourage them to vamp when they're trying to impress a jury?

Similar anti-TV protests—since quieted—were heard from those opposing C-SPAN's congressional telecasts, which have tended to be about as melodramatic as a budget hearing.

Fears of TV's influence would be justified if cameras in courtrooms were as intrusive as cameras frequently are in newscasts and tabloid and "reality" shows, altering behavior by becoming a close-up participant instead of merely a long-range observer. In contrast, the single camera in the Smith courtroom would be a minicam mounted on a stand at the rear of the room. Unobtrusive. Out of the way. Observing from afar.

America's fascination with trials—or what it thinks are trials—is epitomized by the popularity of Perry Mason and other fictional courtroom wizards. But these super-heroes, and even "reality" shows purporting to show actual court cases, distort truth by tailoring it to the needs of TV. Actual telecasts of even sensational criminal trials, on the other hand, have at least the potential to educate viewers about a process few of them will ever encounter in person.

CNN, which has been televising significant portions of sensational trials since 1982 without incident, would cover the opening of the Smith trial and return intermittently depending on what was happening. Courtroom Television Network plans no change in its usual format of virtual gavel-to-gavel coverage, and would also provide pool coverage for the rest of TV.

Oh yes, the rest of TV, especially the media house flies who feed on smelly garbage and the gang of exploiting voyeurs who can't resist lighting the world in neon. They don't need real courtroom testimony to make a juicy story when they can fake it.

But inevitably, opponents of courtroom cameras note, even the most responsible newscasts will air sound bites of only the most titillating testimony, resulting in distorted coverage that is good television but bad journalism. That charge, however, is just as applicable to print reporters, who have no space to regurgitate entire trial transcripts, after all, but instead risk taking things out of context each time they decide about what to include and omit.

No one advocates barring print reporters from courtrooms. Why discriminate against TV?

As camcorders continue their revolutionary expansion into all areas of our lives, increasing the likelihood even of neighbors electronically spying on each other through bedroom windows, there's a natural desire to roll back time by conserving little pockets of privacy beyond the lens of the camera. Trials are not private, however. Cameras or not, they already are open to the public, so the issue is not whether there should be an audience for the Smith trial, but whether TV should be allowed to enlarge it.

"The way to get this story out straight and clear and honorably and true is for the public to have more good solid information, not less," Floyd Abrams, a prominent First Amendment attorney representing Courtroom Television Network, argued this week before Judge Lupo.

Beyond such platitudes there is a simpler truth: TV coverage of trials is allowed under Florida law, and there is no reason to make an exception with William Kennedy Smith.

[1991]

Give bin Laden His (Televised) Day in Court

◆ Despite its limitations and spotty record, television is our best hope for preserving the totality of epic criminal trials on which history may turn.

Much of television news inevitably comes down to its own celebrities and entertainment.

The Fox News Channel has many people covering Afghanistan, for example, but only one starring in his own melodramatic promo. Say hi to Geraldo Rivera, informing viewers that love of country led him to enlist as a foreign correspondent-come-lately in the war against terrorism.

Meanwhile, CNN has granted battle-tested Christiane Amanpour her own nightly show from the war front, glitzily titled "Live from Afghanistan."

That glimmer of show-biz rhetoric aside . . .

The consensus of this week's talking heads is that the following is highly improbable but something to chat about anyway, because the stakes are potentially so high and schmoozing endlessly is cable news networks' preferred way of filling their vast stretches of time:

Osama bin Laden is captured in the mountains of Afghanistan.

He is not executed on the spot by Geraldo.

He is brought to the United States or one of its military bases in the Pacific and tried for terrorism.

You're rolling your eyes because the chances of this man ever touching U.S. soil are remote. If we've learned anything in recent months, though, it's that ruling out the unexpected can be premature.

So . . . extending this hypothetical, what happens if bin Laden does face his U.S. accusers in court?

It's difficult envisioning a scenario in which the bogeyman Americans most despise would be prosecuted in one of those military tribunals that President Bush has evoked in an action drawing criticism from both the left and the right for being against the spirit of U.S. openness. You know, the possible out-of-view trials of foreigners charged with terrorist offenses, proceedings that conservative columnist William Safire predicts would be "military kangaroo courts."

A secret trial followed by a terse public announcement of bin Laden's status, then on to "Survivor" and *Harry Potter*?

Even if lawful, such a trial would not be tolerated by America's collective consciousness. Lesser terrorist suspects could have their cases settled in the shadows probably without large public outcry. But public interest in a bin Laden trial would be too intense for the Feds to bottle and ignore.

His trial would be historic, arguably the most significant of our time, bigger, yes, even than O. J. Simpson's. Even Americans who advocate promptly disemboweling bin Laden and impaling him on a stake believe, surely, that the trial of such a global villain should not play out in secret.

Now that we agree on that . . .

The next logical step would be to obtain maximum public exposure by allowing TV cameras to cover a bin Laden trial.

Yes, that stormy debate again. Cameras in the courtroom? It's a crossroads of the First and Sixth Amendments, where some believe freedom of expression and the public's right to know inevitably collide with a citizen's right to a fair and speedy trial.

Bin Laden is no U.S. citizen, however, and it's hard imagining many Americans being sensitive to the fairness issue when it applies to a reviled foreigner accused of terrorism that includes ordering the September 11 murders of thousands of innocent Americans and others.

So what would be the barrier? This.

Although California and forty-six other states allow trials to be tel-evised at the discretion of presiding judges, cameras are banned from federal criminal trials, and only rarely have federal civil actions been on TV. That's so even though the federal judiciary is as accountable to the public as other courts, and courtroom cameras are unobtrusively small and quiet and can be made stationary so that jurors are never shown.

Quietly driving this no-cameras philosophy at the federal level is the U.S. Supreme Court, which stubbornly refuses to allow its own hearings to be televised, a regressive attitude that robs the public of an opportunity to witness the workings of the highest legal body in the land.

Hello! It's the twenty-first century.

If ever there were a case meriting suspension of archaic rules ban-ning TV from federal courtrooms, it was the trial of Oklahoma City bomber Timothy McVeigh. Even more worthy would be a trial in-volving bin Laden.

The question of whether bin Laden could get a fair trial in the United States—explored by experts without consensus in a Court TV special Thursday night—is better left to the legal crowd. Might the presence of cameras make impaneling an impartial jury even harder? Possibly. Excluding cameras from such a trial, though, would be unfair to the public.

There's a long history of media being bad actors at sensational trials, at least as far back as the frenzy surrounding Bruno Hauptmann's 1935 conviction for the murder of Charles Lindbergh's infant son. Intrusive newsreel cameras were allowed inside that courtroom, and Hauptmann was brutalized by newspapers well before the jury got the case.

Burned into our memories, more recently, are the TV fright wigs and bulb noses who tooted their kazoos at Simpson's criminal trial. Their shrill display triggered what some have called an O. J. "backlash" that curtailed high-profile trials being televised in the 1990s. Judges were clearly more wary, most notably with TV being excluded from Simpson's subsequent civil trial.

Do lawyers showboat for cameras? Possibly, just as they do for juries and for news crews awaiting them outside. In fact, the circus at the first Simpson trial came mostly outside, not inside, and one could argue that Judge Lance Ito's courtroom was unruly because he was unable to control it, not because of TV's presence.

Would even networks and stations carrying a bin Laden trial gavel to gavel twist and knot testimony into provocative sound bites and keep a daily score of who was ahead as if reporting the World Series? Of course. Would Geraldo return from the front in time to cover the trial, and would there be a news show outside the courtroom titled "Live From Osama"? Count on it. That's the messy American way, however, and an acceptable price for the open society we cherish. So the verdict is in, agreed? If there is an Osama bin Laden trial, televise it.

[2001]

One Picture Can Be Worth
a Thousand Clips

◈ *Still pictures versus TV? In many cases, shooting the old-fashioned way still works best.*

What if the great Alfred Eisenstaedt had been born in a later era and had become a television cameraman instead of a photographer?

He might have had an exciting, productive career. But he would not have turned out to be one of the most celebrated pictorial artists of his time, earning universal praise and being hailed in eulogy after eulogy after he died last Wednesday at age ninety-six.

Americans would not be toasting anew his famous photograph of a sailor kissing a nurse in New York's Times Square on V-J Day, a glorious back-bending smooch that epitomized the nation's war-ending euphoria on August 14, 1945. There would be no retrospectives of his work, including a high-strutting drum major trailed across a field by a line of imitative children, their elation and abandon conveyed by laughter and pliant body language. And the *Los Angeles Times* would not have published, as it did Monday in Calendar, his wonderful photograph of Parisian youngsters with joy and fascination on their faces while transfixed by a puppet show.

Eisenstaedt was "a small man with unobtrusive ways who used a small, unimpressive camera, and he did not intimidate those whom he photographed but caught their essence and their actions almost as though by accident," his former *Life* colleague Carl Mydans wrote in the *Times*.

Had Eisenstaedt been a news cameraman, however, *he* would have been the attraction, and those French children, instead of being spontaneous, would have been reacting to his minicam instead of to the slaying of a dragon in the puppet show. That is, if Eisenstaedt would have been there to shoot them in the first place, given the likely agenda of his newscast employer.

His medium would have been television, whose visuals are infinite but rarely indelible, and whose few images that do linger almost always graphically capture the disparaging sadness of human behavior, not the sheer bliss of living.

Mentally replaying those TV pictures, you again see Jack Ruby gunning down Lee Harvey Oswald in Dallas in 1963, two days after the assassination of President John F. Kennedy, which was captured on film by amateur cameraman Abraham Zapruder. You see the *Challenger* exploding shortly after launch. You see Rodney G. King beaten like an animal by Los Angeles Police Department officers. You see dazed Reginald O. Denny pulled from his truck and brutally attacked at Florence and Normandie. You see a white Ford Bronco staying just ahead of pursuing squad cars while traveling Los Angeles freeways with a famous murder suspect. You see doomed skeletal children in Somalia. You see the rubble of a government building in Oklahoma City. You see the Balkans' multitudes of dead, bloodied, and homeless.

All are reflections of violence and misery that, beyond a doubt, were important for the public to witness. What you rarely recall from TV — because violence and misery are its preoccupation — are pictures that affirm the best of humanity. It's the savagery of Denny's attackers whose pictures are most vivid in our memories, for example, not the courage of those who rescued him.

Some famous still photographs also are overwhelmingly grim. Think of Robert Capa's remarkable 1937 photo of a soldier falling in the Spanish civil war, his rifle slipping from his hand a millisecond after being fatally pierced by a bullet. And Bill Reed's shot of tobacco-chewing Neshoba County Sheriff Lawrence Rainey and his deputy, Cecil Price, grinning defiantly in court with their redneck cronies while being arraigned in 1964 for the murders of three Mississippi civil rights workers.

And John P. Filo's 1970 photo of fourteen-year-old Mary Ann Vecchio screaming in anguished horror beside the body of a student slain in a clash between the Ohio National Guard and anti–Vietnam War demonstrators at Kent State University.

Some of these defining images are in a 1973 book of *Life* magazine photos that I happened across after the death of Eisenstaedt, who was a *Life* contributor for many years. Containing samplings of his work and that of dozens of other photographers, it includes sections on soldiers at war, ugly episodes of the African-American struggle for integration, and other images of conflict.

But the great bulk of photos in the book show Americans and others merely getting on with the routine of life: a boy sitting stiff-backed at his piano recital, artist Georgia O'Keeffe doing some deep pondering in New Mexico, an ecstatic, half-immersed woman being baptized in Los Angeles, a Japanese mother tenderly bathing her seventeen-year-old daughter who was born blind and physically disabled as a result of mercury poisoning. And on and on, page after page, they go.

On and on they *don't* go on the most visual of media, television. Or at least you don't recall them.

Of course it's human nature to remember the great disasters. Another problem for TV, notes a news cameraman for a Los Angeles station, is the fleeting quality of its pictures in contrast to still photos—the exceptions being repetitive reruns (the King, Denny, and O. J. Simpson freeway footage being vivid examples) that inevitably accompany every mention of some stories, intensifying the viewer's visceral response.

"You could pull off a good frame from some video that I shot and it would be a memorable picture," said the cameraman, who asked that his name not be mentioned, "but the problem is that the video goes by so fast. Look at the *Challenger* explosion. It blows up, and before you know it the pieces are in the ocean."

Sometimes it takes a still photo to memorialize a worthy TV picture. On a wall in our kitchen, for example, is a 1989 photo—from TV—of a single Chinese dissenter opposing a tank in Tiananmen Square, a constant reminder of a singular moment of bravery that was all too brief on the small screen.

The TV cameraman mentioned dramatic still and TV photos of a fireman cradling a dying infant pulled from the debris of the Oklahoma City bombing that yielded myriad pictures. "You can see the firefighter's face, the emotion. But the video of the exact same thing doesn't give you time to really look at the expression on his face."

That's because television news, impulsively zooming in the fast lane while swept up in the frenzy of the immediate, rarely pauses to let the viewer reflect.

The local news cameraman believes that TV news, by showing pictures in sequences supported by sound, has the potential to provide a context that's beyond still photography. But it rarely takes the time to do so.

I'm reminded of Dorothea Lange's bleak, influential photographs of migrant farm workers and their families in California during the Great Depression, especially her most renowned one of a mother holding her two children. That woman's troubled yet resolute expression is its own context. Hanging in the Library of Congress, "Migrant Mother" is a portrait of a generation's terrible economic plight, and its will to resist adversity and survive.

Would TV linger on such a picture if it got aired? Or would it be reduced to a flash card preceding weather and sports?

[1995]

The Death of Challenger Recalled

◈ *TV did a swell job of memorializing the* Challenger *disaster— when not exploiting it.*

It was corny, maudlin, and overly sentimental. It was mushy and weepy, gushy, gooey and schmaltzy—all the things that are ridiculed in a play, film, or TV movie.

It also was extraordinary and wonderful.

Friday's memorial ceremony in Houston for the seven astronauts who died aboard the shuttle *Challenger*—carried live by ABC, CBS, NBC, and CNN—deserves a longer life than a TV moment. It should be made into a video for Americans who need revving up about their country.

There are two distinct sides to American TV, at once the nation's whoopee cushion and its security blanket. You can forgive its nonsense at times like these when, for however long or short, it helps bond a diverse and often-divided people.

For a week now, tragedy has again been our common denominator and TV our common voice. In terms of numbers, the nation has suffered far greater losses than the explosion of *Challenger*, but few larger when it comes to symbolism. And TV has swelled this American footnote into an unforgettable wake.

You didn't have to be a flag-waver to experience a rush of patriotism and a sense of release and completion—like an enormous sigh— when the seven *Challenger* victims were eulogized Friday by President Reagan and others at Johnson Space Center. There have been few scenes on TV more gripping or pure or spiritual or intensely emotional than the space center throng singing "America the Beautiful" and then "God Bless America" as the president and first lady personally greeted the dead astronauts' families.

And seldom has Reagan, who was visibly moved, had broader shoulders or stood taller. When the tearful daughter of *Challenger* captain Michael Smith put her head on the president's chest, it was enough to make grown men and women choke up. And at least one did.

ABC anchorman Peter Jennings had begun in a quivering voice to describe the healing impact of Reagan's "mere presence" when suddenly he could no longer continue. For perhaps a minute, there was only silence except for what sounded like soft sobbing in the background.

We often underestimate the capacity of network anchors to influence America. Because of TV's immediacy and reach, however, they are the ones most of us look to for an emotional cue during unsettled times. And if they can panic the nation, they also can play a positive role, as Jennings did in Houston. This healthy, human display of feeling by a man unfairly faulted by some as being icy, had a cleansing, almost cathartic effect, as if a surrogate had pulled the plug on our emotions too.

The ceremony was an honest memorial that gave the nation what it needed most—a good cry.

Yet, around the edges at least, TV coverage of the *Challenger* tragedy has occasionally been less honest than manipulative and exploitative. Pictures of the *Challenger* explosion have been used as promos for newscasts, and CBS on Friday used a picture of teacher/astronaut Christa McAuliffe's mother wiping away tears as an early-morning tease for "The CBS Evening News" that was to follow much later.

There was every reason to include footage of the *Challenger* explosion and the reactions of McAuliffe's family and other launch spectators in news coverage on the day of the tragedy. But there was no justification for repeating those pictures again and again over the next two days as if feeding viewers' appetite for violence and misery.

Meanwhile, there are new excesses, including reporters hassling children for their reactions to the *Challenger* disaster, as if kids were human test tubes.

The issue of personal privacy has become a sidebar to the *Challenger* story. While watching NBC's "Today" show Thursday morning, I heard someone shout, "Turn it off! Turn it off!" The voice was mine.

Continuing its *Challenger* coverage, "Today" was replaying a tape of Cincinnati teacher Jim Rowley reacting to seeing the fiery explosion on a TV set in his classroom. A Cincinnati TV crew had been sent to the classroom of Rowley—a semi-finalist to go on the *Challenger* flight—to capture the happy reactions of the bearded teacher and his students to the launching.

Instead, viewers saw Rowley near collapse. He sighed deeply and his entire body seemed to sag in response to the horror he was witnessing on the screen. He was so devastated, so distraught that he could barely speak. "Let's turn off the camera," he muttered emotionally. He obviously wanted to be alone with his thoughts.

But the camera continued to roll. Even worse, it moved in even closer on the teacher's face, then lingered on the shocked faces of students and then trailed the stunned Rowley as he silently walked across the classroom and left through a door.

That's when I shouted at TV to lay off.

ABC's "World News Tonight," "The CBS Evening News," and even NBC's "Nightly News" earlier had used the same footage but clipped it at the point where Rowley made his request for privacy. But not "Today." The incident was fleeting, gone in a flash and hardly representative of most *Challenger* coverage. Yet it represented the ultimate media hypocrisy.

On the one hand, "Today" mournfully lowered its eyes and its voice when referring to the seven shuttle victims. On the other, it freely exploited Rowley's grief over the tragedy.

The people's right to know is not a synonym for the media's right to bully. The camera shouldn't be a voyeur, and Rowley had the right to grieve beyond the scrutiny of millions of TV viewers.

"Today" executive producer Steve Friedman seemed almost to agree when asked about the decision to air the complete Rowley footage. "It was real close, right on the line," he said by phone from New York. "I certainly would not have done it if it was a family member. And in retrospect, after seeing it, I think I would have cut it off after he asked the camera to stop."

There are rare times when the people's right to know outweighs the individual's right to privacy. An example: the memorable footage of the McAuliffe family and other launch spectators reacting to the explosion of *Challenger* at a public occasion. No other pictures—including those of the explosion itself—better conveyed the emotional impact of the shuttle's midair destruction. And no other first-day pictures so vividly defined the nation's loss.

The president called the seven *Challenger* astronauts heroes, and they are. If only there could be so grand and eloquent a testimonial for the many less glamorous American heroes that no one has heard about.

TV cameras poignantly surveyed the anguished faces at the Houston memorial Friday, and the networks showed excerpts of private rites in other areas of the country. And following their hour telecasts, ABC, NBC, and CBS joltingly switched back to their usual morning fare-game shows. That's America too.

[1986]

Columbia: *Freeze This Frame*

◈ *When the space shuttle* Columbia *exploded and its crew died, television anchors and reporters this time rose to the sad occasion.*

"This is my play's last scene."

That line from *Wit*, a play about a college professor dying of cancer, came to mind as U.S. television went to high alert and half-mast Saturday, draping itself in black crepe for hours to report the demise of space shuttle *Columbia* and its crew of seven over Palestine, Texas.

The irony, of course, is that a disaster was required to make *Columbia* cosmic TV. The nation's manned space program had become so routine to many that news of the January 16 launch found scant room in newscasts dominated by the economy, North Korea's nuclear threat, and probable war with Iraq.

Yet speaking to the heart Saturday on CBS was footage of a white column heading earthward against a brilliant blue sky, a sight "so stunning . . . the imperative is to be quiet for the moment," said that old Texan Dan Rather gravely, thick pouches drooping like saddlebags under his puffy eyes.

Any chance of survivors? ABC's capable Lynn Sherr was asked early Saturday. "Absolutely not," she replied.

The calm professionalism of TV anchors and their support teams was admirable, belying a behind-the-scenes clamor for experts, eyewitnesses, and amateur-shot pictures that began even before most viewers had poured their morning coffee.

Immediately preempted across the board—with memories of 9/11 still painfully fresh—was talk of terrorism, bound to be a topic given that *Columbia*'s crew included Israel's first astronaut, Colonel Ilan Ramon. "For this to have been terrorism would require technology not known to exist," said NBC's veteran Pentagon reporter Jim Miklaszewski early on, citing government sources. That reassurance was echoed widely all across TV on a day when whipping up Americans would have been ruinous.

When it came to wild speculation about terrorists taking down or sabotaging *Columbia*, in fact, Americans caught a break because it was the weekend. That meant many of the nation's most polluting talk-radio hosts were off the air, sparing listeners the whiplash of their shrill, inflammatory rhetoric.

If you caught a whiff of déjà vu, join the crowd. Disaster and moving pictures have merged in the public consciousness since newsreel cameras captured the flaming up of the *Hindenburg* in 1937. And much later, our most tragic episodes began to be stamped indelibly as TV stories, from home-camera footage of President Kennedy's assassination and Jack Ruby's nationally televised killing of Lee Harvey Oswald in 1963 to the terrorism that destroyed New York's Twin Towers in 2001.

In between, in 1986, came heart-wrenching TV pictures of an earlier space shuttle disaster, as *Challenger* veered to the right and, after less than two minutes of flight, exploded into a massive fireball that filled two-thirds of the screen. Nothing Saturday matched that sight, or close-ups of Cape Canaveral spectators anticipating a majestic spectacle, their smiles turning to bafflement, then concern, then disbelief, then terror, all seeming to blur as a single emotion.

Perhaps we'll learn the long-range impact of all this someday, whether we're becoming terrified or desensitized or just mentally exhausted by the grimness confronting us daily.

TV's least inquiring minds were otherwise occupied as the live coverage wore on. Inevitably, there was much more time to fill than information to fill it. So bring on the vacant theorizers and babblers. A typical question to guests: "Give me a sense of your thoughts now?" In other words, were they feeling good or bad about *Columbia* and its astronauts disintegrating? And check out this inane CNN question to someone who had witnessed the breakup in the sky: "The fact that you saw five pieces and heard five sonic booms, did you realize immediately there was trouble?"

In the spirit of eulogizing and awarding halos, some of TV's human space helmets seemed also to feel it was their patriotic duty to express support for NASA, no matter the circumstances—before reasons for the shuttle's destruction were known. Meanwhile, Rather worried about Mars. Does anyone really care if he gets to see Americans land there in his lifetime?

Viewers also got the usual profiles galore detailing each molecule in the lives of the dead astronauts, even though in terms of human tragedy, what happened Saturday was hardly more calamitous than everyday passengers perishing aboard a crashing airliner.

Grandiose eulogies are clearly the stuff of contemporary TV, and perhaps even the most overcooked ones have a benefit. As Kevin Merida wrote in the *Washington Post* a few years ago, public death is "one of the binding American experiences, giving strangers something to talk about in a culture in which individuals are increasingly distanced."

If so, consider yourself bound. Despite continuous talk of debris, space modules, vapor trails, and sonic booms, and lots of arcane jargon in the wake of Saturday's NASA press conference, the day was a poignant reminder that even in an age of technology, the human element still matters.

Space is one of the nation's most popular fantasies. For this mission, though, there would be no Captain Kirk or Mr. Spock to make things right in the end. Only TV pictures of this last scene in *Columbia*'s play, and the irony that its Israeli crew member died above a place called Palestine.

[2003]

High Noon in Television's High Court

◈ *Many still disagree about whether it was fair, but no one can say that Clarence Thomas versus Anita Hill was pretty.*

Thank you, Mr. Chairman.

I want to say what a pleasure it is for me to be here among my colleagues whom I loathe as I smile insincerely at an onerous roach like you and begin making a political speech and celebrating myself while pretending to interrogate the witness whose plight I will purport to understand even though I have no sympathy for this disgusting lump who reminds me of both my dear old uncle and auntie whom I despise but will publicly say I adore as I speak in front of the TV camera whose presence of course I don't notice as I try to impress millions of viewers with the spontaneous fairness and earnestness I have been rehearsing for weeks in front of a mirror that reflects the image of someone I worship in this wonderful land whose grand traditions I am dishonoring with my cynical opportunism and pretense of senatorial patriotism. Oh . . . I see my time is up.

Whew!

The Judge Clarence Thomas–Anita Faye Hill duel has been the most raw, tense, and captivating political telecast since the early 1970s, shining hot TV lights on both sexual harassment and political harassment.

Let's face it, their performances were reprehensibly self-serving. They lied. They distorted. They misrepresented. They evaded. They sidestepped. They postured. So much so, in fact, that it was impossible to know who was telling the truth.

And those were just the senators.

Whether the smarmy Biden or the babbling Thurmond or the curiously shrinking Kennedy or the McCarthy-aping Simpson or the histrionic Hatch, it was as ugly and infuriating as it was frequently enthralling. In a sense, the public is rather fortunate. As the grating Hatch delivered another of his haranguing pro-Thomas lectures under the guise of questioning him, you were thankful that you hear these guys only occasionally. They have to listen to each other every day.

After being relatively indifferent to sex harassment as news, and to Thomas's earlier appearance before the Senate Judiciary Committee when it came to live coverage, the Big Three networks have joined CNN, PBS, and C-SPAN in swarming all over this spectacle that was triggered when Oklahoma law professor Hill publicly charged that Thomas had sexually harassed her as her boss at the Education Department and Equal Employment Opportunity Commission in the early 1980s.

Kids' cartoons supplanted by a Saturday saturation of news anchors? "There may be extremely graphic testimony you may not want your children to watch," Dan Rather warned on CBS. "Back and forth they go, alternating the questions," said ABC's Peter Jennings, explaining the Judiciary Committee's political makeup to younger viewers.

Such knowledge was not necessary to be swept up in the emotional fervor of Friday's opening. Surrounded by his entourage and cheered on by government workers and other supporters chanting "Thomas! Thomas! Thomas!," the embattled Supreme Court nominee preceded his accuser into the Senate Caucus Room—and what Senator Joseph R. Biden, Jr., the committee's chairman, called the "blinding light" of publicity—like someone about to fight for the heavyweight championship.

The atmosphere throughout the day and parts of Saturday and Sunday was not only electric but also pathetic, as the shrill din of politics resonated across the airwaves.

Not since the Watergate hearings and Richard Nixon's subsequent resignation as president has TV so acutely focused the nation's attention on such an epic, volatile, high-stakes, nation-polarizing political drama and the issue underlying it. Because of its huge swells of spontaneous emotion—and because it turns entirely on the images of just two people—this event has mesmerized the public via TV in a way not even approached by the ambiguous, tightly choreographed Iran-Contra hearings.

You watched the faces of Hill and Thomas for clues to their believability. She blanched. He twitched. She choked up. He cried. What did it all mean?

In fact, this extraordinary addendum to Thomas's confirmation hearings appears almost to have taken on a life of its own through TV, as if repeated monitoring of the rising and falling credibility/momentum barometer were an end in itself.

CBS correspondent Rita Braver to Dan Rather during a Saturday morning break: "It is considered at this part of the day that the momentum is with his side."

Some of the pictures have conveyed self-contained dramas in themselves:

* The anger of Hill's friend, Ellen Wells, while denying Sunday being part of a plot to sabotage Thomas. Then her emotion in telling Senator Arlen Specter that, based on her own experience, sexual harassment was the sort of act that became "indelibly burned in your brain," thus making note taking unnecessary.

* The contempt on Thomas's face as Senator Howell Heflin told him, "Some of us want to be fair."

* The tears in the eyes of Thomas's wife, Virginia, as Hatch asked him to respond to Hill's charges.

* The faces of some of the Judiciary Committee's Democratic members as Hatch led Thomas through a friendly line of questions designed to let Thomas shine. The Democrats reminded you of a pool player looking on helplessly as his opponent runs the table.

* Senators on both sides quoting newspapers as automatic truth when it was in their best interests, then attacking newspapers when it wasn't.

* Senator Alan Simpson decrying political cynicism the day after he had claimed on TV to be getting calls and letters about Hill—particularly from Oklahoma—saying: "Watch out for this woman!" He gave no details, and refused to do so Sunday in an interview with NBC News.

* Biden drawing a laugh when needing to borrow the spectacles of Senator Strom Thurmond to read a newspaper clipping on which he

was basing a critical question to Thomas. Nowhere was there a more striking example of the variance in the skill levels of the Democratic and Republican interrogators. The former have been frequently inept, the latter frequently brilliant.

* The monolithic maleness and whiteness of the committee members, creating a vivid, powerful metaphor for the nation's historic gender and color imbalance in not only the highest reaches of government but in all corridors of power. It was history repeating itself: men judging a woman, whites judging blacks.

TV strategies—creating visual symbols and seeking the maximum possible audience based on when Thomas or Hill would be in front of the camera—have been especially significant in a conflict hinging on image. But so is how the media choses to characterize the story to Americans who might not have seen it unfold live on TV. On Friday, for example, KNBC's Steve Handelsman reported from Washington that Thomas had been accused of sexually harassing Hill "behind his closed doors." Implicit was the image of Thomas closing the doors to his office and doing something furtive. However, Hill testified that she could not recall if the acts she alleges occurred behind closed doors.

Just as critical was the way others chose to interpret the proceedings when reviewing them outside the hearing room. On Friday and Saturday, for example, Hatch and Simpson repeatedly gave TV interviews in which they were unchallenged while flat-out misrepresenting Hill's testimony. Simpson at one point claimed that Hill had testified that Thomas hadn't sexually harassed her, but only that his alleged actions were "just an annoyance." In reality, Hill said she believed she had been sexually harassed but wasn't sure whether Thomas's alleged actions met the legal definition.

Hatch did get his comeuppance once after telling Peter Jennings that Hill was "caught up in a very clever embroilment," but adding, "I don't want to call her a liar." Jennings: "You already have, senator."

It was Rather, though, who inadvertently summarized the confusion and ambiguity veiling this event that has been captured so remarkably on TV by saying at one point: "Who and where happens next?" Exactly.

[1991]

TV Keeps the Dreams— and Dross—Alive

❧ *On this day a racist spewing hatred on a TV talk show was eclipsed by memories of Martin Luther King, Jr.'s eloquence.*

Epic moments no longer must die or fade, thanks to television. They now live on as important video reference points—aspirations from the past, for example, to be weighed against accomplishments of the present.

Or lack of accomplishments.

Sunday marks the twenty-fifth anniversary of the great march on Washington organized by civil right leaders pledged to peaceful desegregation and equal opportunity for all Americans. The memory lingers in blurry TV pictures of the enormous throng of participants from across the nation and of Martin Luther King, Jr., at the Lincoln Memorial, delivering his stirring "I Have a Dream" speech that still brings chills, even in mental reruns.

So we've come here today to dramatize a shameful condition. In a sense, we have come to our nation's capital to cash a check.

"I will never forget it," Dick Gregory wrote afterward about the exhilarating event that capped a summer of racial violence and political tensions. "It was wall-to-wall black folks and white folks, over a quarter of a million of us. I had never seen so many black folks and white folks together this side of a race riot."

Gregory, the comedian and social activist, went on to give his impression of King on that steamy hot day of jubilation:

"It seemed as if the very cells of his body were charged with new life and renewed spirit. As if the magic of the day, the nobility of the cause had been transformed into a potent elixir and absorbed into the very cells of his body, infusing him with optimism, courage, and joy. It was contagious."

All these years later, it is still contagious.

You can have the TV speeches of George Bush or Michael Dukakis or even Jesse Jackson, each of whom was celebrated in recent weeks for rallying his constituency with oratory. King spoke not from a prepared text or a TelePrompTer but from the heart, spoke words that were his own at a tense time when his leadership was being challenged by militants within the civil rights movement.

And such words.

Go back to Mississippi. Go back to Alabama. Go back to South Carolina. Go back to Georgia. Go back to Louisiana. Go back to the slums and ghettos of our northern cities, knowing that somehow this situation can and will be changed. Let us not wallow in the valley of despair.

I came across a transcript of that speech the other day and began reading it for the first time. Its rhythms, eloquent phrasing, and powerful ideas fused with my memory of King's rich voice and those black-and-white TV pictures of him.

Ironically, a "Donahue" segment happened to be playing on KNBC Channel 4 as I read the speech, a segment as repugnant as the speech was inspiring. There I sat—King's speech on my lap, white supremacist leader Tom Metzger and his mimicking son on the screen spewing hate while denying a former comrade's charge that they had him savagely beaten after he rejected their movement. These marshmallows endorse violence? How could anyone even imagine it?

Phil Donahue was in his fairness mode to a fault that day, being almost nauseatingly polite to the older Metzger as if owing objectivity and dispassion to this dangerous, smooth-talking racist who heads the White American Political Association and the White Aryan Resistance Group.

Despite his abhorrent philosophy, Metzger has the same First Amendment rights of other Americans. So the City Council of Kansas

City, Missouri, was wrong and shortsighted recently in using a disputed legal maneuver to deny Metzger's talk show, "Race and Reason," time on the city's cable access channel merely because of the ideas the show espouses.

That doesn't mean, however, that Donahue should treat Metzger gently and pass the prosecutorial buck to the studio audience, or especially that Donahue should go out of his way to give Metzger or anyone else of his miserable ilk a national stage by having him on as a guest.

What about knowing thine enemy? A far better grasp of the evil potential of white supremacist groups is available from the new Costa-Gavras film *Betrayed*, which, despite being manipulative and deeply flawed as drama, is valuable viewing for Americans.

I don't know why, but I continued listening to the "Donahue" segment while also reading King's speech, at once hearing the voices of Metzger the hate-monger from the set and King the love-monger from within, their clashing messages vying for my attention. It was a mismatch, the twisted logic and tinny diatribes of the smirking racist gradually becoming eclipsed by the more powerful visionary words of the martyred civil rights leader.

I say to you today, my friends, so even though we face the difficulties of today and tomorrow, I still have a dream. It is a dream deeply rooted in the American dream. I have a dream that one day this nation will rise up and live out the true meaning of its creed, "We hold these truths to be self-evident, that all men are created equal."

A twenty-five-year-old black man named Charles Washburn was in a Chicago TV station when rhetoric from the Washington march first reached his ears.

With a bachelor's degree in business from Kentucky State University, a certificate in telecasting from the Milwaukee Institute of Technology, and directing experience at a Milwaukee station behind him, he was being interviewed for a job at NBC-owned WNBQ (now WMAQ).

Friends had told him the station was seeking "a Negro qualified to work there in an assistant directing capacity." They told him the timing was perfect, that the publicity leading to the Washington march had put heat on TV stations to hire blacks. If WNBQ really intended to hire a black assistant director, Washburn reasoned, surely it would hire him, because "it was a rare black in the area who had my credentials."

He recalls the interview with a station executive while a TV in the office was tuned to NBC's live coverage of the march. He recalls the words of marchers coming from the set: "We're marching for jobs and human dignity!" And he recalls thinking: "I'm getting my job, a job that a black has never held before at this station."

Washburn was confident. Without a doubt, his small corner of King's dream was coming true.

This is our hope. This is the faith that I go back to the South with. With this faith we shall be able to transform the jangling discords of our nation into a beautiful symphony of brotherhood.

But the check that King earlier spoke of wasn't to be cashed by Washburn then. Following the interview, he never heard from the station again.

Two months later, he did hear from friends with contacts inside the station that WNBQ "didn't hire anyone for the job, and they never intended to." Washburn concluded from this that his interview was a kind of window dressing intended only to give an impression that the station was moving toward hiring blacks for meaningful positions.

Washburn put it all behind him, going on to earn a master's degree in radio and TV from Syracuse University and ultimately moving to Los Angeles, where he has spent the past decade as a production manager and assistant director in TV and theatrical movies while also writing scripts.

Meanwhile, the color of TV continues to change only in tints. Washburn laments that dramatic stories about blacks remain a near-impossible sale in white-minded Hollywood. An aspiring film director, he wonders if he "would have been whatever I wanted to be in this town by now if that barrier — that sixteenth of an inch of skin — hadn't been so visible."

And he thinks about that day in Chicago twenty-five years ago, when the heady atmosphere of civil rights marchers became the backdrop to his own dream.

And when this happens, and when we allow freedom to ring, when we let it ring from every village and every hamlet, from every state and every city, we will be able to speed up that day when all God's children, black men and white men, Jews and Gentiles, Protestants and Catholics, will be able to join hands and sing in the words of the old Negro spiritual: "Free at last. Free at last. Thank God Almighty, we are free at last."

[1988]

IV

Burying the Hype:
True Heroes and Deities Unmasked

Much of writing about television consists of saying hello and goodbye. Often that means greeting newcomers and bidding adieu to the outgoing, as in a piece here noting Charles Kuralt bowing out from CBS News and those rich "On the Road" TV stories that lingered with many of us indelibly. As I reread that essay and other eulogies I wrote, drifting through my mind was little Brandon de Wilde at the end of *Shane*, desperately calling after Alan Ladd's heroic gunslinger to "come back."

In very different ways, from Shane and from one another, the figures I cite in some of these pieces were heroes too, and television the frontier where they flourished, just as Shane's best qualities surfaced on a Wyoming homestead caught turbulently in a struggle between old ways and new.

There's a widespread yearning in the United States for role models and public figures to admire. So, yes, we do love our icons, even when they're not the gleaming, pure-of-heart Christ figures that doting TV disciples make them out to be when they die tragically.

Mortals in life, there's no dislodging them from divinity once they are airbrushed into history.

Heading this list, naturally, are Princess Diana and John F. Kennedy, Jr., both so indelibly beatified that their twenty-four-karat goodness couldn't be cracked with a jackhammer. Mounting this pedestal more recently was NBC correspondent David Bloom, whose death while covering the invasion of Iraq—a dashing figure riding atop a tank his colleagues nicknamed the Bloommobile—illogically earned him promotion to the rank of News Giant.

As another essay notes here, moreover, Jessica Lynch was not the first American soldier to gain unearned most-worshipped-hero status merely for being captured in combat and rescued later.

How curious that real heroes—those who risk their lives doing the rescuing—nearly always get overlooked.

Big Man, Big Laughs, Big Legacy

◆ *Jackie Gleason's gift to us was a Golden Age of Comedy—his own.*

Jackie Gleason was a show-business extravaganza of awesome punch lines and paunch lines, a legendary schmoozer and boozer who called people "pal." He was Ralph Kramden, the Poor Soul, Joe the Bartender, and Reggie Van Gleason III roly-polied into one.

Jackie loved beautiful women, J&B Scotch, flamboyance, sixty-piece orchestras, luxury, Florida, and comedy—lots and lots of comedy. He died Wednesday of cancer.

A little traveling music, please.

I interviewed him in Beverly Hills in 1986, when he was seventy. You couldn't have predicted then that he would be dead little more than a year later. Impossible!

A former 300-pounder, the Great One was sometimes large enough to be renamed the Great Two. But on this afternoon he was a slenderized 215 pounds—his version of anorexia—and as swanky looking as always, the ever-present red carnation in the lapel of his white silk sports jacket. Although he emptied perhaps half a pack of cigarettes in two hours' time—the smoke continually twisting upward past his pencil mustache and thick-lidded blue eyes—he looked terrific and was tireless.

"Comedy is ten times tougher than drama because it has an immediate critic-laughter," said Gleason, the TV legend-turned-movie actor, who was finishing *Nothing in Common* with Tom Hanks at the time.

"You go out and tell a joke, and the result had better be there. But acting is a cinch. They make a big deal over it, yet it's like the plumber who comes home with lipstick on his cheek and convinces his wife that he was bowling and a broad bent over to give him a drink and brushed him. He makes his wife believe that, so he's a great actor. Everybody acts. You notice there are actors who go to school, but there are no schools for comedians, because it's a gift."

Gleason had the gift. Boy, did he have the gift—the full, 100-proof genius. He was less a comedian than an actor who did comedy, achieving eloquence as much with body language as with words. He gave America layers of fat and layers of laughs. He couldn't tell jokes and didn't create gags; he created characters with gags. And what characters.

It's a 1957 Reggie Van Gleason crack that lingers as a metaphor for the chain-smoking, chain-drinking Jackie. Actually, it was a setup for one of Edward R. Murrow's "Person to Person" interviews. Murrow would interview celebrities in their homes via an enormous TV screen. There was boozy playboy Reggie in his penthouse, wearing his usual silk hat and formal evening clothes, tipsy as always, proudly standing in front of a model-train display.

As Reggie lifted a shot glass, Murrow asked: "Are model trains your hobby, Reggie?"

"No, booze," replied Reggie, downing the whiskey.

Jackie's big looping signature was "The Honeymooners," the hilarious extended sketch of a series that ran in various forms on CBS in the 1950s, 1960s, and briefly in 1971. "The Honeymooners" was Gleason's highest artistry, its continuing reruns granting him immortality and enabling him to leave without vanishing.

Much of the so-called "Golden Age of Television" is golden only in memory. The overwhelming bulk of programs from that era would be dated dinosaurs today, valued as history rather than as art. But Gleason's comedy is timeless. "The Honeymooners" is just as funny today as thirty years ago, the situations still as relevant, the characters eternally fresh.

Gleason chose a blue-collar setting. As an ordinary guy who wasn't making it, though, his Ralph Kramden was a struggling Mr. Everyman, frustrated, angry, and very human. Everything about Ralph was big: his belly, his mouth, his dreams. Everything but his success.

If nothing else, the Kramdens made you feel wealthy. There was the drab two-room flat at 328 Chauncey Street in Brooklyn, where Ralph, the uniformed bus driver, and his nagging wife, Alice, lived in semi-squalor: battered icebox and stove, old chest, round table covered by a checkered table cloth. Upstairs were Ralph's best friend, sewer worker Ed Norton and his wife, Trixie.

The cast didn't need additional props. They had each other as props. Ralph was a roaring, hot-tempered bully who menaced Alice when she pointed out his many failures: "One of these days, one of these days, POW, right on the kisser!" If another threat was needed, he could always fall back on: "BANG-ZOOOOOOM, right to the moon!"

But there would be no pows or bang-zooms, for Ralph was a phony whose threats were a bluff, his gruffness a camouflage for his insecurities. He never lowered the boom on either the guileless Norton or the caustic Alice, who inevitably got in the last wisecracking word. "If you were only my size . . . ," Ralph once threatened, waving his fist. "If I were your size," she replied, "I'd be the fat lady in a circus."

As a TV entrepreneur, Gleason was no softie. He had a reputation as a tyrannical, demanding boss who oversaw every facet of his shows. He reportedly had such disdain for his writers that he wanted no personal contact with many of them, insisting that they slip their scripts under his door. He would return them by passing them under the same door.

More than merely a wonderful performer, though, he was a shrewd performer. He realized that it was in his and his show's best interests for him to share the stage. So scene-swiping Art Carney was given scenes to swipe as Norton. And Audrey Meadows—the most famous and longest-running Alice—was given her moments too, although Ralph's wife was a counterpuncher who rarely initiated action.

It's coincidental that Fred Astaire and Jackie Gleason should die in the same week, one a movie star who dabbled in TV in the twilight of his career, the other a pioneering TV star who later worked in movies. They were so different, yet so alike—one known for his grace, the other for his growl, but both giants whose work defined entire genres of entertainment.

On that afternoon in 1986, Gleason spoke articulately and passion- ately about a broad range of topics, including AIDS, Jerry Falwell, Ronald Reagan, South Africa, and rock music. But the subject always returned to comedy.

"If I went to a producer today and told him I wanted to do a com- edy series where there was no sexual innuendo, no jokes, and one guy's a sewer worker and the other guy is a bus driver, I'd be thrown out be- fore I got started," Gleason said, somewhat bitterly.

He was probably right, which makes us all the luckier to have "The Honeymooners" remaining in circulation—a gift to this generation and others to come—even after Jackie Gleason has left the scene. Bang zoom, straight to the moon.

Bye, pal.

[1987]

Excellence, from "Marty" to the Mafia

◈ *As an actress on the screen, Nancy Marchand was wallflower and witch rolled into one.*

Viewers know her best as Tony Soprano's wretched hag of a mother.

On a Saturday evening in 1953, though, Nancy Marchand is in the arms of Rod Steiger at one of those seedy, second-floor New York City ballrooms that serve as lonely hearts clubs where singles came to dance and drink Coca-Cola.

A pathetic, defeated figure tailored for spinsterhood, she is tall and plain in her black cocktail dress, hair pulled back into a thick brown knob under a net, nose too large for her narrow face, dark eyes gazing vacantly. She is not quite twenty-five, a perfect Clara for Steiger's chunky Italian-American butcher who is resigned to another gloomy night of heartache when encountering this fellow reject in Goodyear Television Playhouse's live production of "Marty," the Paddy Chayefsky play on NBC that two years later will become an Oscar-winning movie.

Marty comes to her out of his own desperation, having been re-buffed by another woman, and out of pity, having refused a crass stranger's offer of five bucks to take this "dog" of a blind date named Clara off of his hands. How low has she sunk? When Marty does ask her to dance after she's been abandoned, she accepts his mercy, buries her head in his shoulder and weeps out of humiliation.

As the shy, gawky wallflower and self-described "fat, ugly little guy" slowly go cheek-to-cheek to canned music, something sweet and magical happens. She pours out her hurts, and he tells her he can recognize pain a mile off.

Then the epiphany. "We ain't such dogs as we think we are," he says. Her eyes hint recognition. Perhaps he's right. Perhaps they have a future together, despite the misogyny of his ever-adolescent cronies whose jokes about homely females make them feel manly.

He promises to phone her tomorrow, she promises to wait for his call. Redemption looms.

It's this wounded Clara—not the accomplished Marchand's more famous TV role as tough, aristocratic newspaper publisher Margaret Pynchon in the CBS drama series "Lou Grant"—who competes most vividly in my mind with the memory of her as Livia Soprano on HBO.

Compete with Livia, a witch for the ages?

I've watched my "Marty" tape at least a dozen times through the years, ever impressed by Marchand and Steiger together, how moving they are absent of cheap emotion, and how persuasive despite the rudimentary production quality of the time. The pain in their characters is palpable under director Delbert Mann, the glints of hope renewing.

Although forty-seven years now separate Clara and Livia, they unite in the actress who played them. How different the characters are, one a vulnerable young schoolteacher eroded by repeated rejection, the other an aging, self-pitying crab who diminishes herself as she diminishes others. One pursuing joy, the other incapable of it.

The irony is that Livia was originally supposed to die at the end of the first season of "The Sopranos" but was kept alive in part because Marchand, in signature work, made her hatefulness so indelible. And now Marchand herself has died, just shy of her seventy-second birthday, losing her battle with lung cancer Sunday not long after completing her second season as an ailing Mafia matriarch with a glacial heart.

If a performance were a gleaming epitaph, Marchand's on "The Sopranos" was it. She won Emmys as Mrs. Pynchon at a time when TV drama was not nearly as good as it is today, and meaty roles for women were rare. But she was even more deserving of the Emmy she was nominated for in 1999 but didn't get.

The eyes that melted poignantly for Marty as Clara were ice as ruthless Livia, who in the show's first season appeared to join her bitter brother-in-law, Uncle Junior (Dominic Chianese), in plotting the murder of her Mafia boss son, Tony (James Gandolfini).

Her own son. Did she really want Tony dead or was she confused or even demented? That loose end unknotted, Livia spent much of the second season despised by Tony while recovering from a stroke, just as Marchand was limited by her cancer.

In this season's next to last episode, however, it was her intensity, steeped in the script's dark absurdity, that drove the hour toward bizarre closure. After Livia's daughter, Janice (Aida Turturro) had shot dead her brutal mobster husband-to-be on the first floor of the house, and Tony had ordered the body fileted and disposed of, here came Livia, descending the stairs ever so slowly in her whirring motorized chair, stringy hair askew, ready for her close-up.

The ensuing clash was memorable, with Livia peering over her glasses as Tony jawed at her for being a cruel mother to Janice, then rising from her chair and defending herself as if she were a sacrificing Stella Dallas: "I wasn't always perfect. But I always tried to do the best I could. . . . And I know you, any of you, didn't like it when I tried to tell you what to do. Babies are like animals. They're no different than dogs. You have to teach 'em right from wrong. But I was your mother. Who else was gonna do it? If you ask me, I did a pretty damn good job."

Hearing that, Tony glared incredulously at the mother who had raised two killers—himself and Janice—as she dabbed at her nose with a limp handkerchief and remarked, curiously: "I suppose now you're not gonna kiss me."

An old lady's madness exposed.

Television "may well be the basic theater of our century," Chayefsky said in 1953. And Marchand may well have been one of its best character actresses, from ballroom reject when TV was very young, to gnarled, scheming shrew after she and the medium had aged together.

[2000]

I Confess! I Did Watch Perry Mason!

◈ *Was there more fun anywhere on television than watching Raymond Burr's Perry slaughter poor Hamilton Burger in court week after week?*

The courtroom is still.

"If you weren't there," the attorney asks somberly, resting his thick, slabby frame on the witness stand, "then how did you know your husband was dead?"

The witness's face hardens. The attorney's unanticipated zinger, worded so precisely and economically, is the spear that impales her. Only moments before, she had been so cool, so confident, so completely in control. But now the woman is aware that the attorney and everyone else in the courtroom are staring at *her*, their eyes accusing *her*, each of them waiting for *her* to speak.

Second by second the pressure builds until finally she can bear it no longer. And besides, the hour is almost up.

"All right, I did it. I killed him. I admit it. But you didn't know what he was like."

Even though he's used to this by now, overmatched prosecutor Hamilton Burger's jaw drops.

The trigger for this little flashback is the death this week of Raymond Burr. Rarely has an actor been so closely linked to a single TV character. That character, of course, is the nearly invincible criminal lawyer Perry Mason.

What a brain. What a courtroom tactician. What a fantasy.

Burr spent nearly eight seasons as a paraplegic chief of detectives in NBC's "Ironside." Yet his prior nine seasons as the star of "Perry Mason" on CBS—followed by years of syndicated reruns and a bunch of popular "Perry Mason" TV movies—are what gave Burr one of the boldest TV signatures any actor ever had.

It was "Perry Mason," moreover—TV's 1957–1966 successor to the radio series, based on novelist Erle Stanley Gardner's charismatic character—that for years had such a profound influence on both television and the nation's opinion of trial lawyers.

In 1973, CBS brought back the series with Monte Markham as Perry, a revival that lasted only a season. Only Raymond Burr could be Perry Mason.

The impact of the small screen's original "Perry Mason" on television can be measured by the crush of subsequent courtroom dramas and series that imitated the style and rhythms of the series, especially the trademark, predictable confession sequence that was TV's caviar of camp.

Perry was part defense attorney, part detective. In the courtroom he was uncanny, he was tricky, he was full of histrionics that, to Burger's dismay, judges allowed ("but get to the point as soon as possible, Mr. Mason") because he was, well, Perry Mason.

He defended his despairing, seemingly hapless clients (who were always innocent, of course) by publicly exposing the real perpetrators. Nearly every "Perry Mason" began by designating a likely victim. Then came the body, followed by an investigation, with the episode culminating in a trial that ended with the guilty party breaking down and confessing under Perry's measured but relentless attack.

Usually it happened on the witness stand, sometimes in the spectators' section of the courtroom, where the murderer, feeling the pinch of Perry's remarkable reasoning, would jump to his feet and voluntarily blab all. Inevitably the slayer was "glad" that he did it because, of course, the rest of us didn't know what a monster the victim was. Either that or the death had been an accident. "I didn't mean to do it. . . ."

No one on the bench ever cautioned the confessor, never advised him of his rights, never advised him to consult an attorney before publicly pouring out his guilt. The judge was apparently too enthralled himself to think of legal niceties. And poor Burger (William Talman) and his police alter ego, Lieutenant Tragg (Ray Collins), who was usually the one who had smugly arrested Perry's framed client in the first place. They could do nothing but watch helplessly as their opponent ran the table like a pool shark, their awed resignation a silent acknowledgment of Perry's vastly superior brain.

The pathetic Burger and Tragg (who at times appeared to be the only homicide detective working for LAPD) masochistically persisted in moving against Perry's clients. But you had to wonder why.

According to published "Perry Mason" lore, Perry lost only one courtroom tiff—"The Case of the Deadly Verdict" in 1963—in 271 episodes. No wonder, then, that the public got from "Perry Mason" a skewed image of criminal attorneys and the way cases were tried in court, leading to lofty expectations that had no foundation in reality. The fact is, most criminal trials are tedious, and trial attorneys are more like Hamilton Burger than Perry Mason. As for courtroom confessions? They happen probably about as often as lunar or solar eclipses.

We're living in an era in which sound bites from sensational criminal trials are daily grist for newscasts, and there's even a cable network— Court TV—devoted to nothing but trials. Yet so ingrained is "Perry Mason" in popular culture that even today potential jurors are sometimes cautioned in court not to expect trials that feature dramatic confessions a la Perry.

Beyond all of this, though, the legacy of Raymond Burr is a "Perry Mason" that was and always will be extraordinary fun, to be taken seriously only at your own risk. You had to love Perry's sessions with his loyal secretary, Della Street (Barbara Hale), and faithful private eye, Paul Drake (William Hopper).

Paul, in particular, was a real sketch. Although he employed numerous faceless "operatives" of his own, Paul seemed to have only one client. He would be summoned by Perry (you had the feeling that Paul was hanging on a hook in the closet) and sent off to San Diego or somewhere else at a moment's notice, as if he had no other life. And it was Paul who frequently was yanked into the courtroom at the last moment to hand Perry an important clue, which sometimes turned out to be a ruse, a bit of Perry-style theatrics to hasten the murderer's court-room confession.

Afterward, Perry, Della, and Paul would gather in the legal wizard's office as Perry guided them—and viewers—through the subtle com-plexities of the case that they had been unable to grasp. Then the trio would go out to dinner.

Although the subsequent "Perry Mason" movies never quite recap-tured the old charm, Raymond Burr's original Perry was a great big wonderful hoot. All right, I watched him. I admit it. But you didn't know what he was like.

[1993]

A Toast for Kuralt and
One for the Road

◆ *Three years before he died, television's most-traveled man pulled the plug on his news career and left the road for good.*

Every kid in Belmont, North Carolina, seems to be riding a bike, and that's the story I want to tell you next. The one thing kids want, and parents want to be able to give them, is a bike. But here in this little town, as elsewhere, there are parents who just can't afford to do it. It hurt Jethro Mann to see kids growing up without bikes. See, he grew up without a bike.

Thus did Charles Kuralt introduce "The Bicycle Man," his memorable television profile of a kindly old fellow who maintained a "lending library" of thirty-five bicycles, all of them throwaways that he salvaged himself and made available to any kid who wanted one. They signed them out, then signed them in the same evening. With a dog barking in the background, Kuralt ended his story this way:

"Good night, Mr. Mann."

Like so many of Kuralt's signature "On the Road" pieces, this one hovered in your thoughts as television rarely does, a bright orb of honest sentimentality that radiated hope and warmth while almost moving you to tears. How invigorating—a few minutes that choked you up instead of making you choke.

Kuralt spent two decades being television's Norman Rockwell. He and his crew were all over the U.S. map, becoming a prototype for all the junior Charlies who sprang up like weed patches at local stations everywhere in the '70s and early '80s—reporters assigned to unearth the Americana in their own back yards the way one digs up some soil and discovers the fascinating insect life teeming just below the top layer.

They were mostly less-talented, soft-news copycats, the human pet rocks and Hula-Hoops who were destined to vanish like fads when their bosses got bored with them and turned to techno toys and other journalistic gimmicks. Yet Kuralt endured, remaining a road warrior on "The CBS Evening News" until 1987 while also anchoring "CBS News Sunday Morning" since its inception in 1979 and hosting one of the many CBS News morning show experiments in 1980–1981.

When he retires from CBS News at age fifty-nine after Sunday morning's telecast, he'll pass the "On the Road" torch to . . . to . . . well, no one. In an era when news on television increasingly consists of everything gory and gossipy that's fit to articulate in nine seconds, and when thoughtfulness is confined to fine print, an eloquent calligrapher like Kuralt is tragically out of place and archaic in a traditional newscast, a medieval scribe in the wrong century.

From Eric Sevareid to Bill Moyers, there have been many capable writers in television news and documentaries through the years. Still on my wall is a quote from a script by Marshall Frady for a 1985 ABC News program on the possibility of nuclear holocaust, because it captured for me the essence of despair and the utter desolation facing a globe whose superpowers had whipped themselves into an arms-race frenzy. John Leonard's media criticism continues to flourish on "CBS News Sunday Morning," and let's also be thankful for Roger Rosenblatt, Richard Rodriguez, and some of the other regulars who contribute sparkling essays to "The MacNeil/Lehrer NewsHour" on PBS.

Yet no one in television has had Kuralt's talent for word-and-picture coordination, his gift not only for meticulously crafting and delivering exquisitely simple, minimalist narrations but also for applying these words to pictures in ways that recall the shapes-and-colors perfection of a Matisse. Everything just fit.

You think of Walter Misenheimer's garden, "a paradise, a beautiful garden of thirteen acres, bright with azaleas, thousands of them, and bordered by dogwoods in bloom, and laced by a mile of paths in the shade of tall pines." And the old prospector who staked out his mine in 1962, proving to Kuralt that "the dream of gold dies hard. There are a few old dreamers who haven't quite given up, living in a few old towns that haven't quite fallen down. I'm in one now. It has a name, but we cannot tell you what it is. We promised not to."

You remember eighty-nine-year-old Ansel Toney, who "turned to a pleasure of his boyhood: flying kites." And Arkansas dirt farmer Eddie Lovett, whose library—a lifetime accumulation of thousands of books—"transformed the unlettered son of a sharecropper into an educated man." And, of course, the Thanksgiving reunion of the Chandler family of Prairie, Mississippi, where nine offspring of a sharecropper couple had risen from the cotton fields to become college-trained teachers and academics and were now returning home to celebrate their parents' fiftieth anniversary.

In the future, Kuralt said, when he hears that the family is a dying institution, "I'll think of them. Whenever I hear anything in America is impossible, I'll think of them."

So rich were Kuralt's "On the Road" pieces, so infused with feeling and eye-misting poignancy, that watching the occasional CBS specials that gathered bunches of them in a single hour was almost too much to digest. It was like tripping out on chocolate fudge. Better to experience and savor them separately.

There is no indication at all that Kuralt was forcibly evicted from CBS. He says he's leaving to write a book and to try new ventures. Nonetheless, his departure is a powerful metaphor. These are not happy times for old guards in television news. The faces are ever younger, the resumés ever shorter, and, correspondingly, the payrolls on regular newscasts ever smaller, give or take a few multimillion-dollar superstars.

Age and experience are unfashionable. On April 18, former CBS News correspondent John Sheahan's age-discrimination suit against the network is scheduled to go to trial in New York. Sheahan claims he was unjustly fired in 1991 at age fifty-three, after a twenty-three-year career with CBS, during which he won numerous awards and was the network's bureau chief in Warsaw from 1983 to 1985 and in Beijing for six years after that.

In a letter to the *Los Angeles Times* from his home in Germany, Sheahan says his witness list includes eight former on-air colleagues "who will testify that they, too, were fired or forced to retire because of age." He asks: "How many of us over fifty does CBS News have left?"

After Sunday, one less.

Just as it hurt Jethro Mann to see kids growing up without bikes, it hurts to see CBS News growing older without the man behind "The Bird Lady," "The Singing Mailman," "The Canoe Maker," "The Prospector," "The Gumball King," "The Kite Flyer," "The Balloon Man," "The Toy Fixing Man," and "The Bicycle Man." You think about the stories he would want to tell you next.

Good night, Mr. Kuralt.

[1994]

Contemplating Cosell

◈ *More than someone I loved to hate, pompous, overbearing, supercilious Howard Cosell was someone I hated to love.*

Howwwwww-ward! *Cohhhhhh*-sell! Wherever you are, listen up!

You didn't earn our affection. Many times, though, you earned our respect.

It was obvious from the start that you weren't meant for the sandlot. Big television programs like ABC's "Monday Night Football" and "Wide World of Sports" were your stage, as were foolish ones like "Battle of the Network Stars." But so were big issues.

You sought them, never shrunk from them, in and out of sports. For a time, you even discussed books with their authors on radio. From your support of civil rights to your support of Muhammad Ali's refusal to serve in the military during the Vietnam War, you were that rare TV sports figure who transcended sports. To many, that alone won you a pedestal. NBC's Bob Costas has some space on it too, for adoring and working in sports without becoming a myopic sports zombie. As does Roy Firestone for the depth of some of his ESPN interviews. Perhaps Jim Lampley and a few others are there, as well.

Now calm down, Howard. You may be right about them being shrimps compared with you. But here's the part you'll like. They may have a corner of it, but you own that pedestal.

You're right, Howard. That is telling it like it is.

But some of your eulogizers should get a grip. These embalmers, Howard, are pumping you with enough helium to launch a blimp. TV news reports have described your death Sunday as marking the end of an era. That's the brand of extravagant puffery from sportscasters that you would have condemned as a totality of ignorance. If there was anything approaching a Cosell era, it was a lone-man era, one that ended not with your death but much earlier—with your withdrawal from full-time broadcasting. After that, TV sports reporting resumed being routine, snapping back like a piece of elastic that had been briefly stretched.

On Sunday, Howard, someone with a wand anointed you "the father of serious sports reporting on television." Yes, yes, you're nodding your approval while lighting that blasted cigar. Yet if you sired a movement, where are your progeny, all the crusading little Cosellians who by now would have been going forth on the airwaves and spreading your gospel? As you know, Howard, they either don't exist or are so minuscule that they don't even register.

Cable has brought ESPN, ESPN2, and smaller, specialized sports networks, but their mandate is to go wider, not deeper. It's true that there's a mouth on ESPN named Dick Vitale who is your match when it comes to eclipsing the event he's covering (college basketball). And get this, Howard, he screams even louder than you did while covering Olympic boxing, when you earned the gold medal for gall. But unlike you, all he does is scream.

Oh, here's something you'll like, Howard. Just recently HBO launched a highly promising program titled "Real Sports with Bryant Gumbel," staffed by such real reporters as Lampley, Sonya Steptoe, and Frank Deford, whose segment depicting golf's snooty Masters tournament as a quasi-anachronism would have made you proud. Perhaps (excuse the impertinence) even envious. As if it were an academic journal, however, "Real Sports" is scheduled to air only quarterly.

You're right, Howard. That's totally inexcusable.

The fact is that with few exceptions, TV sportscasting today is not significantly tougher than when you entered the business full time in the 1960s and began building your reputation as an opinionated broadcaster with the reporting instincts of a good newspaper sportswriter and a fancy vocabulary that you wielded like an ice pick. When it comes to sports, the digging in the '80s and '90s has come mainly in print, from such journalist-authors as Ron Powers and John Feinstein and others. There's the occasional attacker and an entire legion of smirking smart-alecks in TV sportscasting today, as the United States has become a society increasingly skeptical of large institutions and increasingly ravenous for gossip about celebrities, sports or otherwise. But the essence of sportscasting hasn't really changed very much.

What's that, Howard? You can cite a plethora of reasons for the status quo?

All right, all right, slow down. You may be right. Yes, yes, sorry about that. You're always right. But here's one you probably haven't considered: Because your grating, condescending arrogance and constant showboating made it easy for your critics to dismiss your serious achievements, your impact as a sports journalist was fleeting. Even at your zenith, you were an object of ridicule, one largely of your own making.

How ironic that someone who correctly savaged jock journalists and others who covered sports on tiptoe as if they were extensions of the industry, should undermine himself by becoming a self-mocking extension of the entertainment industry. What you once wrote about pro football commentator John Madden when he was with CBS — "He's allowed himself to become an overblown parody of himself" — also applied to you, Howard.

Still, you were a character, an original, someone everyone remembers, and that is an achievement in itself. As great as your vocabulary was, though, the one word you never comprehended was *humility*. The more spotlight you got, Howard, the more you wanted. You sought fame like a miser burying himself in coins. You tried on too many hats. When you strayed from sports and serious issues, you were a New Yorker at a dude ranch, falling from your horse. You epitomized camp while toadying up to prime-time's VIPs on those "Battles of the Network Stars" faux athletic events. Your ABC variety show, "Saturday Night Live with Howard Cosell," was a quagmire of inanity on which you attempted — big mistake — to be lovable. Your appearances as yourself in sitcoms, to say nothing of two Woody

Allen movies, nourished your ego, your celebrity, and your bank account, but not your reputation as a sober critic and observer of sports journalism.

In other words, you could have been taken even more seriously than you were, and should have been, Howard. If only you hadn't been you.

[1995]

The Life of a National Hero
Has Its Perils

◈ *This is where I inform a celebrated air force pilot what's ahead for him as an object of worship in the United States.*

You may have heard about the reported late-night talk-show battle between CBS's David Letterman and NBC's Jay Leno over who gets first dibs on Captain Scott F. O'Grady, the rescued air force pilot who became a national hero by surviving on ants and grass for nearly six days after his F-16 was shot down over Bosnia-Herzegovina.

With that kind of resume, the twenty-nine-year-old O'Grady is naturally the guest everyone wants. While Letterman and Leno were competing for him, though, they were unaware that (in my dreams) he already had exclusively granted this column his first in-depth interview, an offer that we swiftly snapped up.

H.R.: We can't tell you how honored we are that you'd pick this column over those television superstars, Letterman and Leno. This is our first interview with a national hero.

s.o.: You see, that's the thing. I can't quite understand why being shot down and getting saved makes a guy a national hero, with President Clinton saying that I represent "what is very best about our country." I'm flattered by all the attention, and grateful, but I'm not Sergeant York, you know. I mean, I ate some insects, munched some weeds, and hid from Serbs who were searching for me.

As I see it, all I did was stay alive until I was found by our own people. Does that make me a national hero? If so, then why aren't the ones who risked their lives saving me—the two dozen Marines who manned the rescue choppers and were on the ground eight minutes and came under fire as they pulled out—also national heroes? Coming and going, they could have been blown out of the skies by surface-to-air missiles. Why didn't President Clinton invite them to lunch at the White House, too?

H.R.: The humility you display, in repeatedly seeking to shun the spotlight, is commendable. You're obviously a fine young man, and we're all happy to have you back. But do something about that naiveté. You're a national hero because the president desperately needed a shining symbol to divert attention from criticism of his embattled Bosnian policy. So you, a clean-cut American in jeopardy, a survivor against heavy odds, a resourceful bug eater, became his designated "true national hero," a theme picked up and drummed home by the obliging news media virtually without questioning its veracity. TV, in particular, is always itching to throw a parade.

S.O.: I can't believe all the TV coverage I've received.

H.R.: The pictures, the sound bites—you were tailor-made for all of it. A national hero, one personally anointed by the president, is great TV. And so is the hero's family.

S.O.: Wouldn't my rescuers be great TV too?

H.R.: You still don't get it. That would be too complex, too confusing, too cumbersome. Too many halos for the media and public to salute. Too many people for Katie and Bryant to interview. Too many people for Clinton to have over for lunch. Better one singer—whose name everyone can easily remember and celebrate—than a chorus.

S.O.: So what happens now?

H.R.: *You've* done nothing wrong. You've handled yourself with dignity. Unlike Kato Kaelin, you're not trading on someone else's tragedy. So take your fame and run with it. The morning shows you've done so far are only a taste of what's coming. They'll need somebody to throw out the first ball at the World Series. Do it. They'll want you to guest host "Saturday Night Live." Do it. Jay or Dave will slap you on the back and turn you into a punch line. Accept it. Even more offers will pour in. But do be careful. Predators are everywhere.

s.o.: Would you help me sort through it all?

H.R.: Sure. Have you been sexually abused or beaten by your parents, screamed at your mother for wearing see-through blouses and tight miniskirts, had sex with underage boys, had a penile enlargement, hung out with the Ku Klux Klan, attempted to murder a sibling, gotten mad at a white roommate for dating African Americans, worn a bra and panties, been held hostage aboard a spaceship from Pluto, appeared in home porno movies, been married to a movie or TV star who mistreated you, promoted bestiality on the Internet, tattooed your private parts, been a bigamist, stalked celebrities, or had a secret crush on a heterosexual man you'd like to horrify by giving him a French kiss on national television?

s.o.: No.

H.R.: Then forget about daytime talk shows.

s.o.: And if Barbara Walters calls?

H.R.: Skip her. She'll make you cry.

s.o.: Howard Stern?

H.R.: No way. He'll urge you to strip.

s.o.: Rush Limbaugh?

H.R.: Nope. He'll want you to be Phil Gramm's running mate.

s.o.: "Hard Copy" has already been by. A camera crew jumped out of the bushes and demanded that I comment on rumors that, while hiding in Bosnian Serb territory, I fantasized about having sex with Princess Di.

H.R.: You didn't talk to them?

s.o.: Only to say it wasn't true.

H.R.: Big mistake. I can hear the intro now: "National Hero Denies Sleeping with Princess Di."

s.o.: I'm also getting pressured by producers wanting to buy movie rights to my story.

H.R.: With Tom Cruise playing you? Yeah, the rumors are flying.

s.o.: Some people from Fox called too.

H.R.: With Fox's demographics? Expect to see yourself on the screen as a sixteen-year-old African American or as a swinger in a singles soap opera.

s.o.: Actually, they mentioned a comedy series, with my character rooming with a Latino gang counselor.

H.R.: Swell. "O'Grady & Gregorio." And you thought the Bosnian Serbs were scary.

s.o.: Another producer mentioned a sitcom that would combine the whimsy of "Seinfeld" and "Friends" with the gravity of global politics.

H.R.: Oh, sure. A bunch of young U.S. pilots crash in Bosnia, then sit around and schmooze about nothing while waiting to be rescued. This is getting serious. I can see your present situation is more perilous than I thought.

s.o.: I haven't even told you about the book.

H.R.: Already, you're doing a book?

s.o.: Not me, actually. It was commissioned without my knowledge by Dove Books and completed by the time I had lunch with the president. It's called *Six Days in June: How Scott O'Grady Would Have Told It Had He Not Been Otherwise Occupied While Hiding from the Serbs*.

H.R.: A serious work. I didn't realize. Look, all of this can be very important to you down the road. Many in the media delight in tearing down what they build up. On the first anniversary of your rescue, there will be stories galore reviewing what you've done in the interim, and if you don't meet the media's high expectations, they'll clobber you just as zealously as they now are glorifying you.

s.o.: I'm jittery.

H.R.: You should be. If you thought getting shot down over enemy territory was tough, wait till you see what it's like being a national hero.

[1995]

A "Masterpiece Theatre" of Pomp and Puff

◈ *If Diana was my "queen of hearts," as the TV people said, why didn't I know it?*

Of course they'll title it the funeral of the century.

Hillary Rodham Clinton mingled with Britain's stiffest upper lips. We sent our own royalty too, with Dan Rather, Peter Jennings, Tom Brokaw, and other sovereigns of the airwaves pouring into London last week and bonging like Big Ben in advance of Saturday's memorably regal farewell to Princess Diana.

It was quite a show.

If your taste in funerals runs to "Masterpiece Theatre," this one was for you. Sporting rich tradition and royals with pomp and protocol coursing through their veins, Diana's funeral was aired live on more than a dozen outlets in Los Angeles, then available on tape later in the morning.

Television itself seemed in mourning during the lengthy procession and service inside historic Westminster Abbey. Those who tuned in the coverage found TV anchors, reporters, and commentators draped in black, their grieving faces at half-staff, their words falling like tears as Diana's funeral cortege edged across London in a scene of heavy solemnity.

"The flowers are lilies," noted ABC's tremorous Barbara Walters, who has made getting people to cry her life's work.

Epic funerals do strange things to people. This one brought out the archaic in CNN anchor Bernard Shaw: "This is such a sad occasion, would that we not be here to cover this, but be here we must." And brought out the ponderous poet in Rather, who kept hoisting himself like the Union Jack: "Through the arch, and onward they march." And brought out the overstatement in just about everyone. Working for ABC, Diana biographer Andrew Morton said about her death in Paris: "I find it one of the most awful tragedies of the late twentieth century, if not the greatest." Veterans of the Balkans, the Middle East, and other hot spots might disagree. Why, even Mother Teresa's death might rival Diana's.

There were, indeed, some indelible sights Saturday, none more so than red-coated Welsh Guardsmen carrying Diana's casket inside Westminster, their steps clacking on the black-and-white floor, organ music and choir voices resonating in the background. You didn't have to be an Anglophile to feel the emotional steam. Moreover, CBS and NBC showed that they knew how to jerk tears when they ran soft, fuzzy, slow-mo footage of Diana as Elton John played and sang the re-worked "Candle in the Wind." While departing from traditional news practice, it was in keeping with newscasters presenting even the soberest events as a kind of entertainment.

And once again you heard emotional speeches by reporters and anchors about Diana being "the people's princess," "our princess," and "our queen of hearts."

Say what? Well, you know, being a spoilsport is a dirty job, but somebody has to do it.

I regret the catastrophic Paris crash and its fatalities. Diana seemed to be a nice person, and what a shame that she'll now remain thirty-six forever. But she wasn't my princess. She wasn't my princess of hearts. I didn't love her. In fact, until she died, I never ran into anyone who did. Honestly, no one.

What is this sainthood stuff, anyway? She was just a stylish, pretty celebrity and survivor of royal wars who many of us felt was prominent in far too many newscasts. You know, too much attention to her and other celebrities, too little to events and issues that affect our lives in more meaningful ways.

How ironic that it was Diana's brother, Earl Spencer, who set the record straight Saturday in a stunning eulogy that was less euphemistic and more honest than most of the coverage of his sister's death. She shouldn't be canonized or "seen as a saint," he said. Unfortunately, his sage words come too late. The real Diana, with the flaws and blem-ishes that her brother candidly recalled with affection, already has been expunged by the wattage of her gleaming legend.

Who wouldn't be amazed by the depth of genuine feeling about Diana in England on Saturday? It was evident on the faces and in the tears of throngs along the cortege route, in London's Hyde Park and elsewhere. Much more boggling, though, is the attention that has been given her death in the United States, another case of media telling the public what to think about, then using the interest they've created to justify their inflated coverage.

A spate of locals pursued the Diana story across the sea. Talk about skewed priorities. I mean, you must be kidding. Los Angeles stations that won't spend a dime to send someone to Sacramento to cover Cal-ifornia government have jetted reporters and camera crews to Paris and London for post-mortems on Diana, princess of Wales?

Yet, naturally, not to Calcutta to cover the death of Mother Teresa. She doesn't merit that spotlight, of course, because she was no regular on "Entertainment Tonight." No interest. She'd hung around too long with lepers and the poor.

Many covering this story also have sought mightily to create or in-crease sympathy for Diana's two sons. Losing their mother is a tragedy for them, of course, and you wondered what emotions simmered beneath the stoniness they displayed during the funeral. But to me, they're as much abstractions as the other royals. I feel much worse for motherless, fatherless, and parentless kids who are virtually alone in the world and have no support systems at all. Let's direct our compassion toward them.

The funeral and the Brits' response to it were quite a spectacle. But even more awesome was the crush of TV treating Diana's life and death as if they were biblical in size and she had parted the Red Sea.

"We have never seen anything quite like it," Brokaw said when Sat-urday's event ended. And that includes the media coverage.

[1997]

When the Coverage Is as Senseless as the Tragedy

◈ *Mayday! That was my response to television's schmaltzy homage to John F. Kennedy, Jr., after his plane plunged into the sea.*

If you dare to raise questions about any of this, you're immediately branded a heartless, soulless, mindless cretin. However . . .

Now that John F. Kennedy, Jr., and his wife and sister-in-law have been buried at sea on live television—delivered there Thursday like heads of state and eulogized by somber celebrity anchors against a medley of chopper pictures from the heavens and file footage of a toddling John-John—doesn't this set a precedent?

The thunderous homage to the late Princess Diana notwithstanding, these are really uncharted waters.

It's a grim thought, and, of course, here's hoping it doesn't happen. But holy hypothetical! What if Ron Reagan, Jr.—son and namesake of another beloved president—should die as prematurely as John F. Kennedy, Jr., and his family would want to have him buried at sea too?

Would this spectacle recur? Would we go through this again . . . and again, with the cameras, commentators, and choppers on call as the occasion demands? Or would the media say no, because the Reagan family's record of suffering doesn't match the Kennedys'?

In other words, this is all a bit crazy and hysterical, don't you think? To say nothing of manipulative.

Television had already explored to the hilt the Kennedys' perilous, oft-lethal encounters with flying. Now, on to something else.

The sea.

"And John Kennedy, Jr., goes down to the sea for the last time," concluded a Thursday profile on CNN set to melancholy music. To music.

Because their staffs have to shut their yaps once in a while, some of the networks on Thursday also reran an audiotape of John F. Kennedy, Sr.'s monologue about humankind coming from the sea and "going back from whence we came." In case you didn't catch the irony—the adult son's death and burial now giving meaning to the father's words—MSNBC delivered it with a sledgehammer by simultaneously showing grainy footage of two-year-old John-John at the wheel of a boat.

If only some of these TV people would go back from whence they came, for this was one more cheap emotional whirlpool in a sea of them.

Moments later, ever-present *New York Daily News* columnist Mike Barnicle, a neighbor and friend of the Kennedys—as many reporting and commenting on this story on TV appear to be—said he was sure that JFK Jr.'s uncle, Senator Edward Kennedy, the senator from Massachusetts, could "hear his family's history on the wind." That is, if he could hear anything above the roar of inflated rhetoric.

And you wonder why they call the Kennedys mythic.

The facts are that John F. Kennedy, Jr., his wife, Carolyn, and her sister, Lauren Bessette, died tragically, delivering an unthinkable blow to their families and causing much of the nation to feel very sad about the loss of this trio of beautiful, accomplished thirty-somethings.

It's the shameless litter of the surrounding coverage that's so maddening. That includes TV reporters repeatedly asking the obligatory question: "Who will carry the Kennedy banner now?" As if JFK Jr. had done that. And as if his uncle's senatorial career were chopped liver.

It also includes TV dwelling on long lines of bouquet-bearing mourners sadly queuing up in long lines outside Kennedy's residence in New York's TriBeCa district. As if they represented mainstream America.

On Thursday, CNN read the signs some had brought with them, including: "John-John, God has voted you president in heaven." Now there's perspective.

You look at these long faces and see, in essence, the same worshipful pilgrims who travel annually to Elvis Presley's Graceland mansion in Memphis to tearfully light candles on the anniversary of his death. The same ones who continue to hang out at the graves of James Dean and Marilyn Monroe. The ones who stand outside and shout at stars arriving for the Emmy and Oscar ceremonies. The ones who because of some internal void find meaning and personal expression only through the lives of celebrities, instead of living fully themselves.

If Kennedy was as grounded and straight-thinking as many now say he was, he would have despised all of this. That includes the relentless fawning over his image.

CNN's star reporter, Christiane Amanpour, who also works for CBS, was on "60 Minutes" Sunday, being interviewed by Mike Wallace about her close friendship with JFK Jr. since college. And her easy, relaxed way of recalling him as someone she adored, without elevating him to divinity, was not only full of intimate insights but also departed refreshingly from the swollen verbiage of many other newscasters.

Yet her appearance also symbolized a media phenomenon of the last couple of decades that may explain some of TV's detail-by-detail obsession with JFK Jr. as a person who transcends his family's long litany of personal tragedies dating to World War II. One that transcends, also, the high ratings that this coverage is drawing.

Publishers and network owners have always rubbed shoulders with the high and mighty. But now, through television, has come the wealthy celebrity journalist, the Diane Sawyers, Barbara Walters, Tom Brokaws, Peter Jennings, Dan Rathers, and Mike Wallaces, who find themselves covering the same VIPs they live near, socialize with, and bump into at swank restaurants. In effect they're reporting on themselves, royalty covering royalty.

It happens even on the lower rungs, indicated by Thursday's introduction granted Jonathan Alter, the *Newsweek* writer who also works for NBC and MSNBC: "You're a journalist, but you also have friends in the Kennedy family."

Meanwhile, the burial of the plane victims and journalistic standards continued.

"When you think of how much the Kennedy family loves the water," a CNN anchor said gravely, "it all makes sense." Actually, none of it makes sense.

[1999]

Index

ABC: Olympics coverage, 37; and Pearl Harbor anniversary, 77, 79, 80
ABC News: and bin Laden videos, 69–70; capable writers for, 239; and fall of Berlin Wall, 56, 58; foreign news coverage, 32–33, 56; and Laci Peterson case, 17; and Linda Ellerbee, 24; and Paula Jones story, 21–22; and Pearl Harbor anniversary, 77, 79, 80; and political campaign debates, 153; and political conventions, 131–133, 134; and presidential photo-ops, 152, 155, 157; and presidential press conferences, 141; and Princess Diana's funeral, 251; and reality programs, 48; self-promotion as news on, 45; September 11 coverage, 63; and shuttle disasters, 209, 210, 211, 212, 213; and Simpson trial, 192, 193; and tabloids, 21–22; and Thomas-Hill hearings, 217. *See also* "Good Morning America" (ABC); "World News Tonight" (ABC).
Abraham, F. Murray, 110
Abrams, Floyd, 200
Academy of Television Arts and Sciences, 171
Acevedo, Kirk, 163
Ackroyd, Dan, 80
Advertising: and celebrity spokespeople, 98–100, 101–104; and war on terrorism, 170–173; and wildlife programs, 95–96
Affleck, Ben, 78, 79, 80

Afghanistan, U.S. war in: and Al Qaeda propaganda videos, 69–70; war reporting, 69–70, 162–165, 171, 172–173, 201. *See also* Bin Laden, Osama.
Ahmann-Leighton, Crissy, 38
Ailes, Roger, 40
Aldrich, Jody, 159–160
Ali, Muhammad, 242
Alice in Wonderland (film), 112
Alter, Jonathan, 255
Alvarez, Linda, 15, 53
Amanpour, Christiane, 165, 201, 255
Amedure, Scott, 90–93
"An American Family" (PBS), 48
American Terrorist: Timothy McVeigh and the Oklahoma City Bombing (Michel and Herbeck), 187
Amezcua, Carlos, 75
Anderson, Bonnie, 13
Animals and television, 81–82, 94–97
Antenne 2 (French television), 113
Arnold, Tom, 74
Arnot, Robert, 45
Ashcroft, John D., 186–187
Ashe, Arthur, 23–24
Asman, David, 39, 41
Associated Press, 22
Astaire, Fred, 229
Atlanta child murders, 27
Atlanta Journal-Constitution, 12
Aumont, Jean-Pierre, 114
Avalon (film), xiii

A NOTE ON THE AUTHOR

Howard Rosenberg was born in Kansas City, Missouri, grew up there, and studied history and political science at the University of Oklahoma and the University of Minnesota. He began his newspaper career as editor of the *White Bear Press* in White Bear Lake, Minnesota, then worked as a reporter for the *Moline Daily Dispatch* and the *Louisville Times*, where he was named television critic in 1971. From 1978 to 2003 he wrote television criticism for the *Los Angeles Times*, winning a Pulitzer Prize (in 1985) and two National Headliner awards. Mr. Rosenberg is adjunct professor at the University of Southern California, where he teaches news ethics in the Annenberg School and criticism in the film-television school. He lives in Los Angeles with his wife, Carol.